D0175651

David B.
Nocturnal conspiracies

Nineteen Dreams
From december 1979 to september 1994.

A T NIGHT, MY DREAMS ARE FILLED WITH CONSPIRACIES, CHASES, TERRORIST ATTACKS. POLICEMEN, SPIES, AND BANDITS MEET ME FOR WEIRD SHOOTOUTS. IN MY SLEEP, I FIND ONCE AGAIN MY LIKING FOR GANGSTER STORIES AND DREAMING MORPHS MY DAILY LIFE INTO A POLICE INVESTIGATION. THE REPETITION OF THESE THEMES MADE ME WANT TO DRAW THOSE DREAMS. I LOVE THEIR CHAOTIC AND POETIC STRUCTURE. I LOVE THEIR MYSTERIOUS LOGIC. I LOVE THEIR ENIGMAS WITHOUT SOLUTIONS. EACH OF THESE DREAMS IS A CHAPTER IN MY DARK NOVEL.

DAVID B.

For Ilaria, about whom I often dreamed while drawing this book.

ISBN 10: 1-56163-541-3
ISBN 13: 978-1-56163-541-2
© Futuropolis, 2005
© NBM 2008 for the English translation
Translation by Joe Johnson
Lettering by Ortho
Printed in China

Comicslit is an imprint
and trademark of

NANTIER · BEALL · MINOUSTCHINE
Publishing inc.
new york

1 • The Leper

A DREAM WITHOUT A PRECISE DATE. THE END OF 1979, BEGINNING OF 1980.

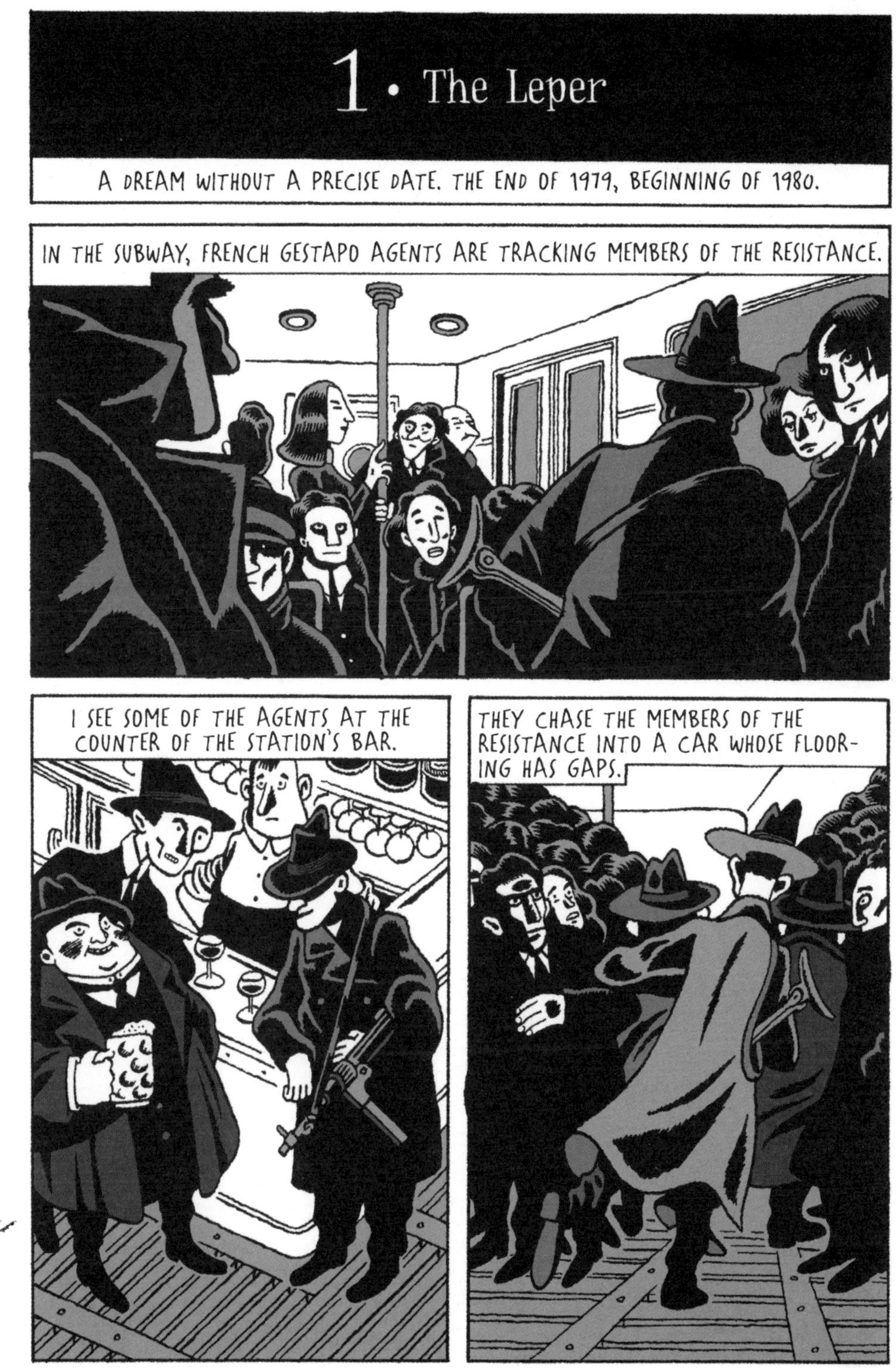
IN THE SUBWAY, FRENCH GESTAPO AGENTS ARE TRACKING MEMBERS OF THE RESISTANCE.
I SEE SOME OF THE AGENTS AT THE COUNTER OF THE STATION'S BAR.
THEY CHASE THE MEMBERS OF THE RESISTANCE INTO A CAR WHOSE FLOORING HAS GAPS.

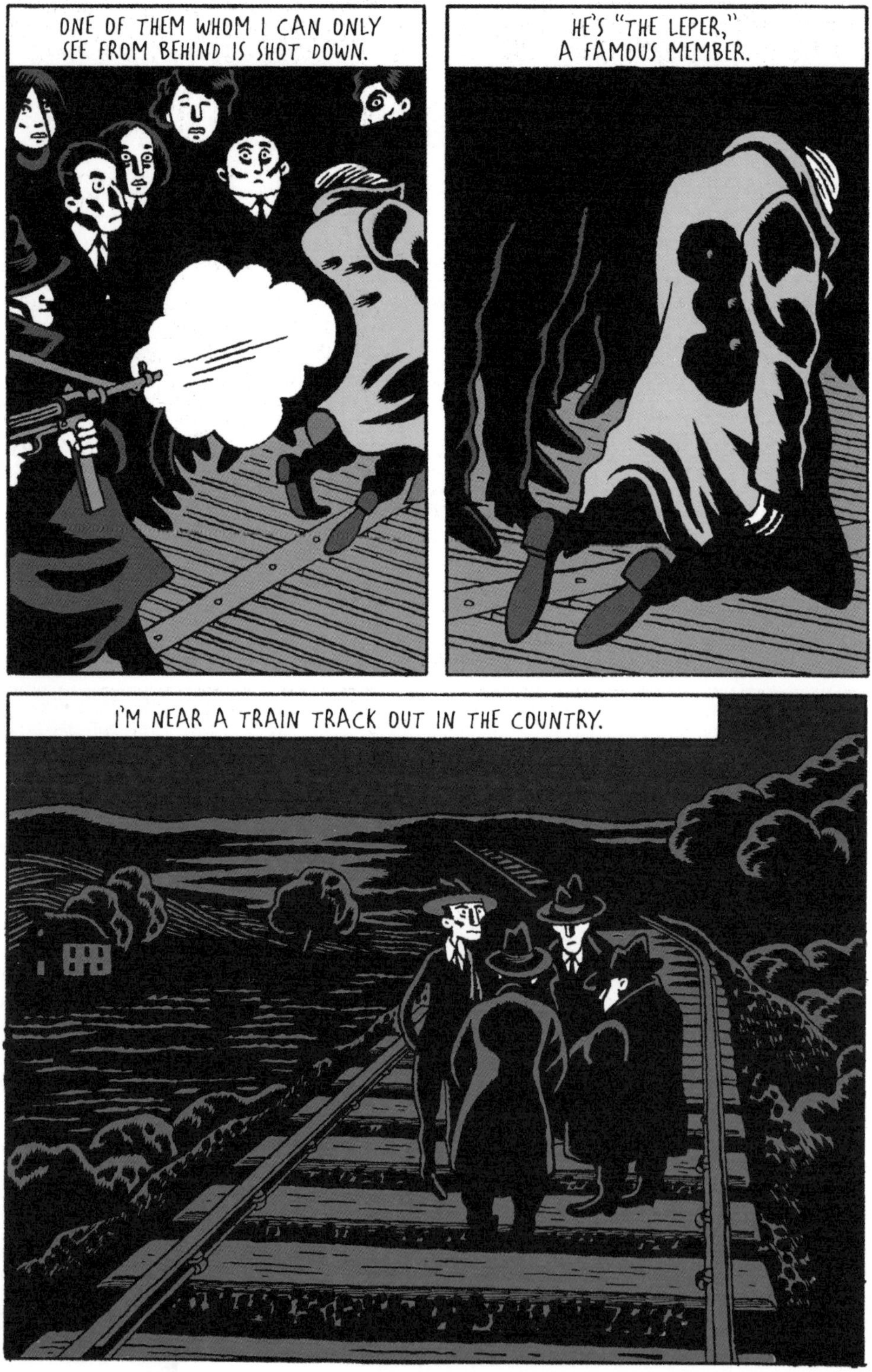
ONE OF THEM WHOM I CAN ONLY SEE FROM BEHIND IS SHOT DOWN.
HE'S "THE LEPER," A FAMOUS MEMBER.
I'M NEAR A TRAIN TRACK OUT IN THE COUNTRY.

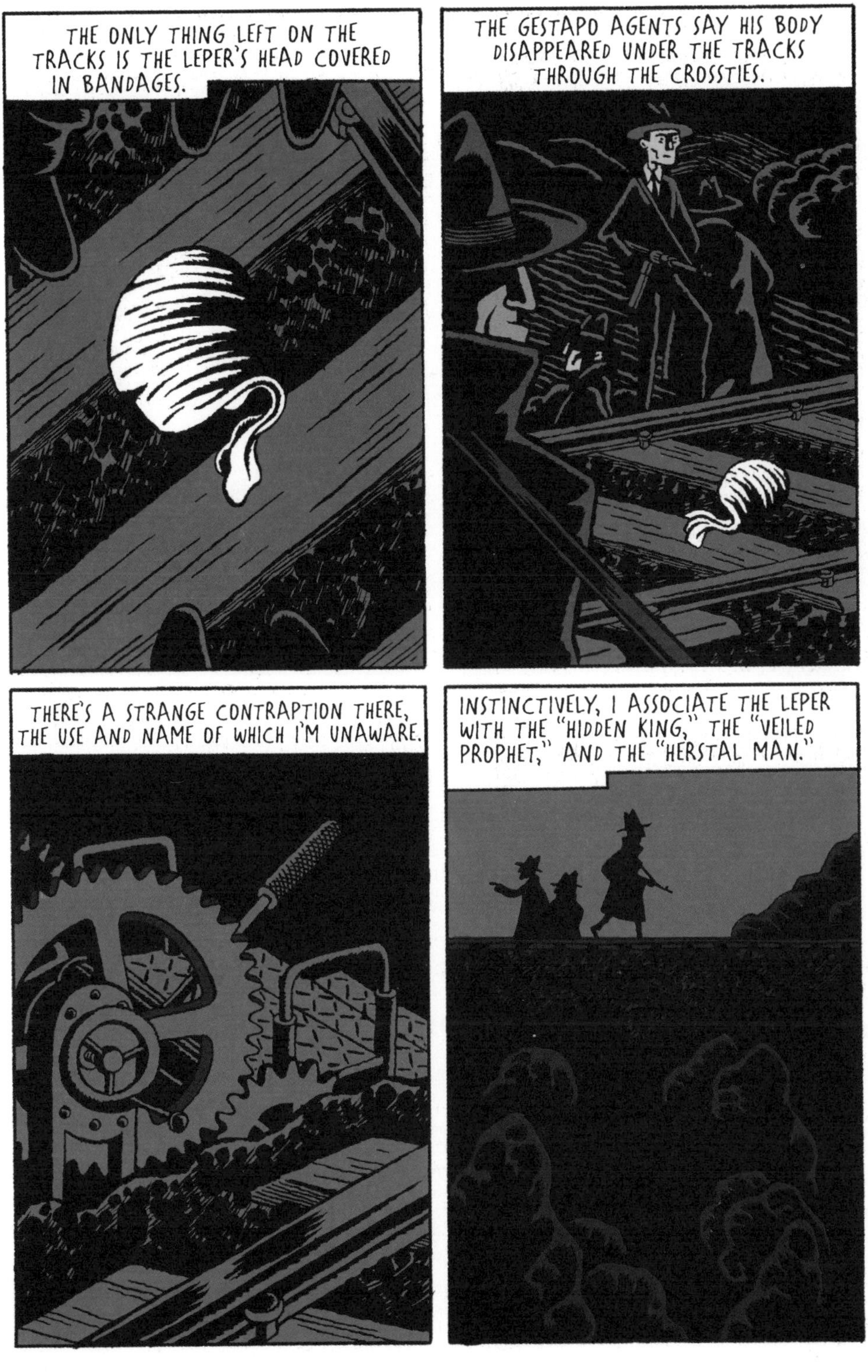
THE ONLY THING LEFT ON THE TRACKS IS THE LEPER'S HEAD COVERED IN BANDAGES.
THE GESTAPO AGENTS SAY HIS BODY DISAPPEARED UNDER THE TRACKS THROUGH THE CROSSTIES.
THERE'S A STRANGE CONTRAPTION THERE, THE USE AND NAME OF WHICH I'M UNAWARE.
INSTINCTIVELY, I ASSOCIATE THE LEPER WITH THE "HIDDEN KING," THE "VEILED PROPHET," AND THE "HERSTAL MAN."

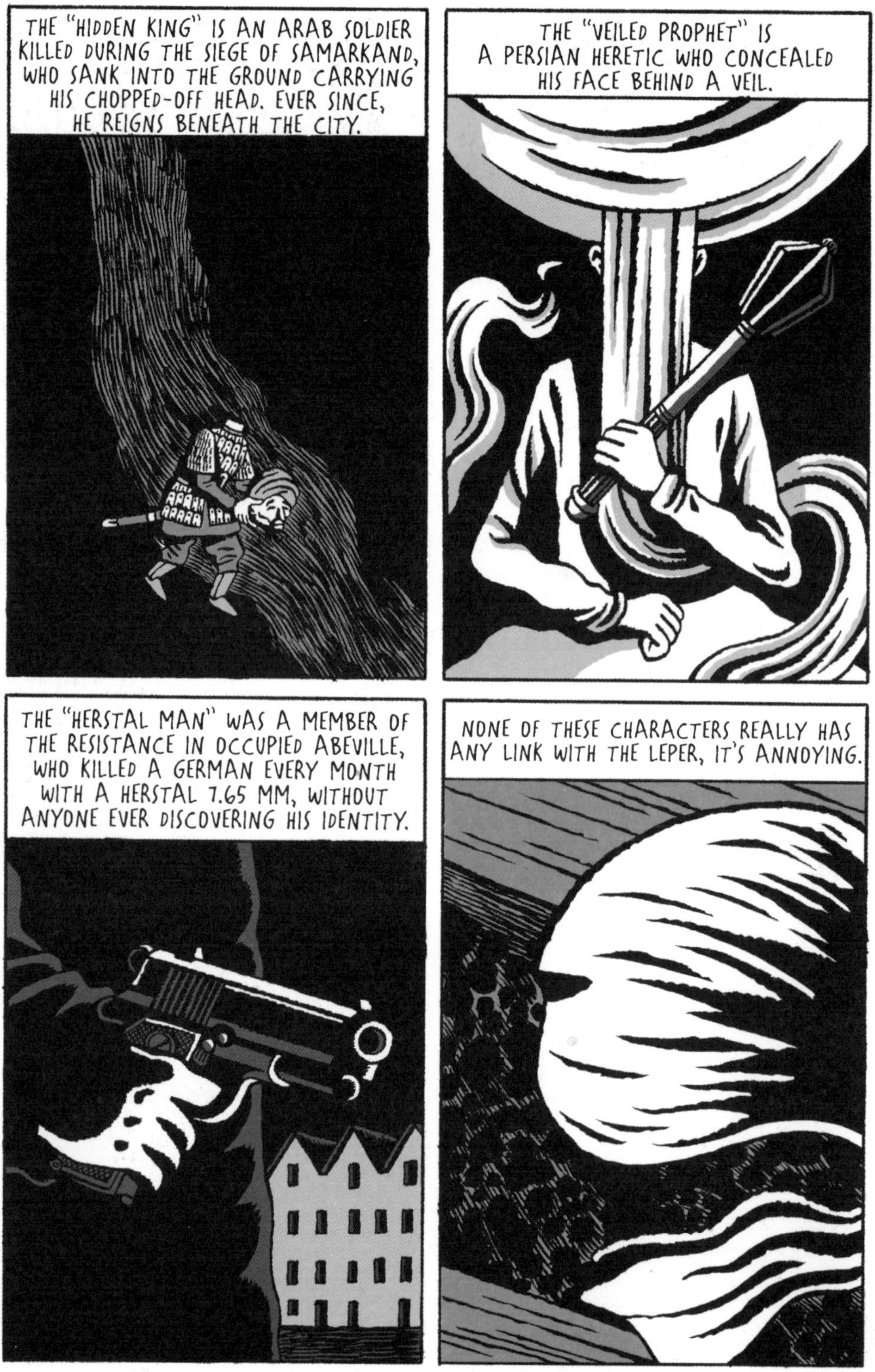
THE "HIDDEN KING" IS AN ARAB SOLDIER KILLED DURING THE SIEGE OF SAMARKAND, WHO SANK INTO THE GROUND CARRYING HIS CHOPPED-OFF HEAD. EVER SINCE, HE REIGNS BENEATH THE CITY.
THE "VEILED PROPHET" IS A PERSIAN HERETIC WHO CONCEALED HIS FACE BEHIND A VEIL.
THE "HERSTAL MAN" WAS A MEMBER OF THE RESISTANCE IN OCCUPIED ABEVILLE, WHO KILLED A GERMAN EVERY MONTH WITH A HERSTAL 7.65 MM, WITHOUT ANYONE EVER DISCOVERING HIS IDENTITY.
NONE OF THESE CHARACTERS REALLY HAS ANY LINK WITH THE LEPER, IT'S ANNOYING.

2 • The Cemetery

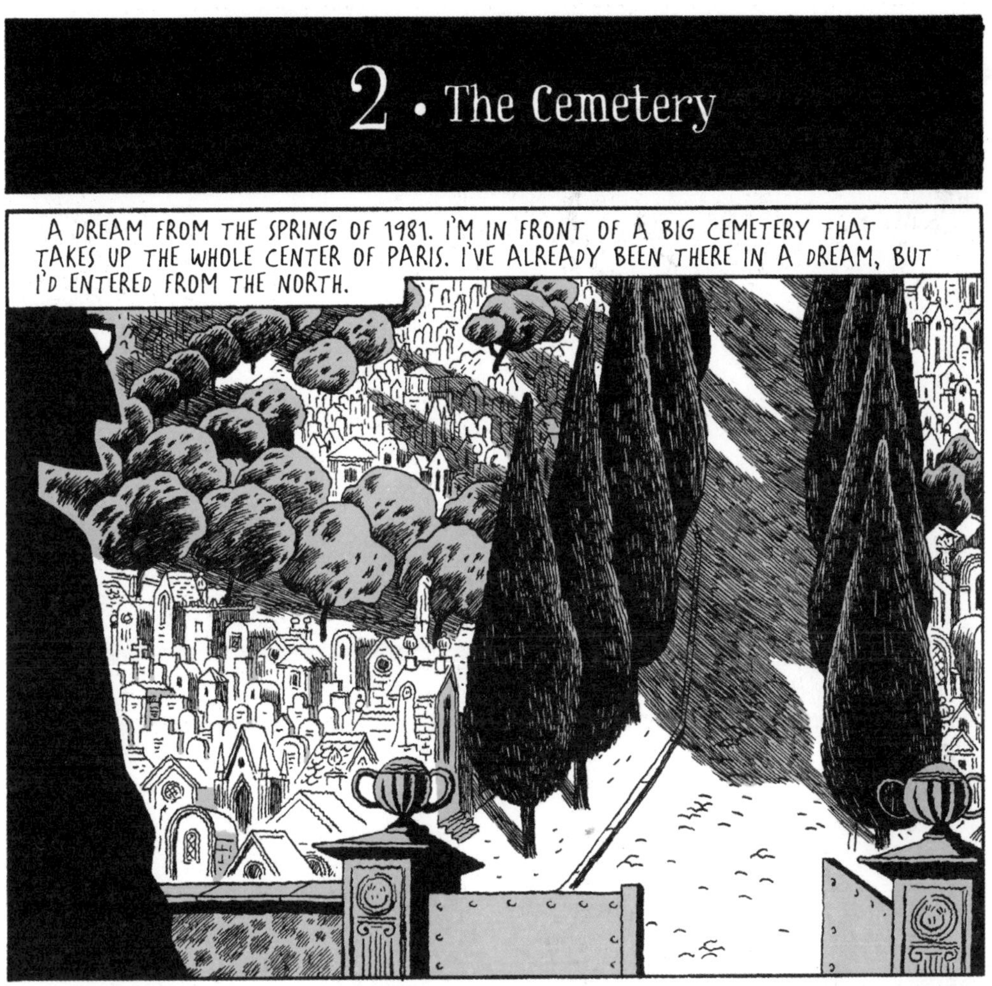
A DREAM FROM THE SPRING OF 1981. I'M IN FRONT OF A BIG CEMETERY THAT TAKES UP THE WHOLE CENTER OF PARIS. I'VE ALREADY BEEN THERE IN A DREAM, BUT I'D ENTERED FROM THE NORTH.

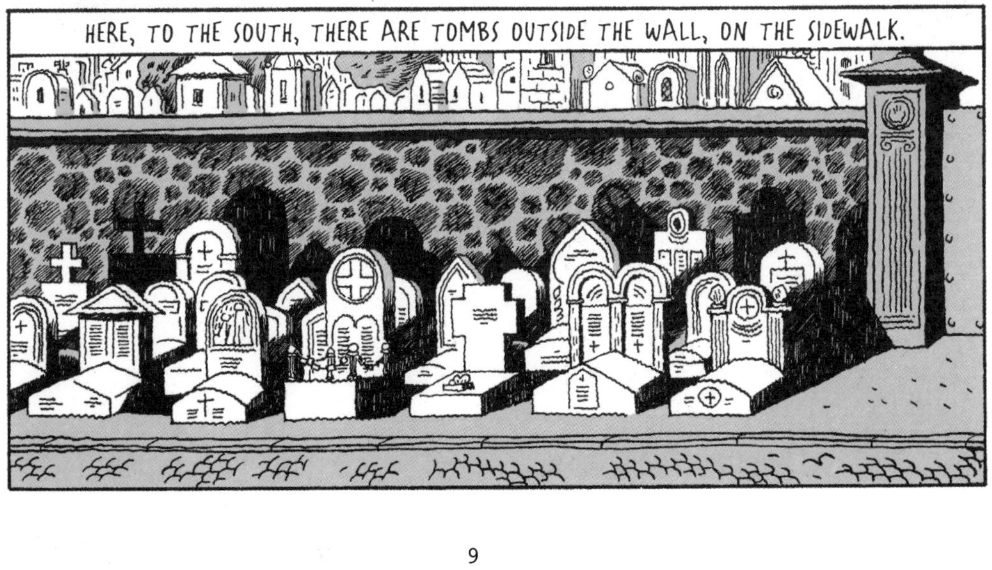
HERE, TO THE SOUTH, THERE ARE TOMBS OUTSIDE THE WALL, ON THE SIDEWALK.

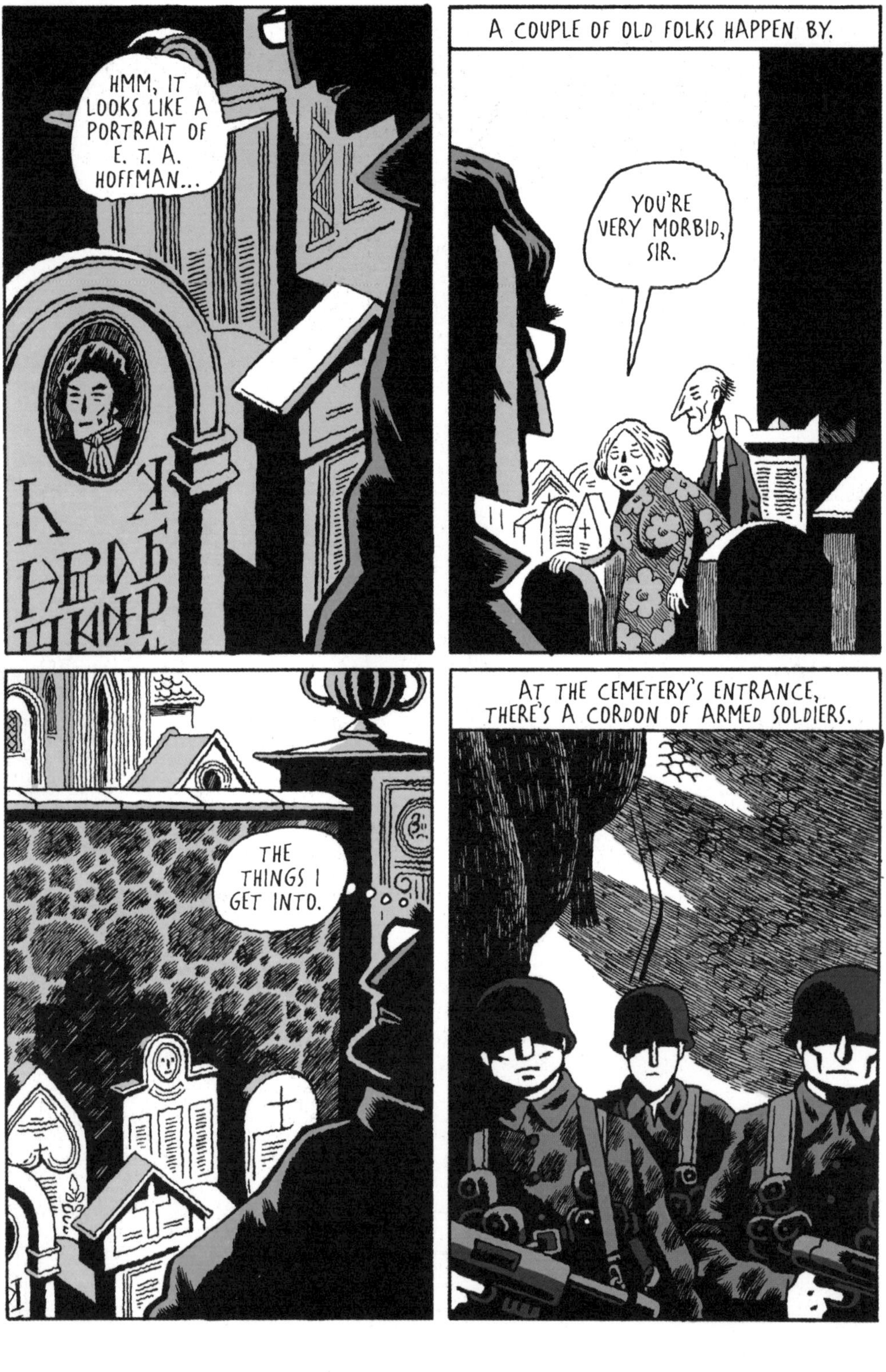
HMM, IT LOOKS LIKE A PORTRAIT OF E. T. A. HOFFMAN...
A COUPLE OF OLD FOLKS HAPPEN BY.
YOU'RE VERY MORBID, SIR.
THE THINGS I GET INTO.
AT THE CEMETERY'S ENTRANCE, THERE'S A CORDON OF ARMED SOLDIERS.

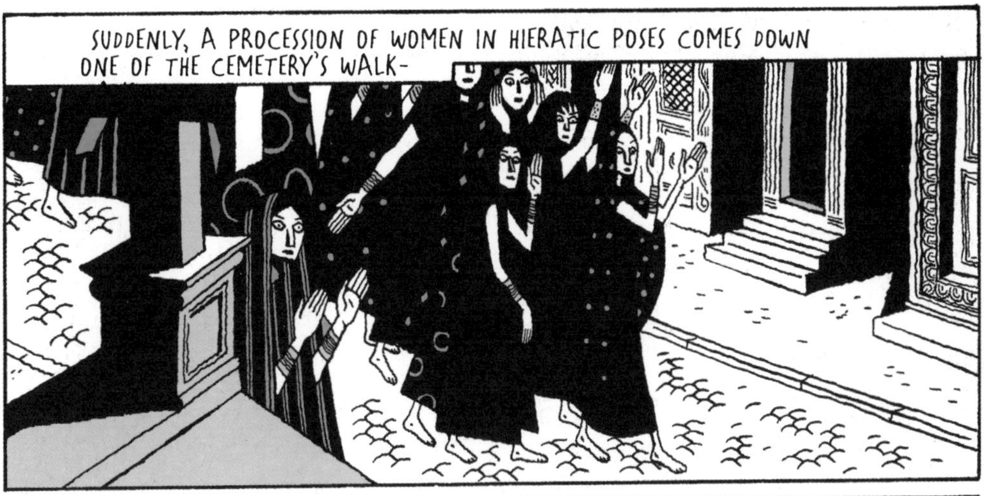
SUDDENLY, A PROCESSION OF WOMEN IN HIERATIC POSES COMES DOWN ONE OF THE CEMETERY'S WALK-

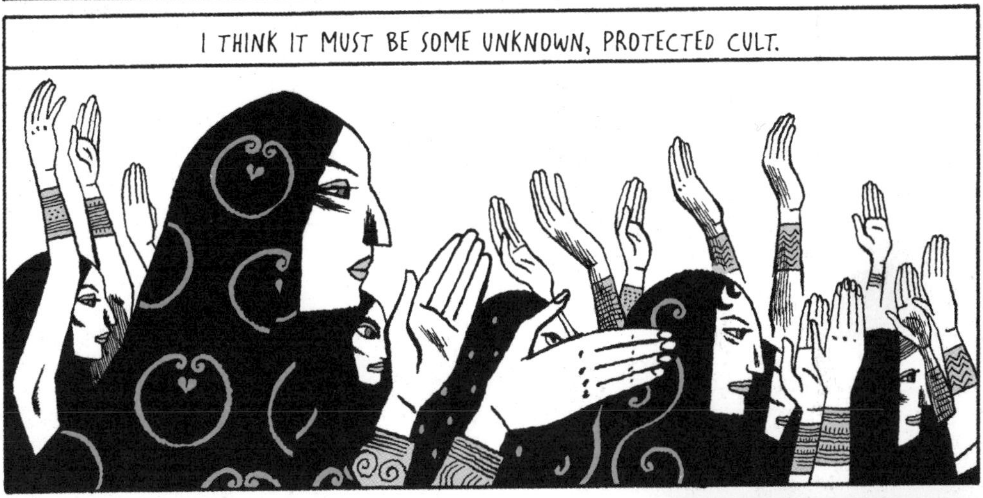
I THINK IT MUST BE SOME UNKNOWN, PROTECTED CULT.

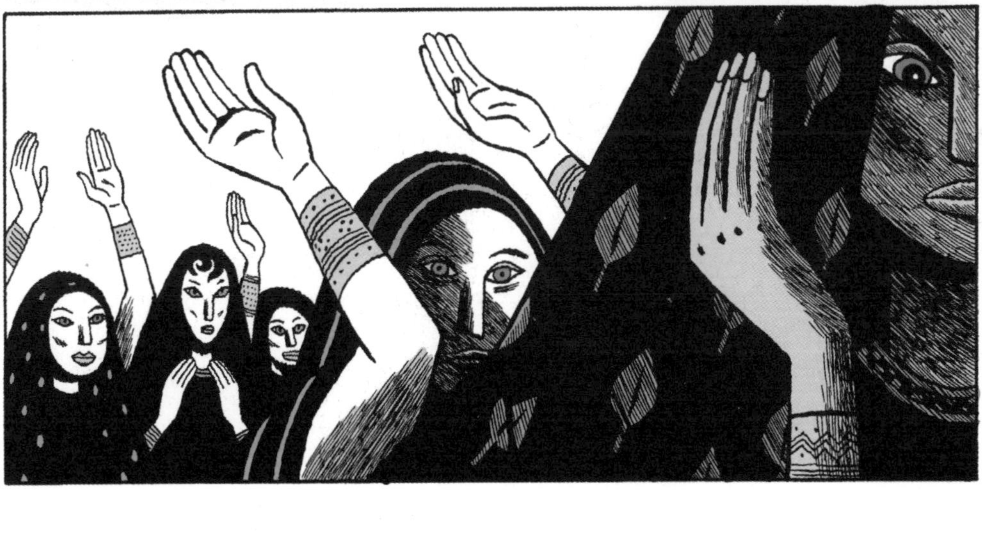

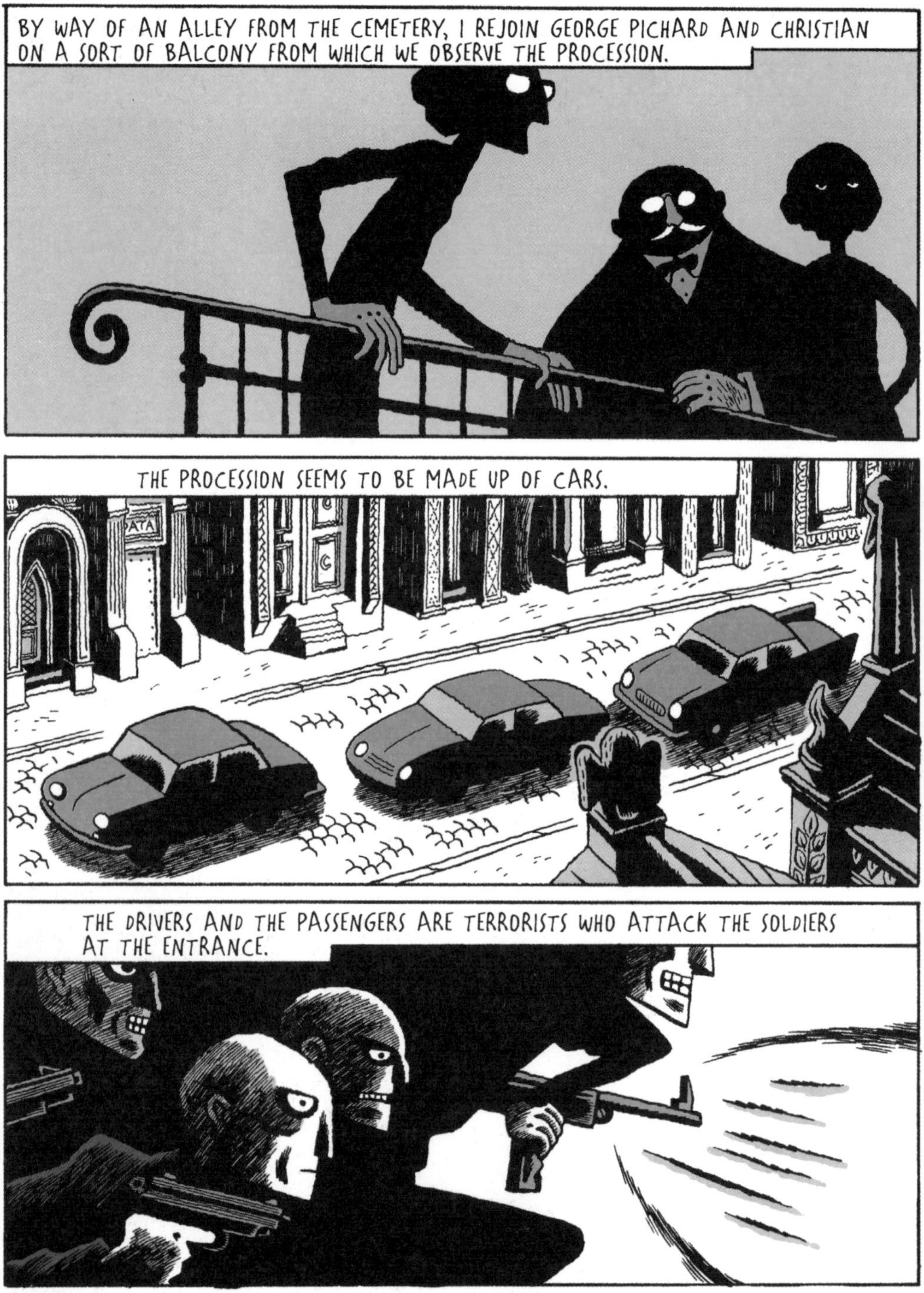
BY WAY OF AN ALLEY FROM THE CEMETERY, I REJOIN GEORGE PICHARD AND CHRISTIAN ON A SORT OF BALCONY FROM WHICH WE OBSERVE THE PROCESSION.
THE PROCESSION SEEMS TO BE MADE UP OF CARS.
THE DRIVERS AND THE PASSENGERS ARE TERRORISTS WHO ATTACK THE SOLDIERS AT THE ENTRANCE.

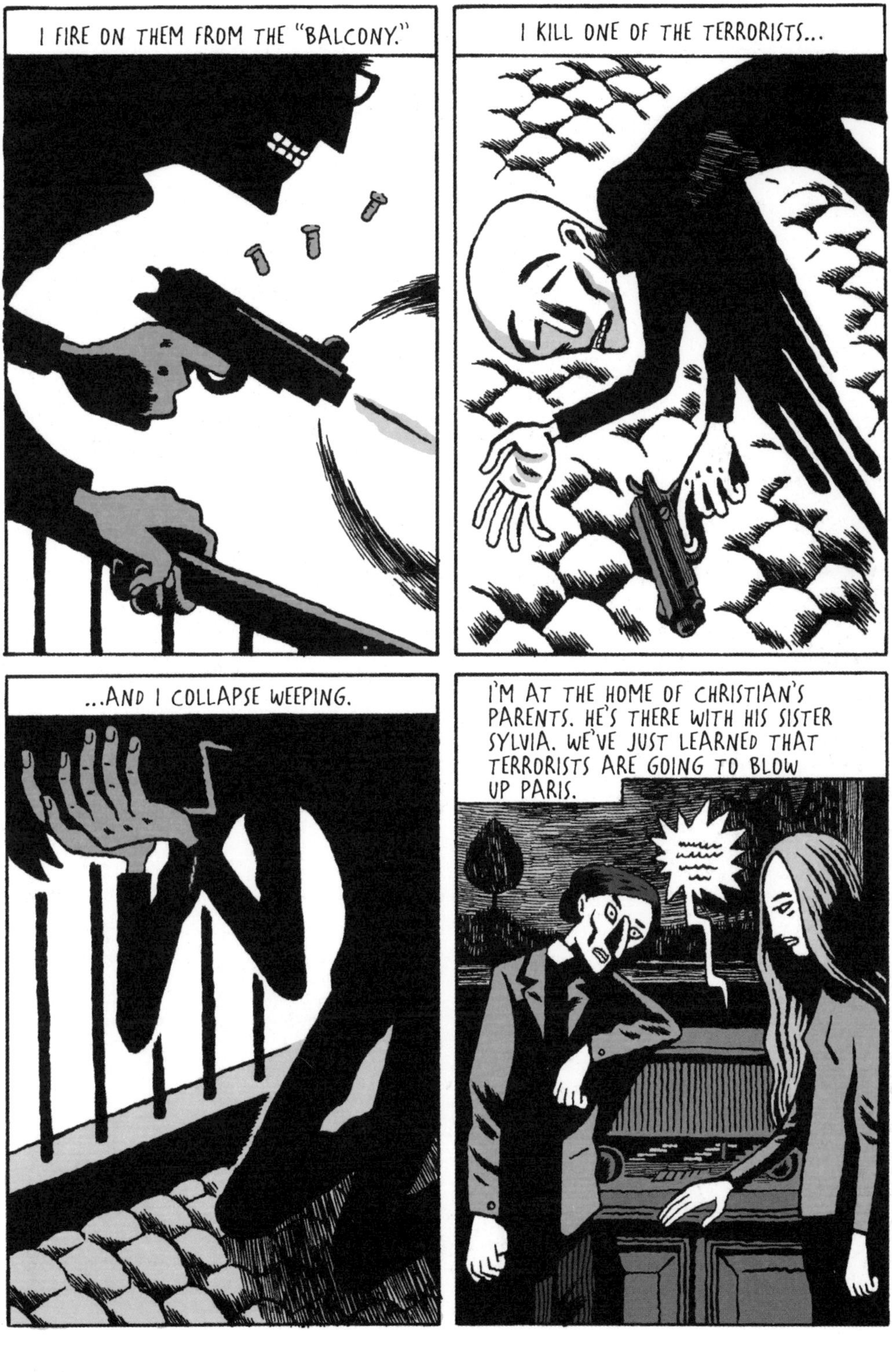
I FIRE ON THEM FROM THE "BALCONY."
I KILL ONE OF THE TERRORISTS...
...AND I COLLAPSE WEEPING.
I'M AT THE HOME OF CHRISTIAN'S PARENTS. HE'S THERE WITH HIS SISTER SYLVIA. WE'VE JUST LEARNED THAT TERRORISTS ARE GOING TO BLOW UP PARIS.

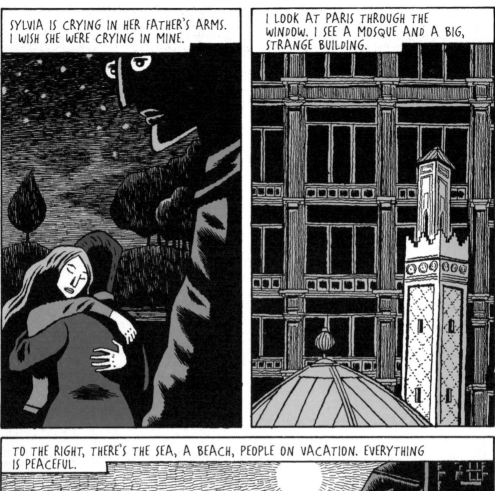

SYLVIA IS CRYING IN HER FATHER'S ARMS. I WISH SHE WERE CRYING IN MINE.

I LOOK AT PARIS THROUGH THE WINDOW. I SEE A MOSQUE AND A BIG, STRANGE BUILDING.

TO THE RIGHT, THERE'S THE SEA, A BEACH, PEOPLE ON VACATION. EVERYTHING IS PEACEFUL.

3 • Eyes

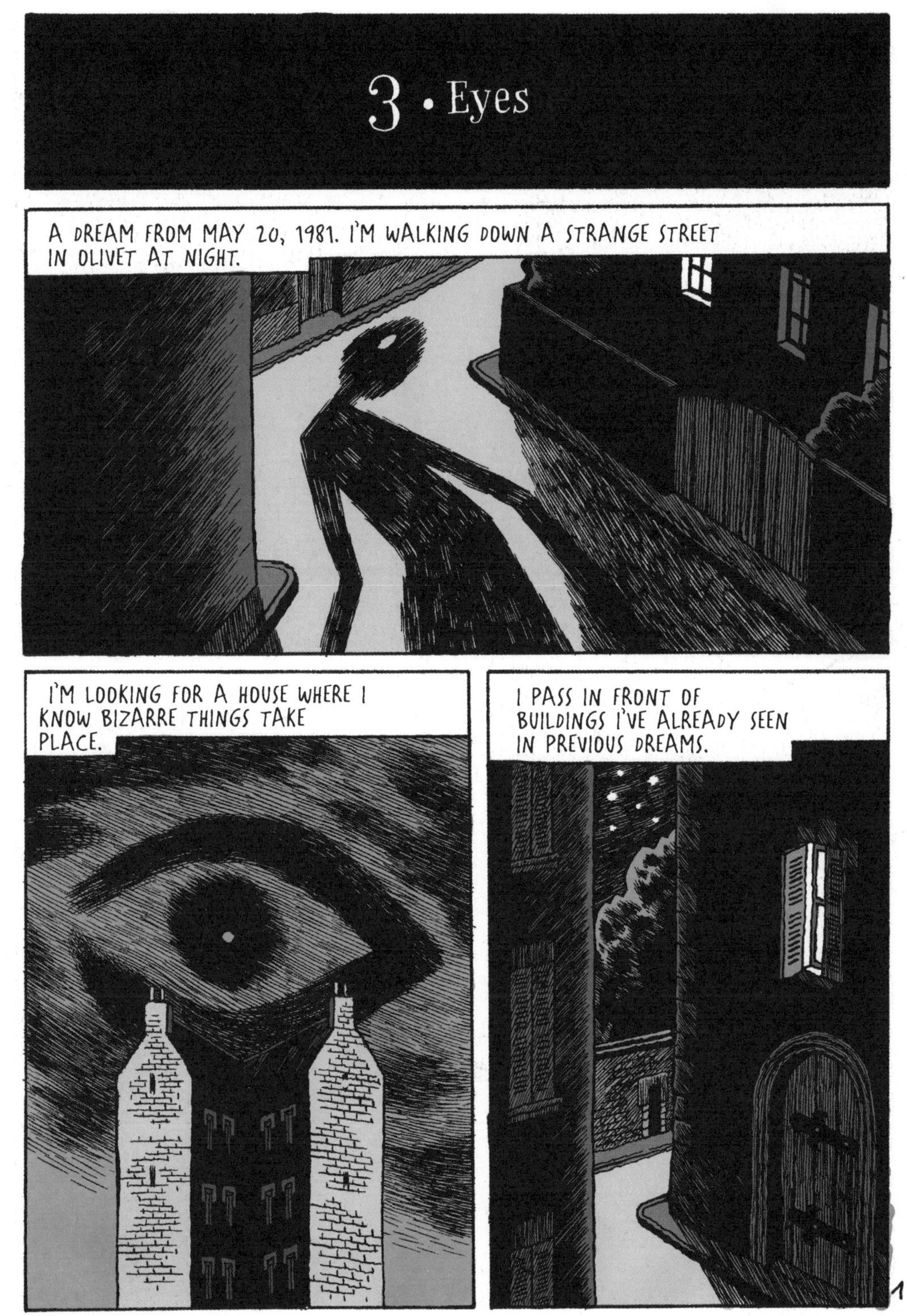
A DREAM FROM MAY 20, 1981. I'M WALKING DOWN A STRANGE STREET IN OLIVET AT NIGHT.
I'M LOOKING FOR A HOUSE WHERE I KNOW BIZARRE THINGS TAKE PLACE.
I PASS IN FRONT OF BUILDINGS I'VE ALREADY SEEN IN PREVIOUS DREAMS.

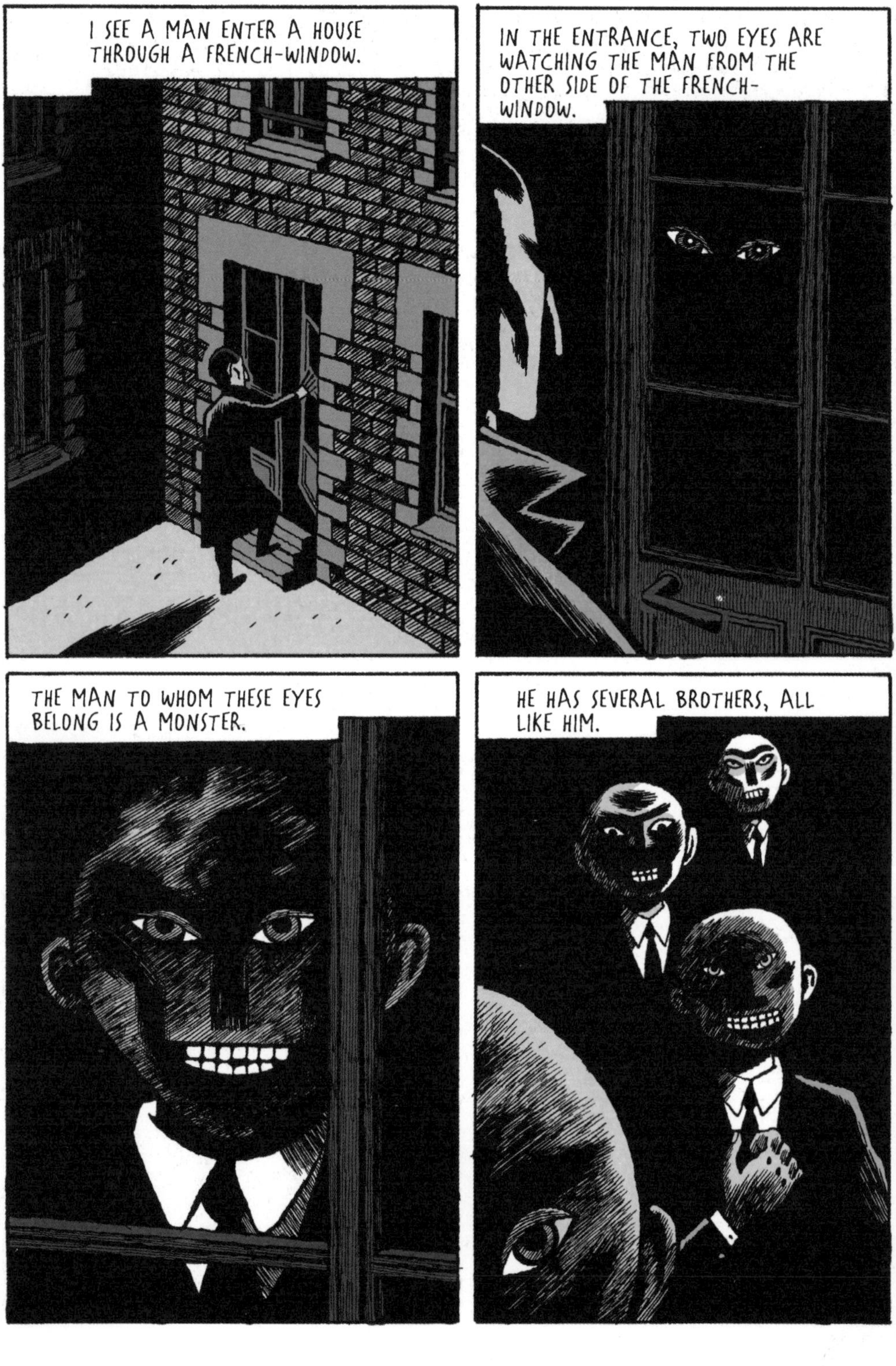
I SEE A MAN ENTER A HOUSE THROUGH A FRENCH-WINDOW.
IN THE ENTRANCE, TWO EYES ARE WATCHING THE MAN FROM THE OTHER SIDE OF THE FRENCH-WINDOW.
THE MAN TO WHOM THESE EYES BELONG IS A MONSTER.
HE HAS SEVERAL BROTHERS, ALL LIKE HIM.

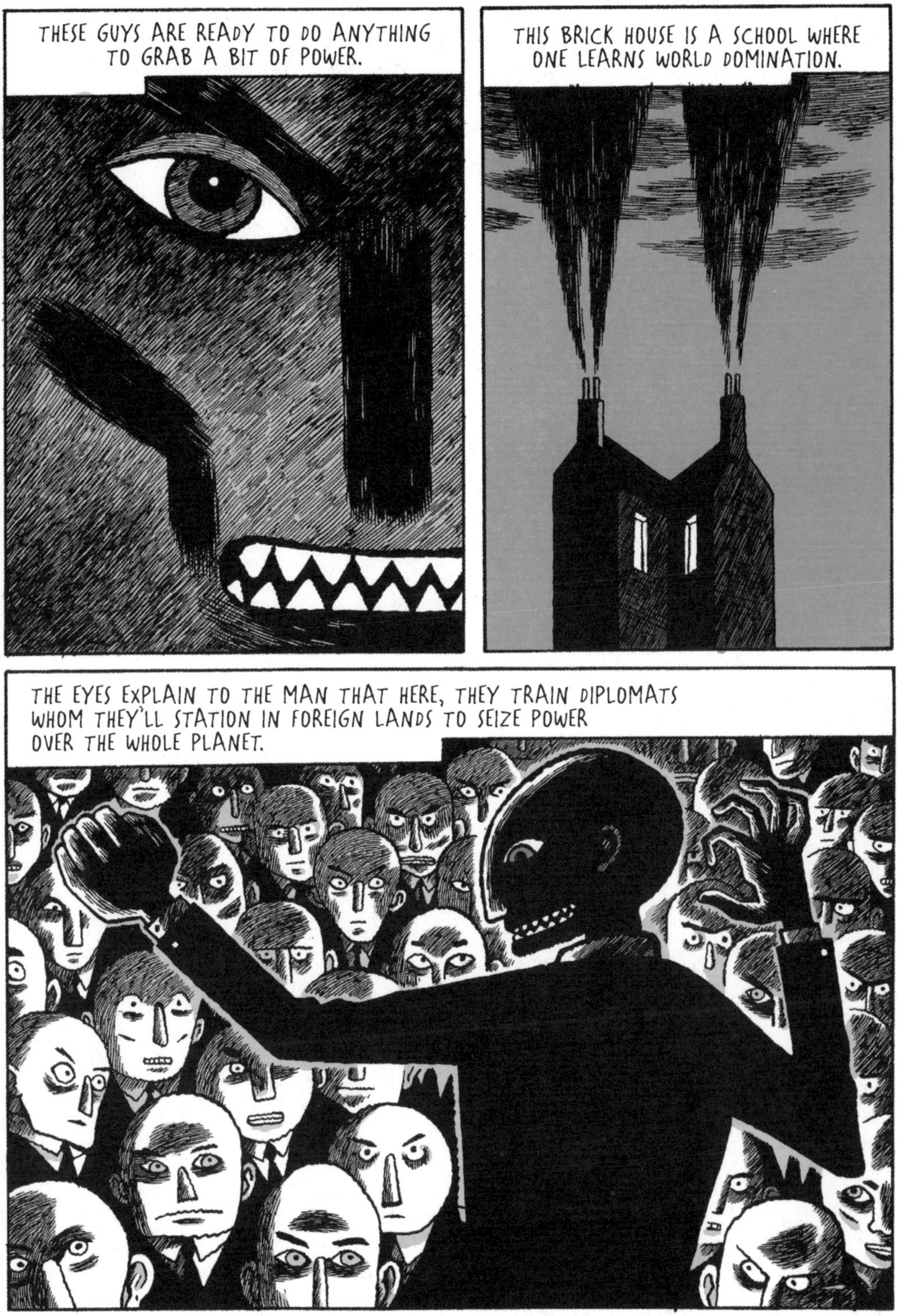
THESE GUYS ARE READY TO DO ANYTHING TO GRAB A BIT OF POWER.
THIS BRICK HOUSE IS A SCHOOL WHERE ONE LEARNS WORLD DOMINATION.
THE EYES EXPLAIN TO THE MAN THAT HERE, THEY TRAIN DIPLOMATS WHOM THEY'LL STATION IN FOREIGN LANDS TO SEIZE POWER OVER THE WHOLE PLANET.

4 • Windows

A DREAM FROM MAY 28, 1981

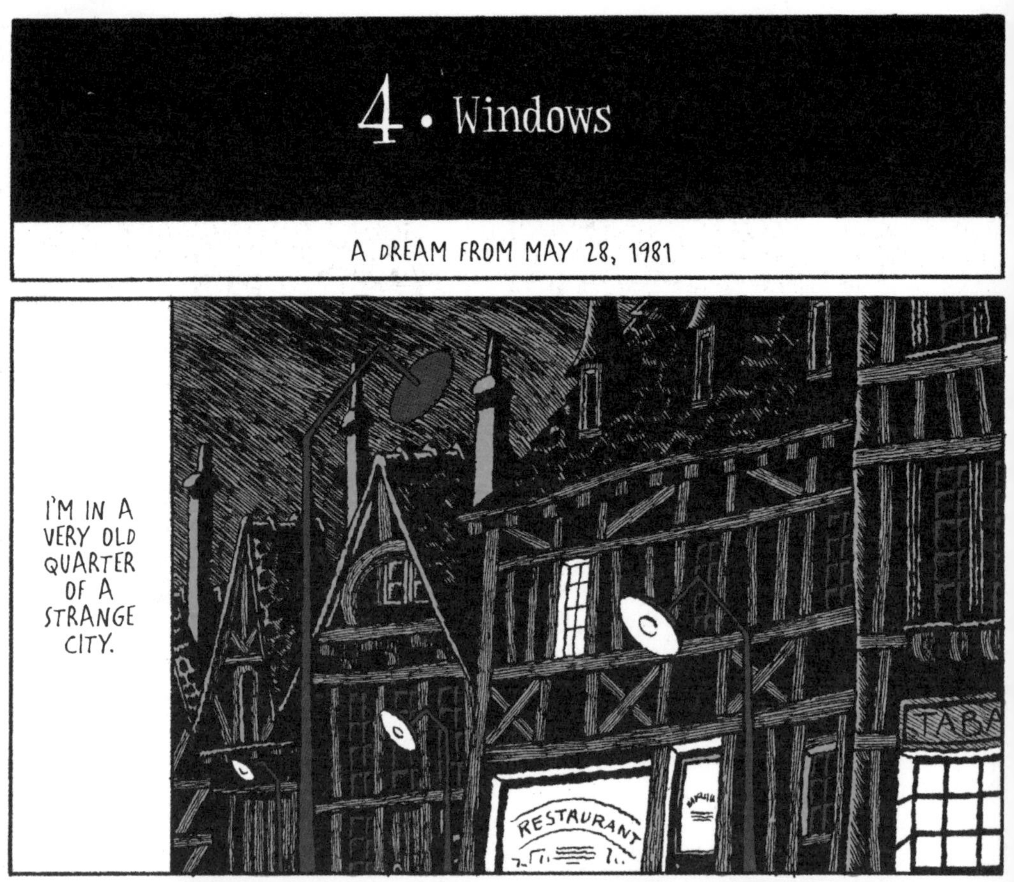
I'M IN A VERY OLD QUARTER OF A STRANGE CITY.
RESTAURANT
TABA

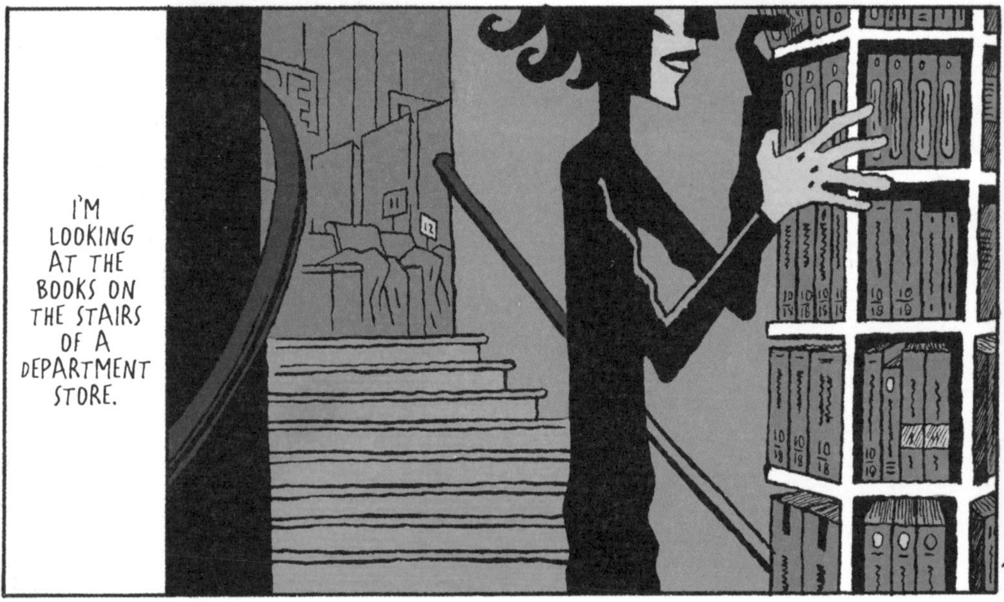
I'M LOOKING AT THE BOOKS ON THE STAIRS OF A DEPARTMENT STORE.

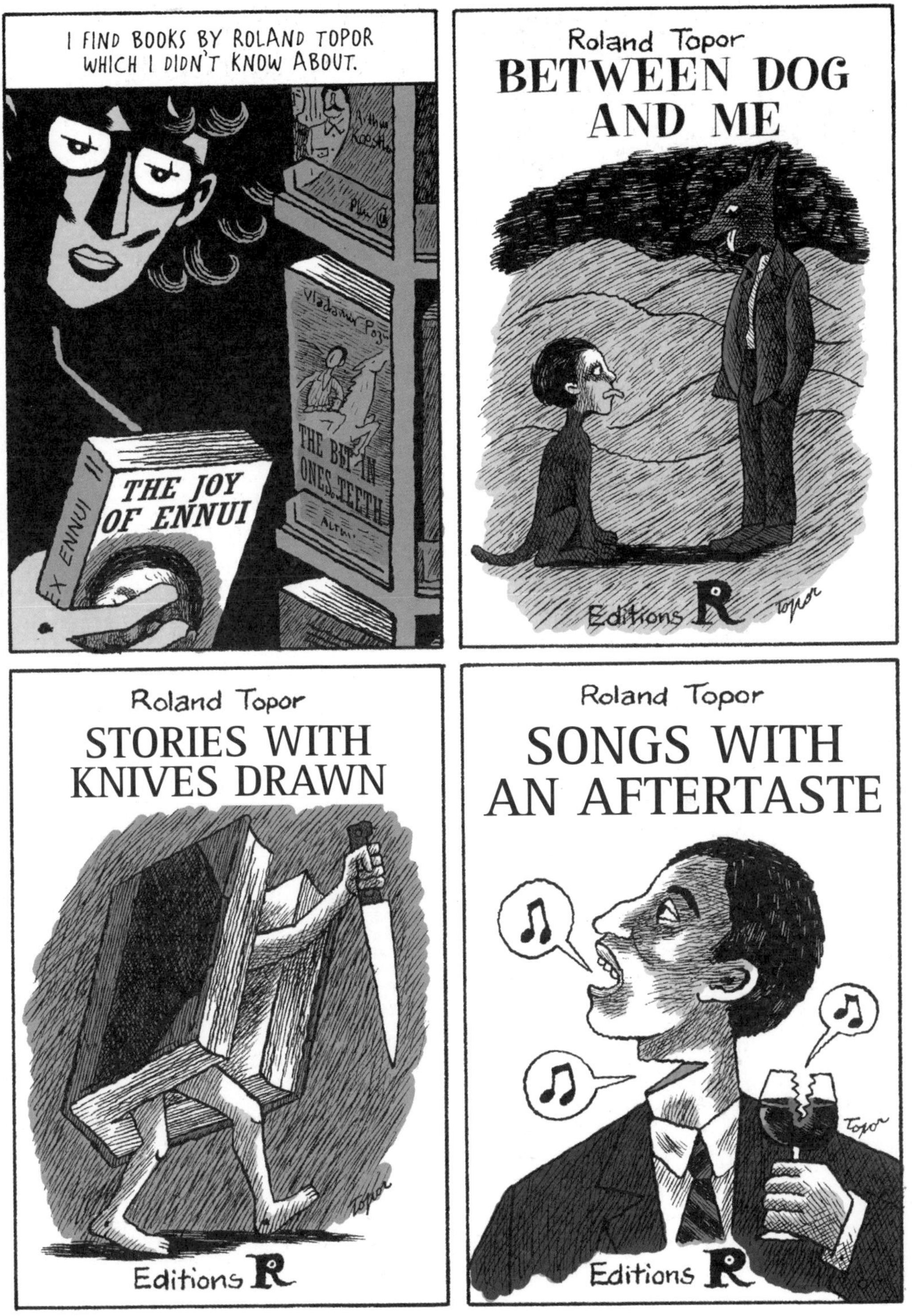
I FIND BOOKS BY ROLAND TOPOR WHICH I DIDN'T KNOW ABOUT.
THE JOY OF ENNUI
Roland Topor
BETWEEN DOG AND ME
Editions R
Roland Topor
STORIES WITH KNIVES DRAWN
Editions R
Roland Topor
SONGS WITH AN AFTERTASTE
Editions R

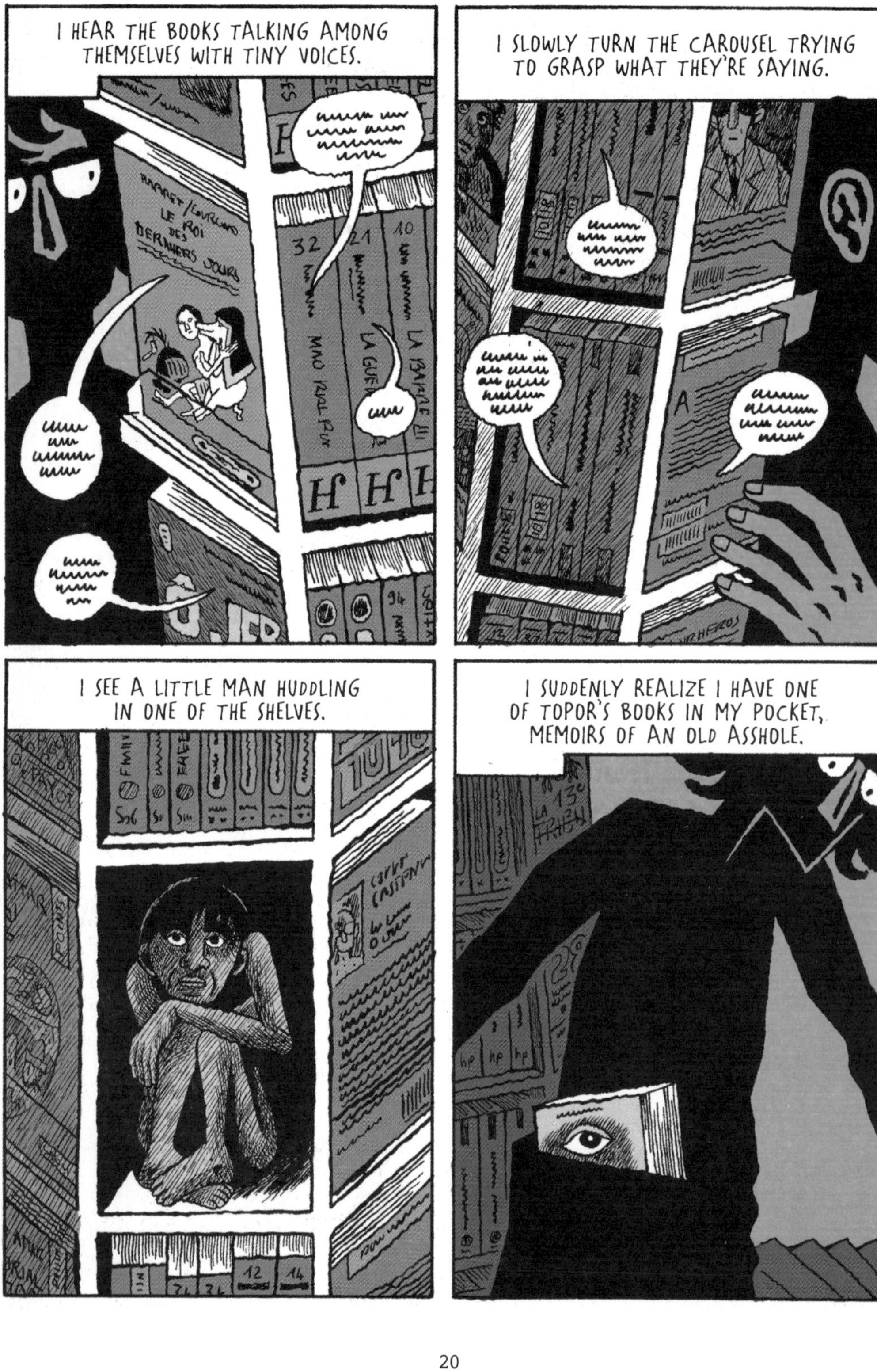
I HEAR THE BOOKS TALKING AMONG THEMSELVES WITH TINY VOICES.
I SLOWLY TURN THE CAROUSEL TRYING TO GRASP WHAT THEY'RE SAYING.
I SEE A LITTLE MAN HUDDLING IN ONE OF THE SHELVES.
I SUDDENLY REALIZE I HAVE ONE OF TOPOR'S BOOKS IN MY POCKET, MEMOIRS OF AN OLD ASSHOLE.

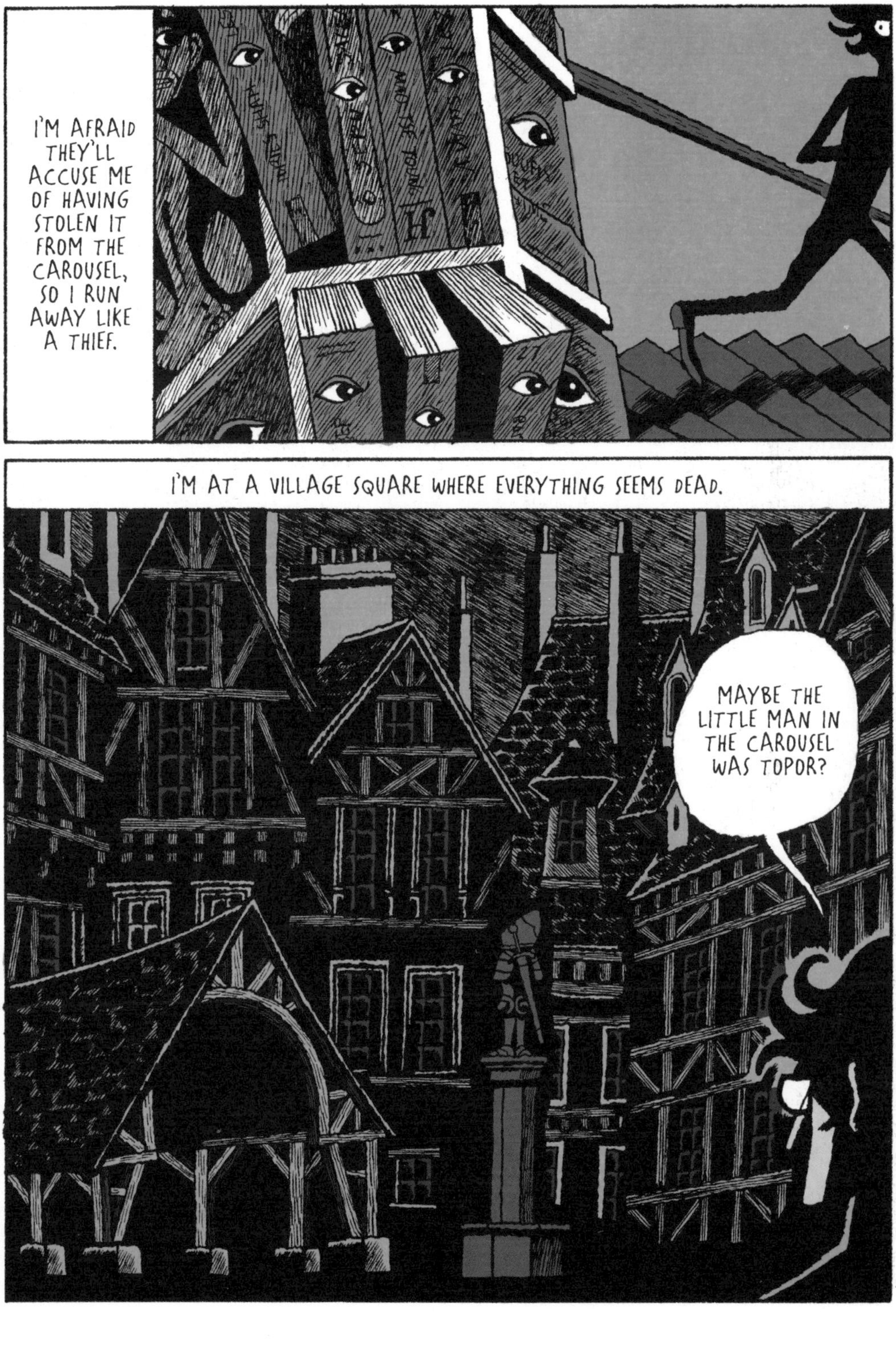
I'M AFRAID THEY'LL ACCUSE ME OF HAVING STOLEN IT FROM THE CAROUSEL, SO I RUN AWAY LIKE A THIEF.
I'M AT A VILLAGE SQUARE WHERE EVERYTHING SEEMS DEAD.
MAYBE THE LITTLE MAN IN THE CAROUSEL WAS TOPOR?

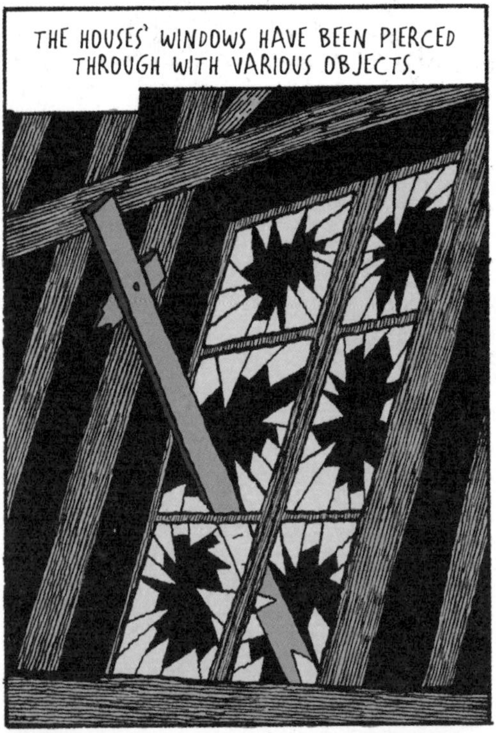
THE HOUSES' WINDOWS HAVE BEEN PIERCED THROUGH WITH VARIOUS OBJECTS.
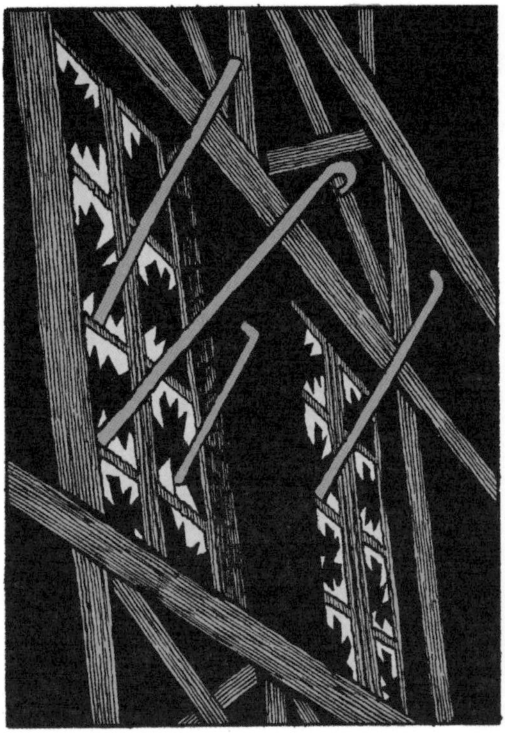
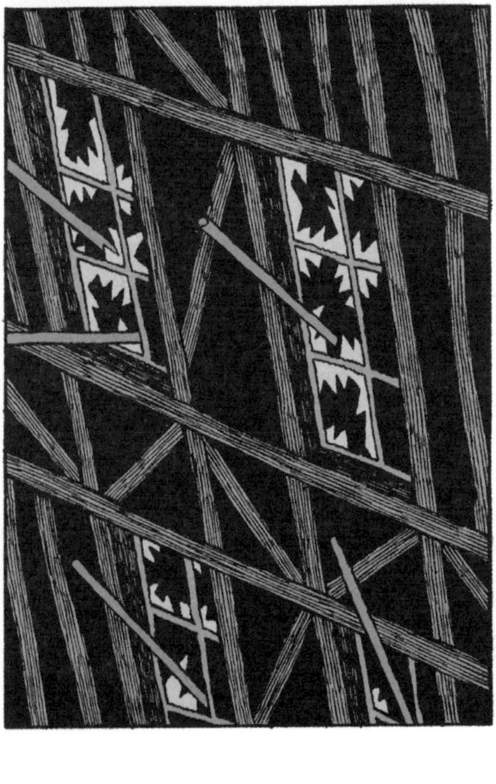
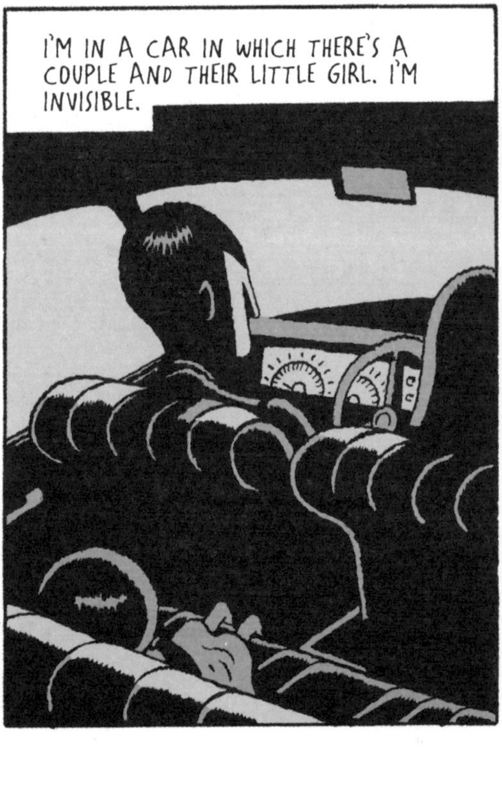
I'M IN A CAR IN WHICH THERE'S A COUPLE AND THEIR LITTLE GIRL. I'M INVISIBLE.

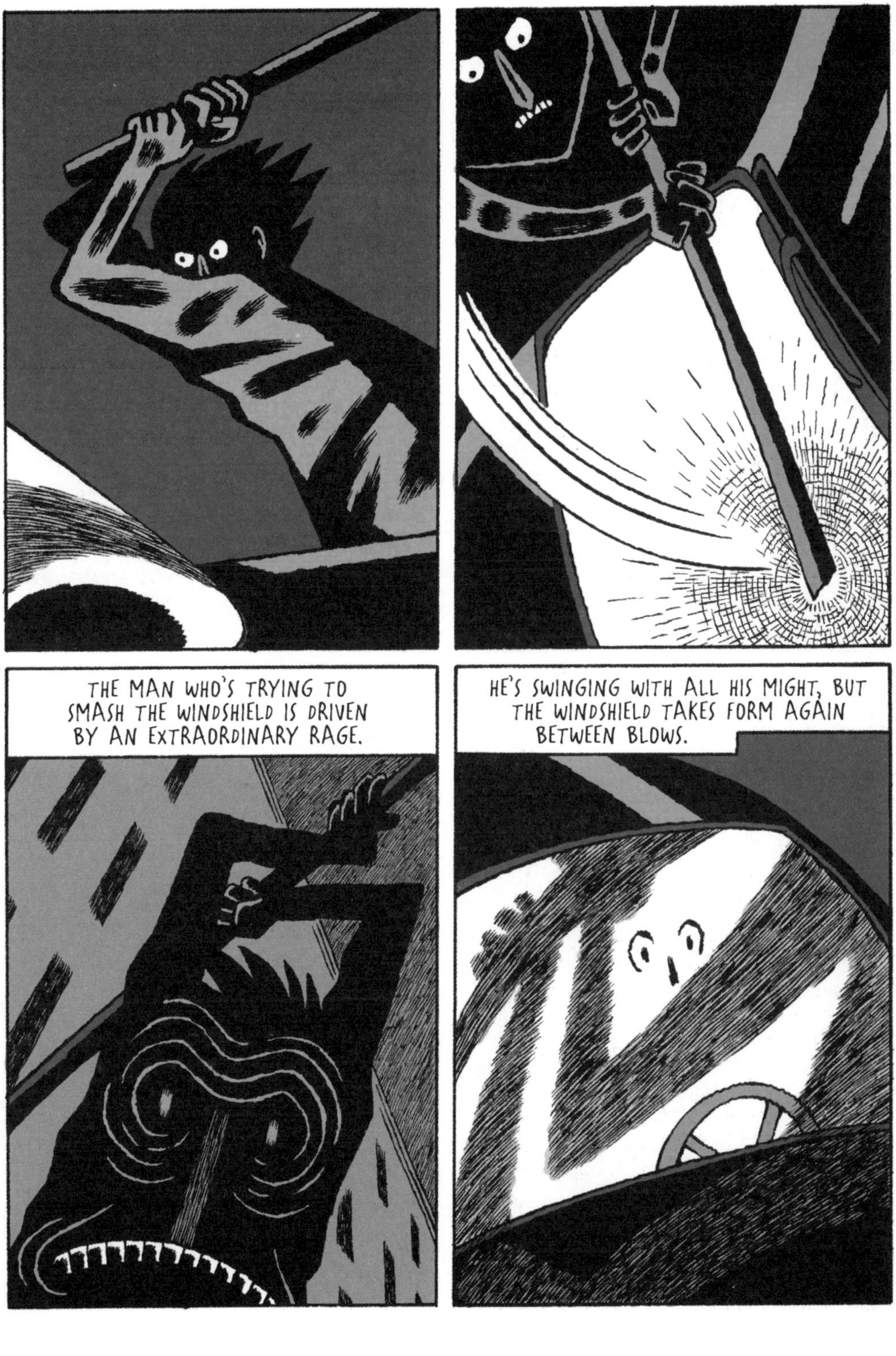
THE MAN WHO'S TRYING TO SMASH THE WINDSHIELD IS DRIVEN BY AN EXTRAORDINARY RAGE.
HE'S SWINGING WITH ALL HIS MIGHT, BUT THE WINDSHIELD TAKES FORM AGAIN BETWEEN BLOWS.

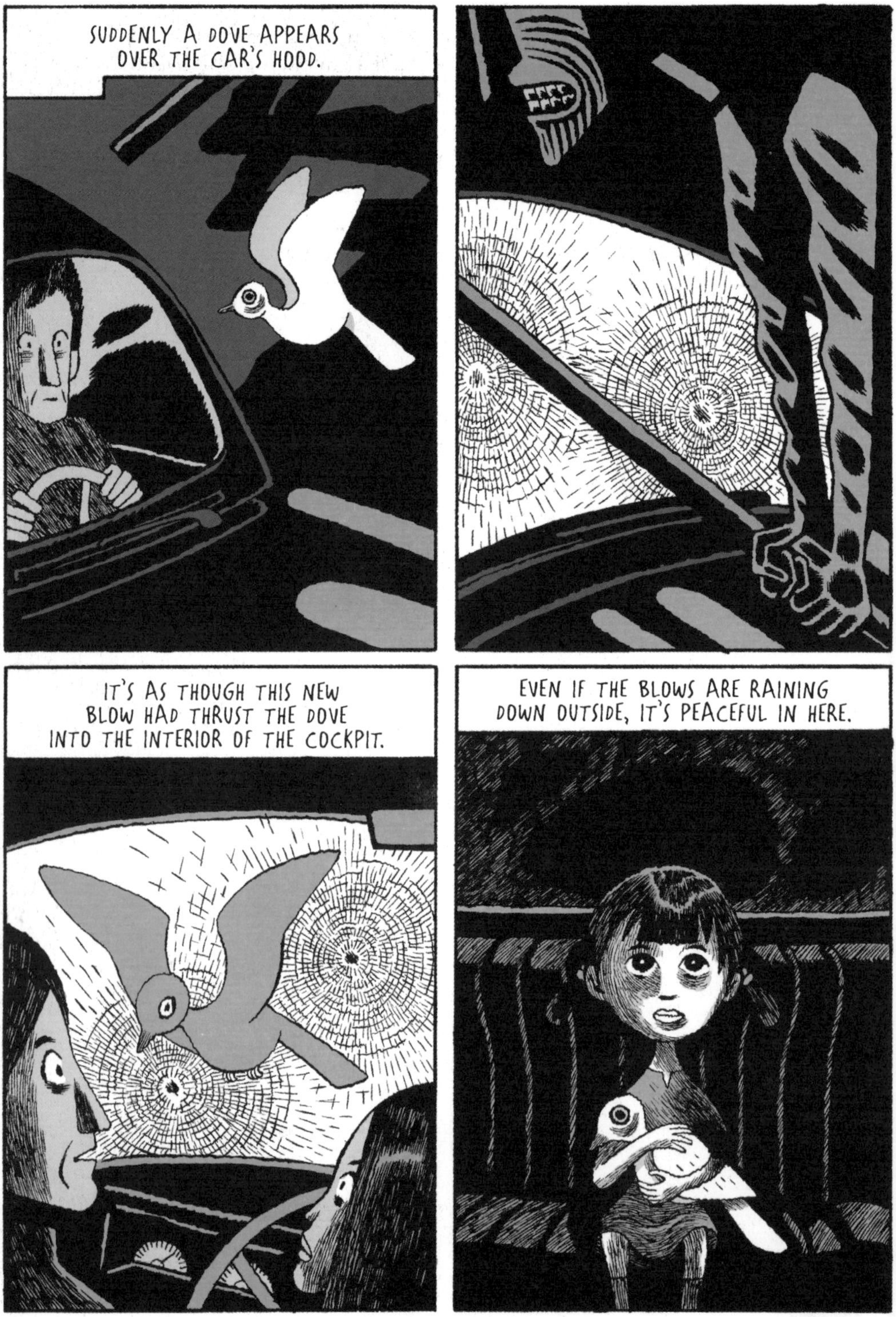
SUDDENLY A DOVE APPEARS OVER THE CAR'S HOOD.
IT'S AS THOUGH THIS NEW BLOW HAD THRUST THE DOVE INTO THE INTERIOR OF THE COCKPIT.
EVEN IF THE BLOWS ARE RAINING DOWN OUTSIDE, IT'S PEACEFUL IN HERE.

5 · Paris

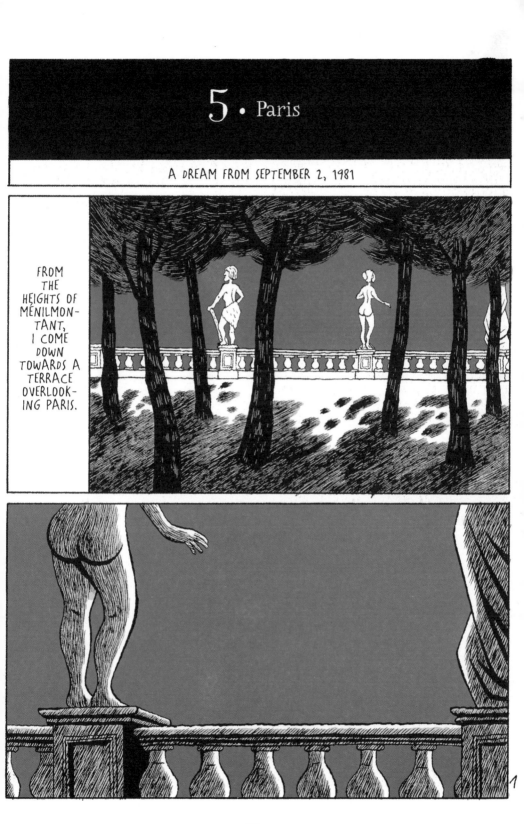

FROM THE HEIGHTS OF MÉNILMONTANT, I COME DOWN TOWARDS A TERRACE OVERLOOKING PARIS.

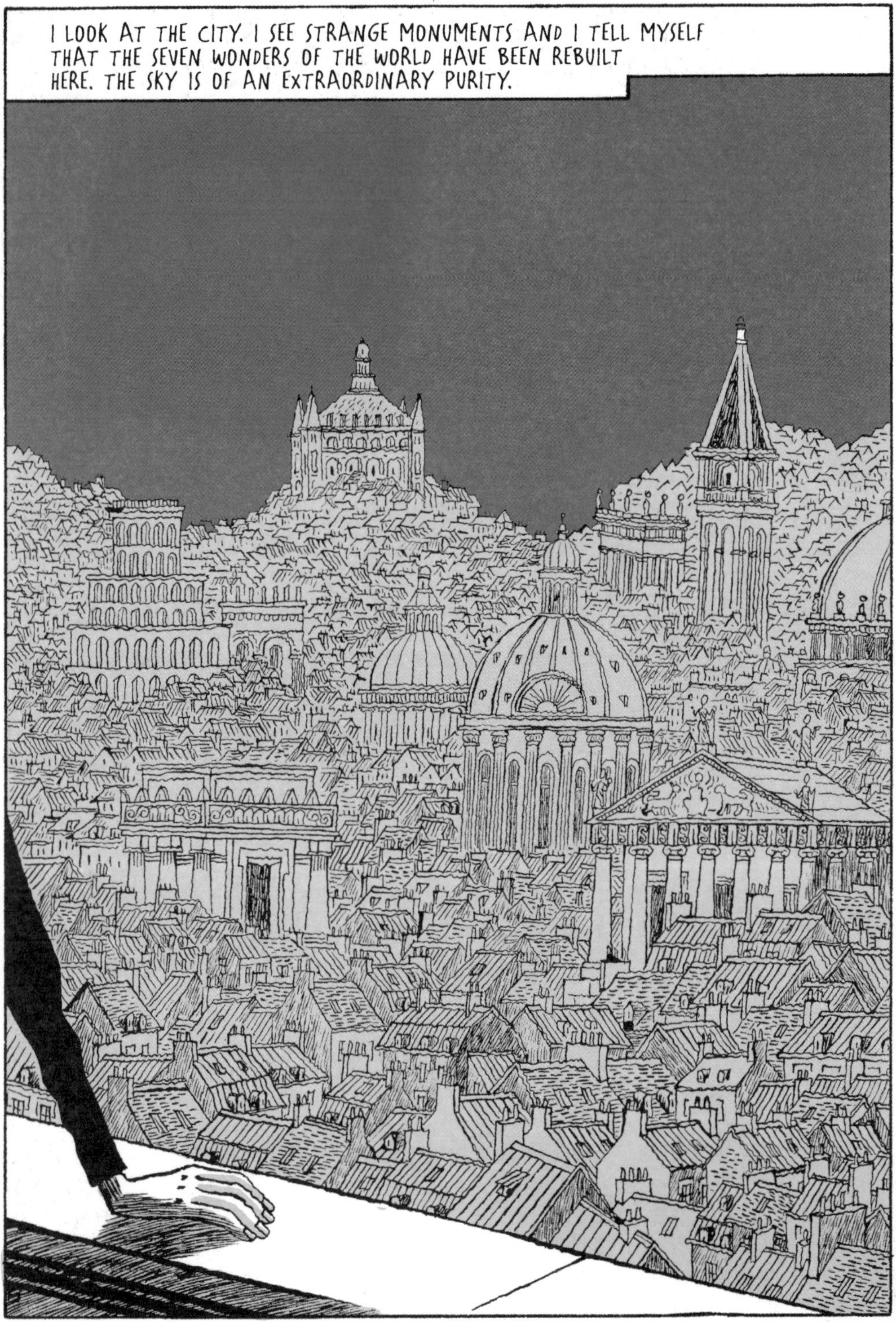
I LOOK AT THE CITY. I SEE STRANGE MONUMENTS AND I TELL MYSELF THAT THE SEVEN WONDERS OF THE WORLD HAVE BEEN REBUILT HERE. THE SKY IS OF AN EXTRAORDINARY PURITY.

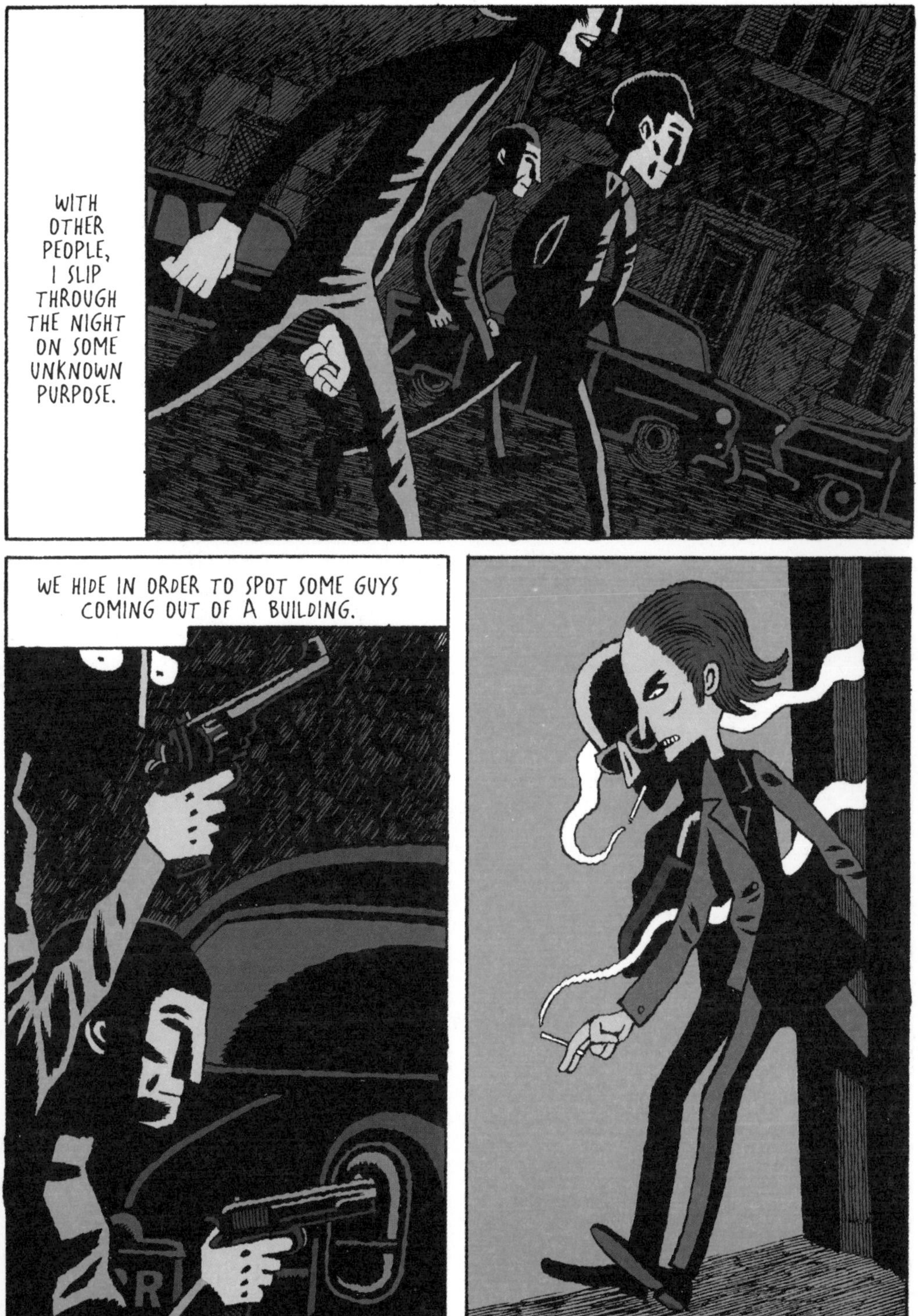
WITH OTHER PEOPLE, I SLIP THROUGH THE NIGHT ON SOME UNKNOWN PURPOSE.
WE HIDE IN ORDER TO SPOT SOME GUYS COMING OUT OF A BUILDING.

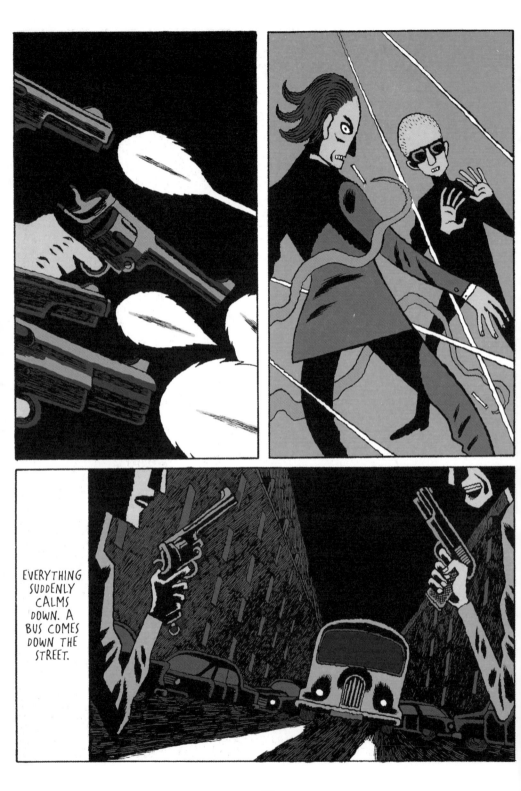

EVERYTHING SUDDENLY CALMS DOWN. A BUS COMES DOWN THE STREET.

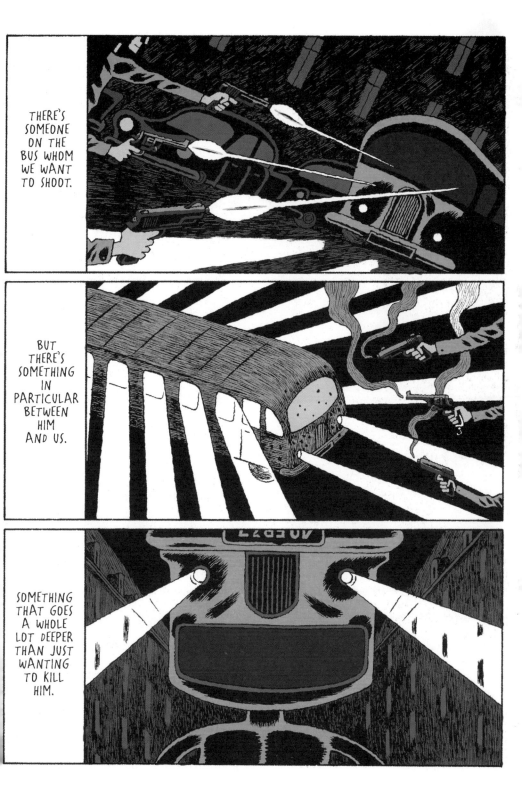

THERE'S SOMEONE ON THE BUS WHOM WE WANT TO SHOOT.

BUT THERE'S SOMETHING IN PARTICULAR BETWEEN HIM AND US.

SOMETHING THAT GOES A WHOLE LOT DEEPER THAN JUST WANTING TO KILL HIM.

6 • The Attic

A DREAM FROM THE NIGHT OF AUGUST 29, 1983.

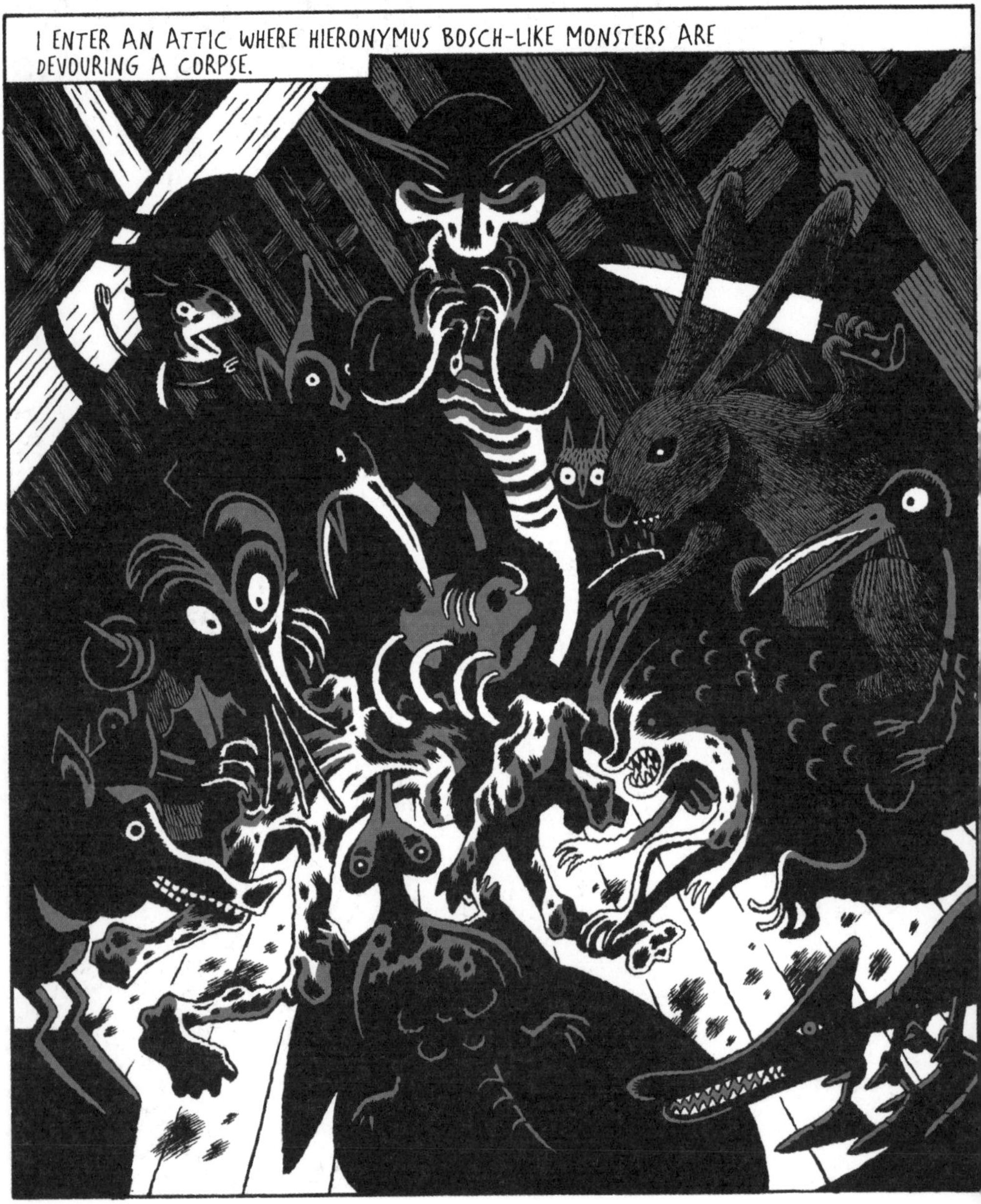
I ENTER AN ATTIC WHERE HIERONYMUS BOSCH-LIKE MONSTERS ARE DEVOURING A CORPSE.

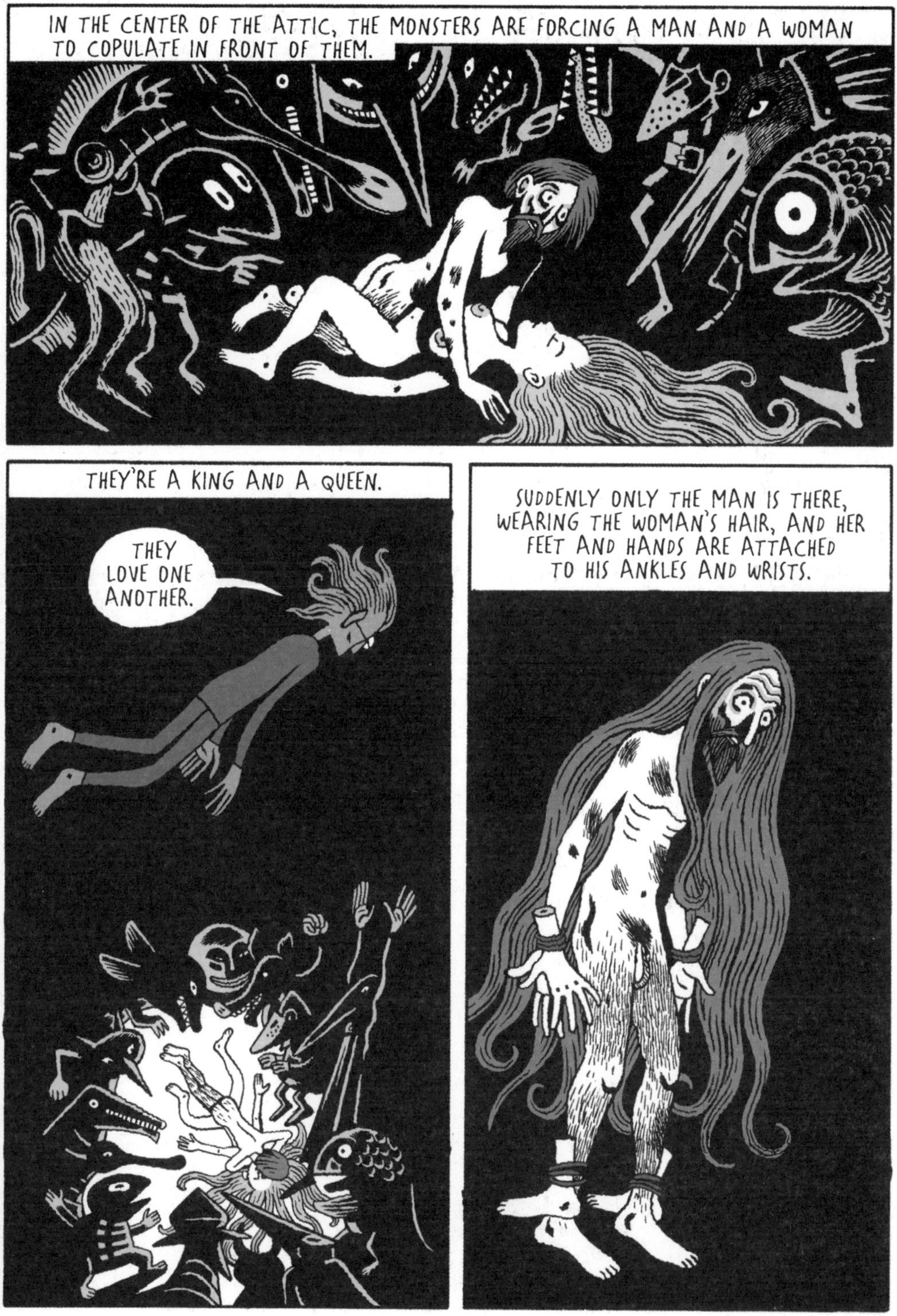
IN THE CENTER OF THE ATTIC, THE MONSTERS ARE FORCING A MAN AND A WOMAN TO COPULATE IN FRONT OF THEM.
THEY'RE A KING AND A QUEEN.
THEY LOVE ONE ANOTHER.
SUDDENLY ONLY THE MAN IS THERE, WEARING THE WOMAN'S HAIR, AND HER FEET AND HANDS ARE ATTACHED TO HIS ANKLES AND WRISTS.

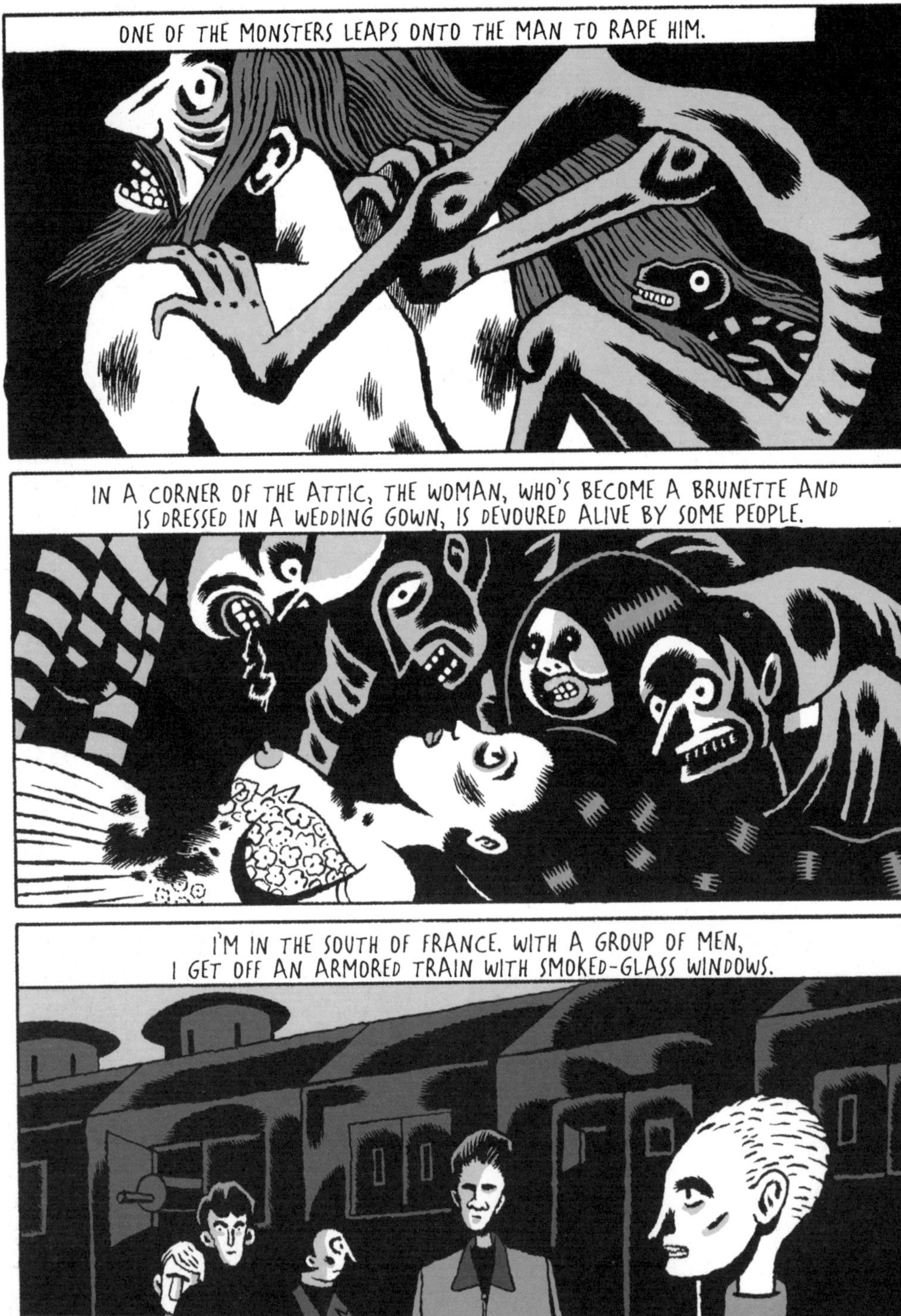
ONE OF THE MONSTERS LEAPS ONTO THE MAN TO RAPE HIM.
IN A CORNER OF THE ATTIC, THE WOMAN, WHO'S BECOME A BRUNETTE AND IS DRESSED IN A WEDDING GOWN, IS DEVOURED ALIVE BY SOME PEOPLE.
I'M IN THE SOUTH OF FRANCE. WITH A GROUP OF MEN, I GET OFF AN ARMORED TRAIN WITH SMOKED-GLASS WINDOWS.

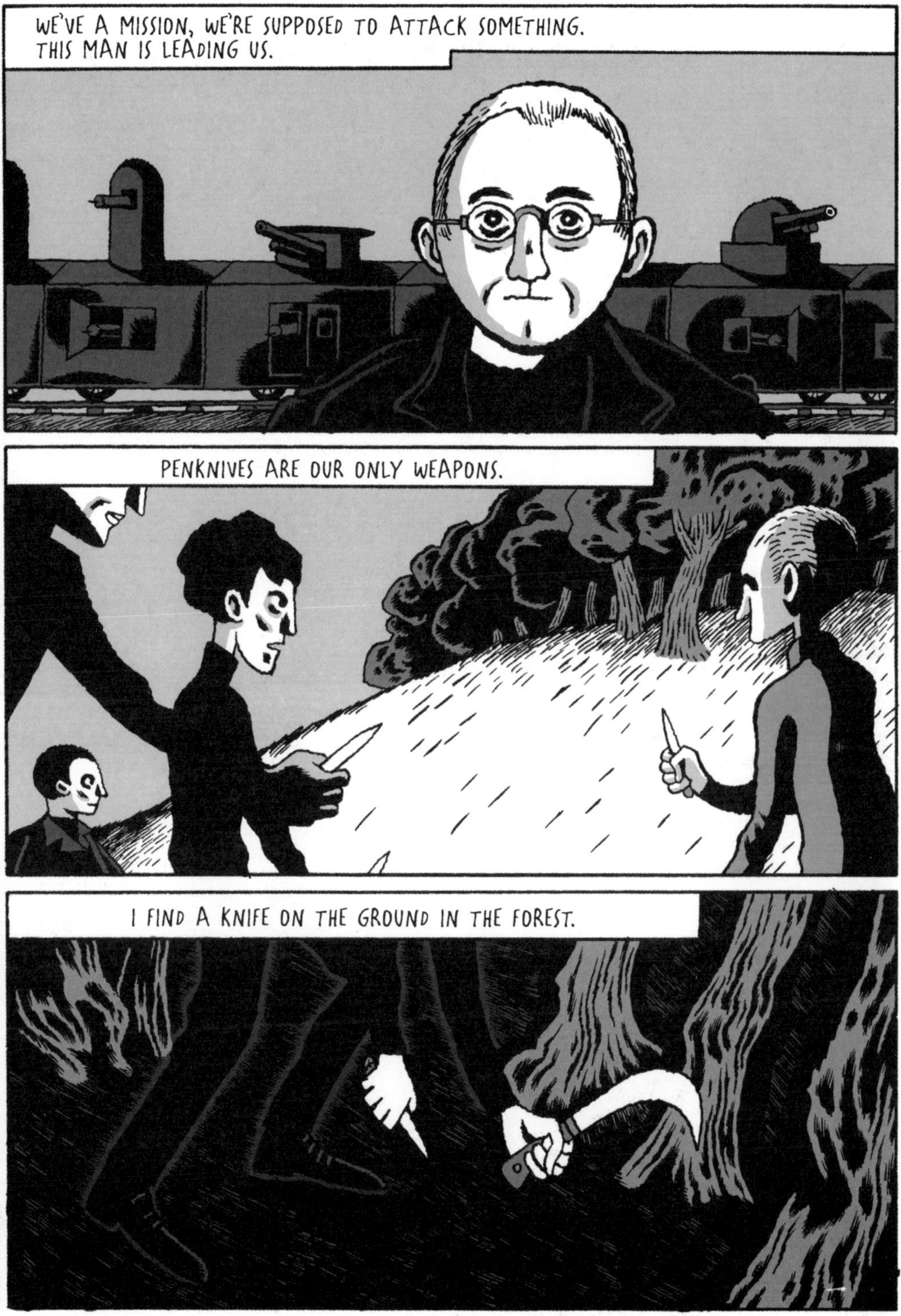
WE'VE A MISSION, WE'RE SUPPOSED TO ATTACK SOMETHING. THIS MAN IS LEADING US.
PENKNIVES ARE OUR ONLY WEAPONS.
I FIND A KNIFE ON THE GROUND IN THE FOREST.

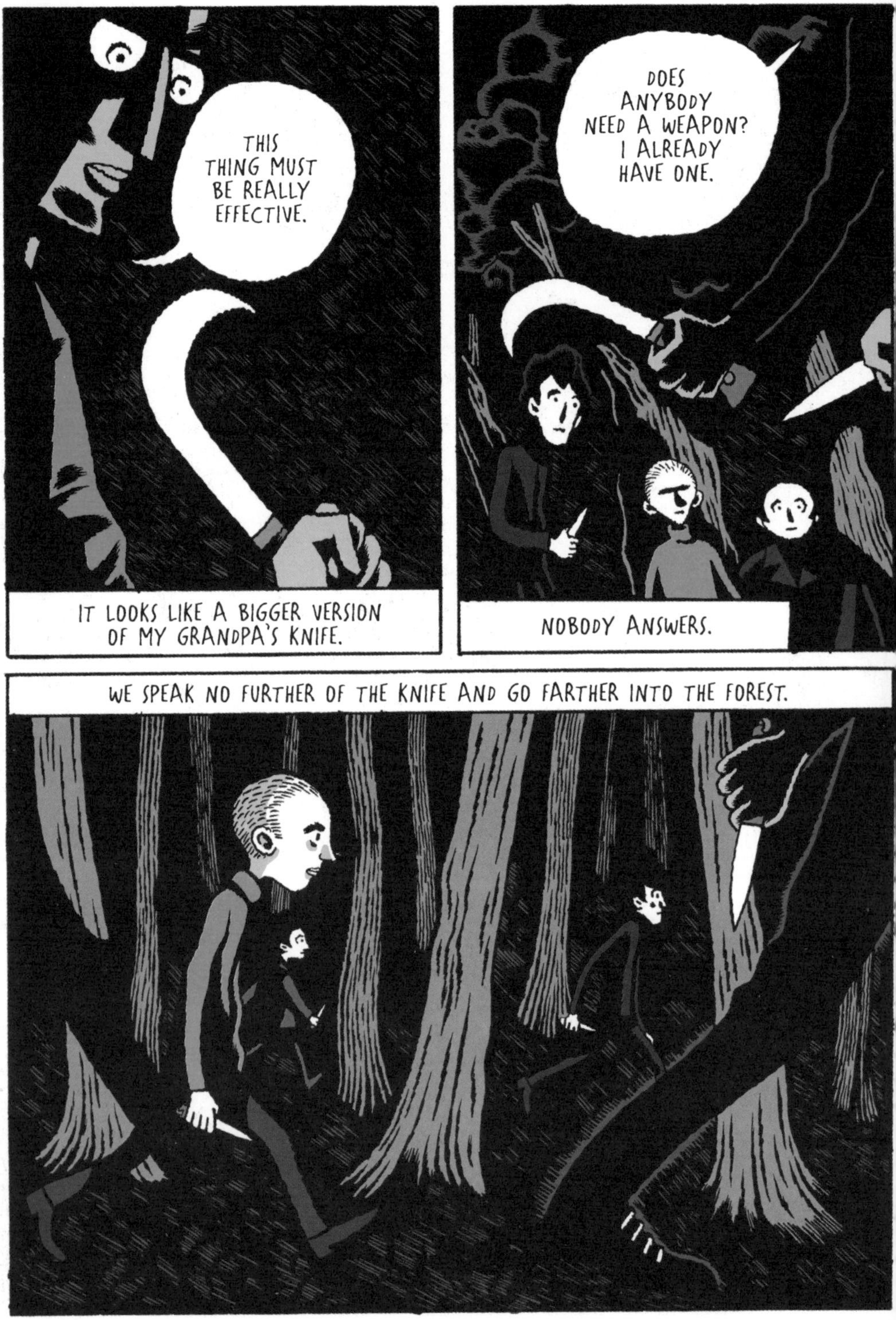
THIS THING MUST BE REALLY EFFECTIVE.
IT LOOKS LIKE A BIGGER VERSION OF MY GRANDPA'S KNIFE.
DOES ANYBODY NEED A WEAPON? I ALREADY HAVE ONE.
NOBODY ANSWERS.
WE SPEAK NO FURTHER OF THE KNIFE AND GO FARTHER INTO THE FOREST.

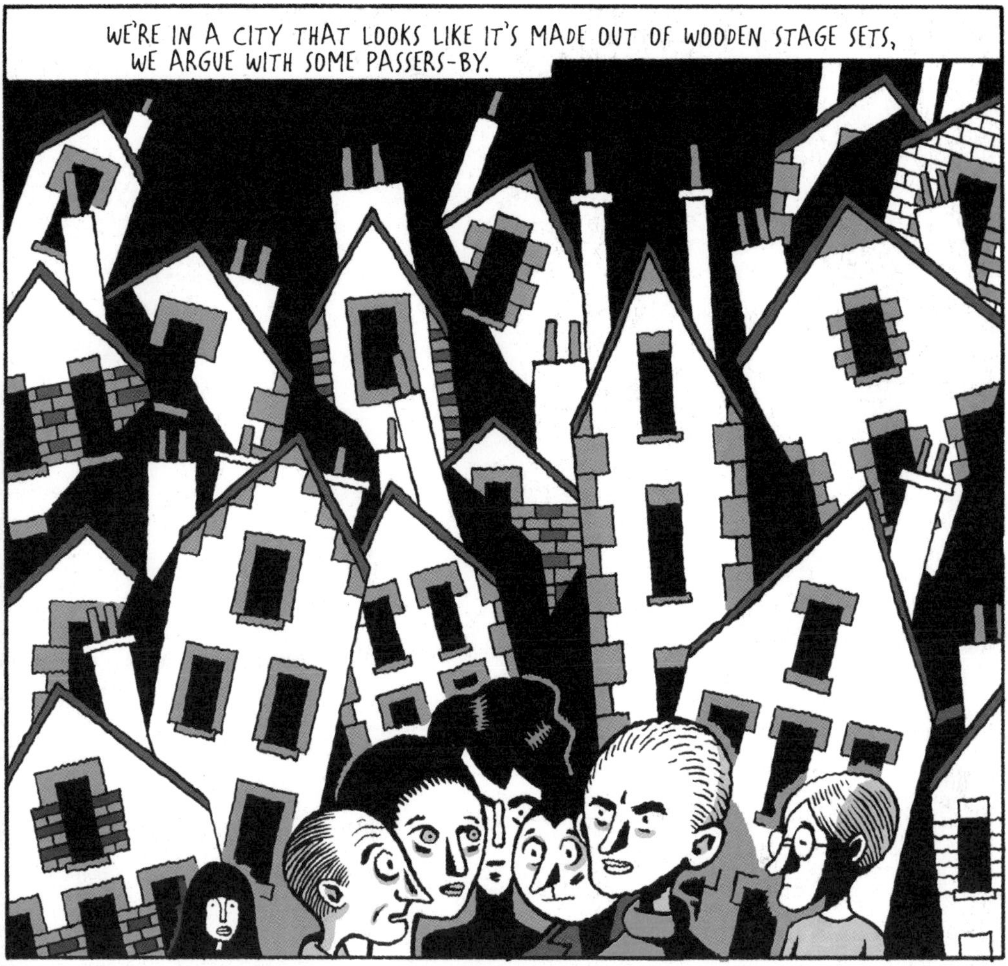
WE'RE IN A CITY THAT LOOKS LIKE IT'S MADE OUT OF WOODEN STAGE SETS, WE ARGUE WITH SOME PASSERS-BY.

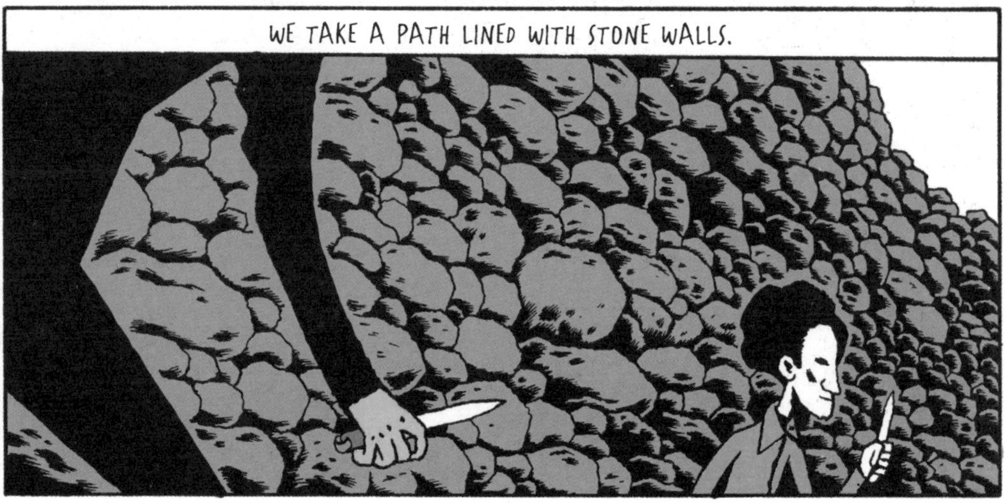
WE TAKE A PATH LINED WITH STONE WALLS.

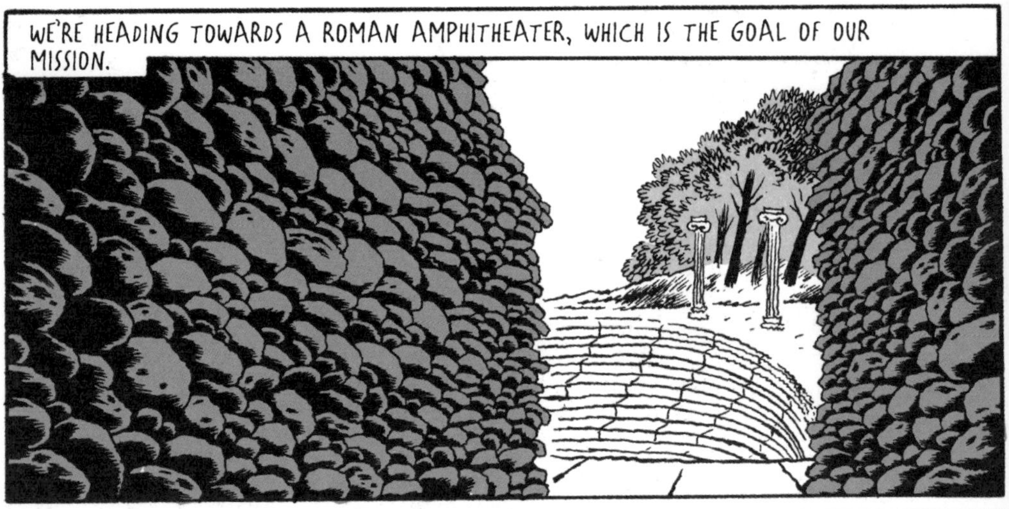
WE'RE HEADING TOWARDS A ROMAN AMPHITHEATER, WHICH IS THE GOAL OF OUR MISSION.

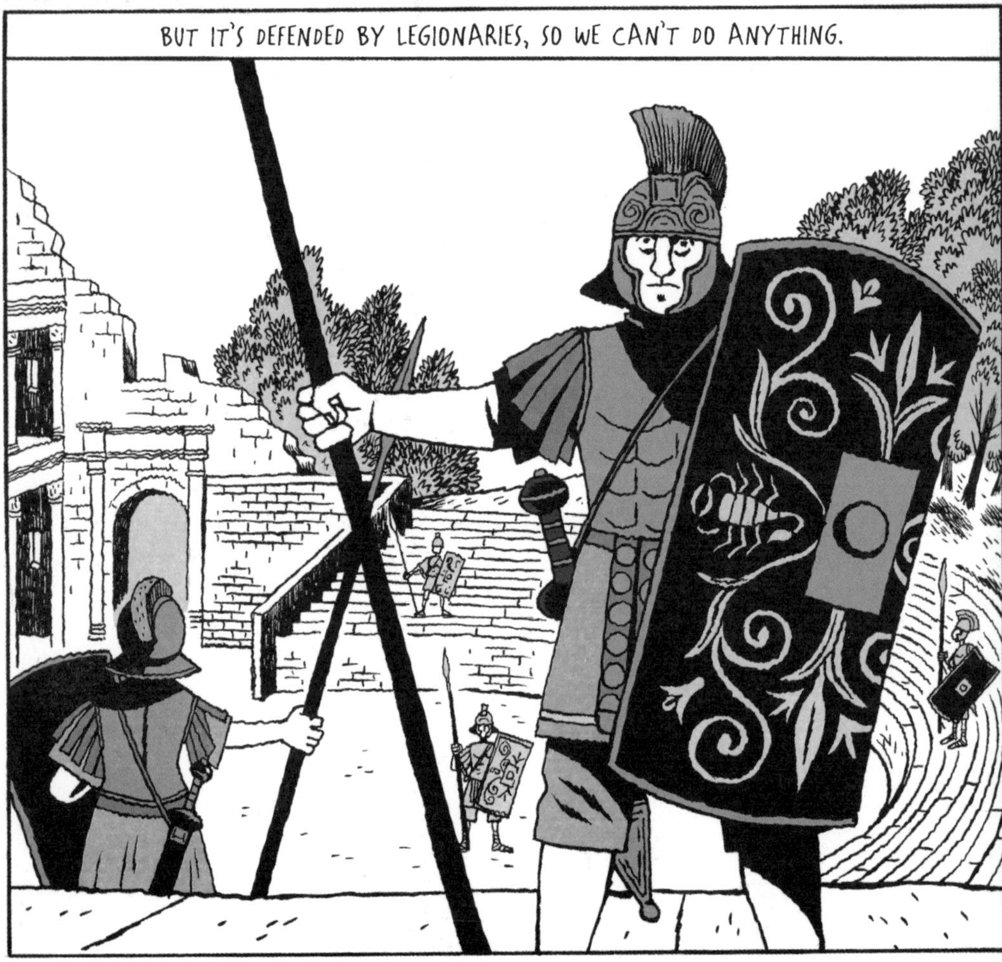
BUT IT'S DEFENDED BY LEGIONARIES, SO WE CAN'T DO ANYTHING.

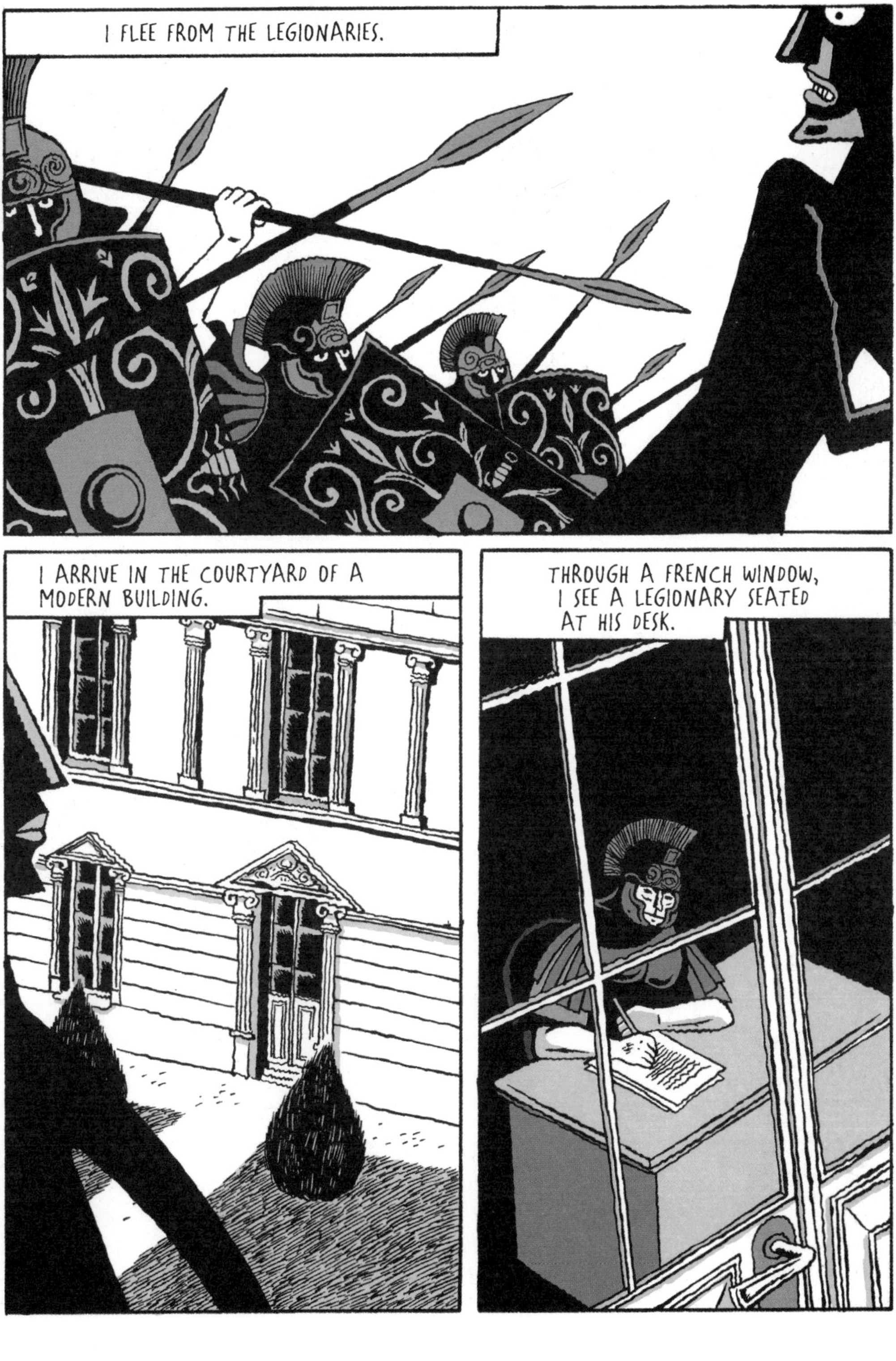
I FLEE FROM THE LEGIONARIES.
I ARRIVE IN THE COURTYARD OF A MODERN BUILDING.
THROUGH A FRENCH WINDOW, I SEE A LEGIONARY SEATED AT HIS DESK.

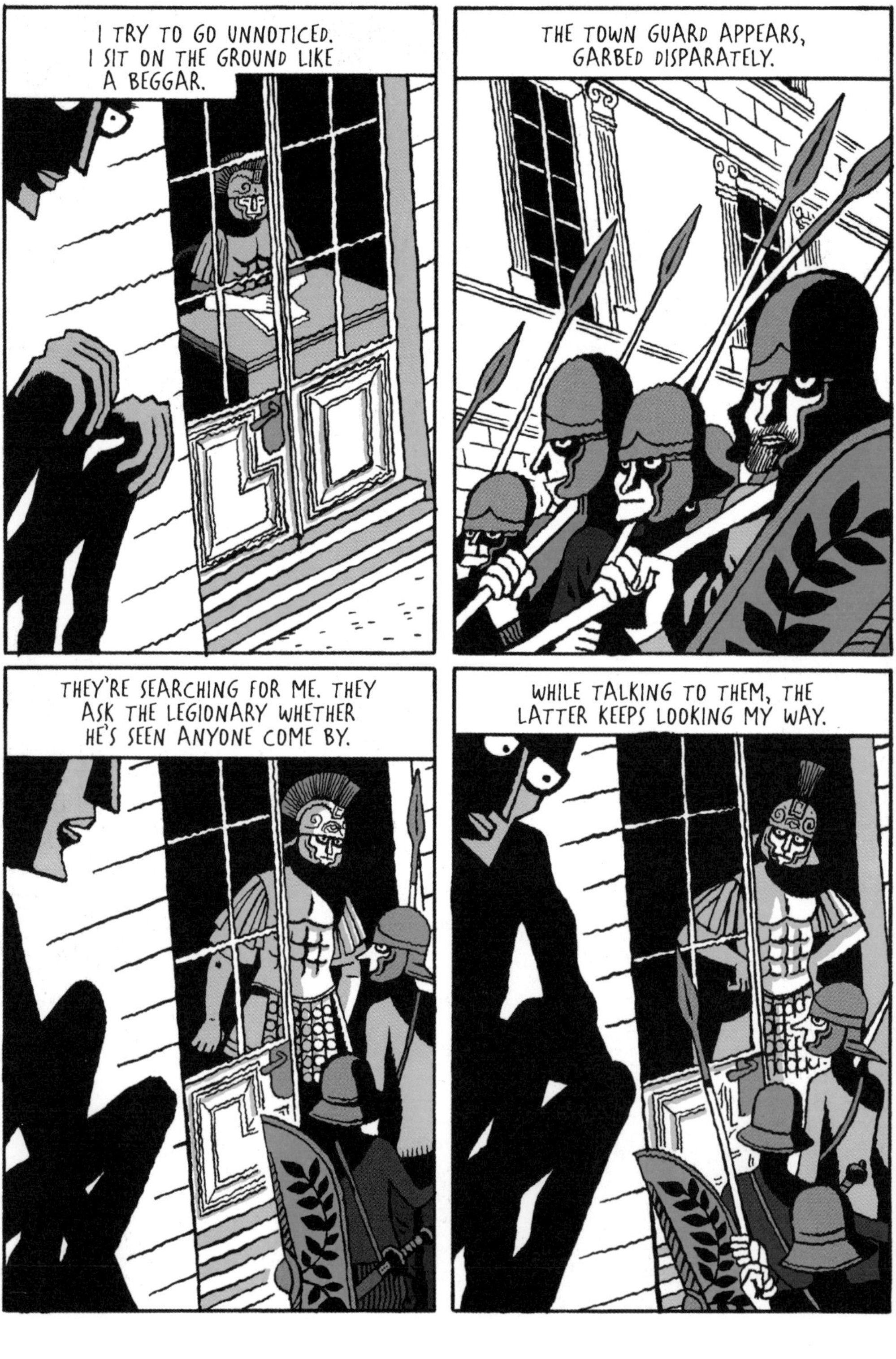
I TRY TO GO UNNOTICED. I SIT ON THE GROUND LIKE A BEGGAR.
THE TOWN GUARD APPEARS, GARBED DISPARATELY.
THEY'RE SEARCHING FOR ME. THEY ASK THE LEGIONARY WHETHER HE'S SEEN ANYONE COME BY.
WHILE TALKING TO THEM, THE LATTER KEEPS LOOKING MY WAY.

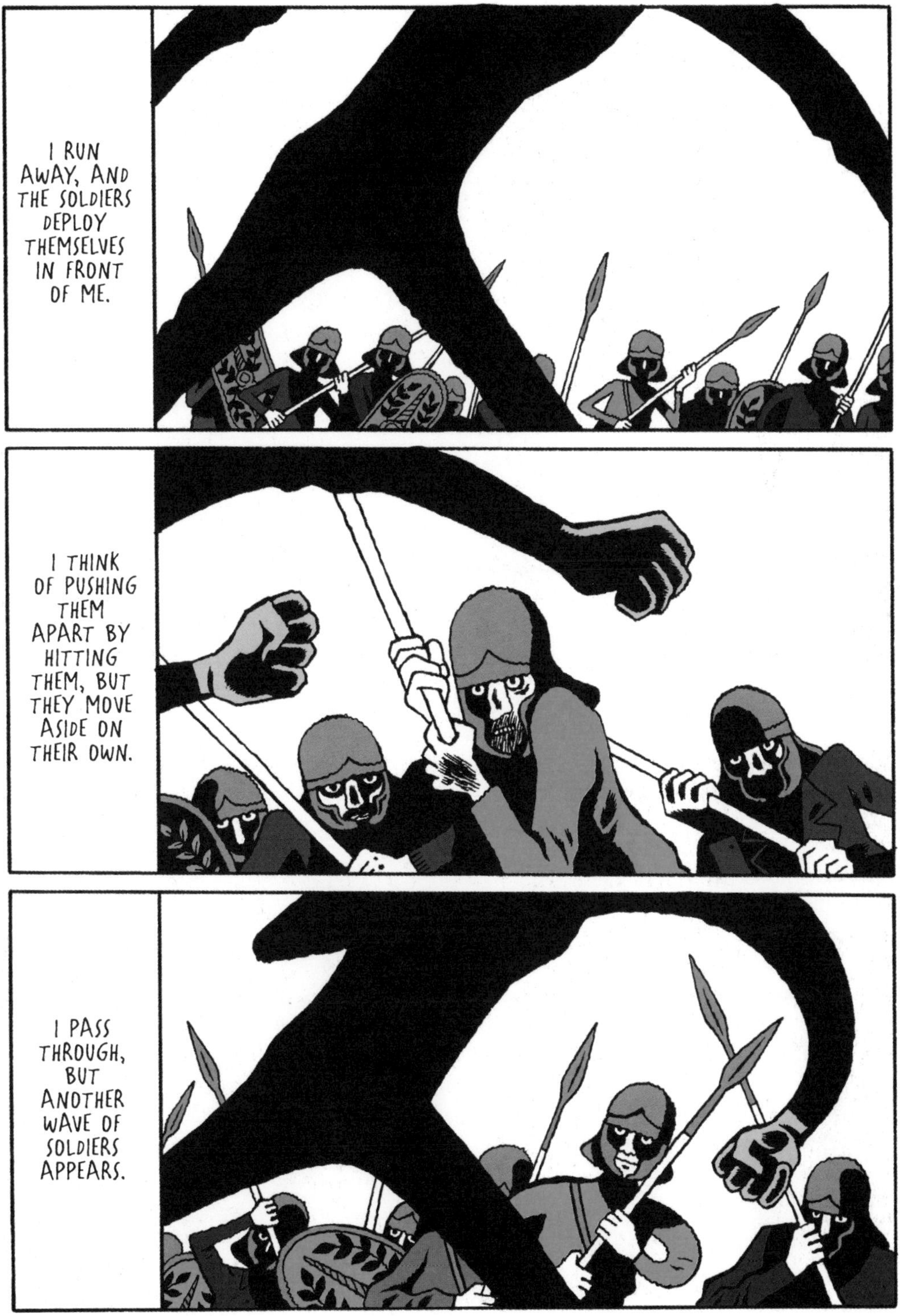
I RUN AWAY, AND THE SOLDIERS DEPLOY THEMSELVES IN FRONT OF ME.
I THINK OF PUSHING THEM APART BY HITTING THEM, BUT THEY MOVE ASIDE ON THEIR OWN.
I PASS THROUGH, BUT ANOTHER WAVE OF SOLDIERS APPEARS.

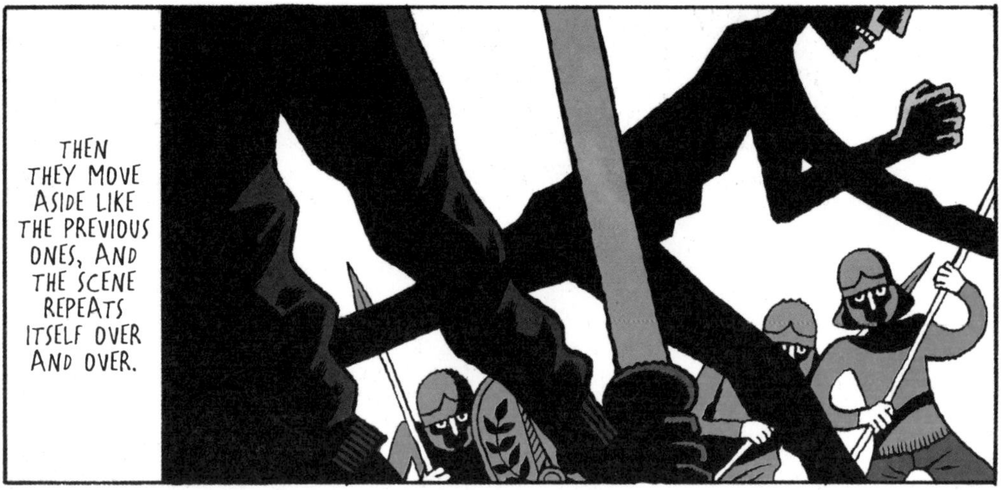
THEN THEY MOVE ASIDE LIKE THE PREVIOUS ONES, AND THE SCENE REPEATS ITSELF OVER AND OVER.

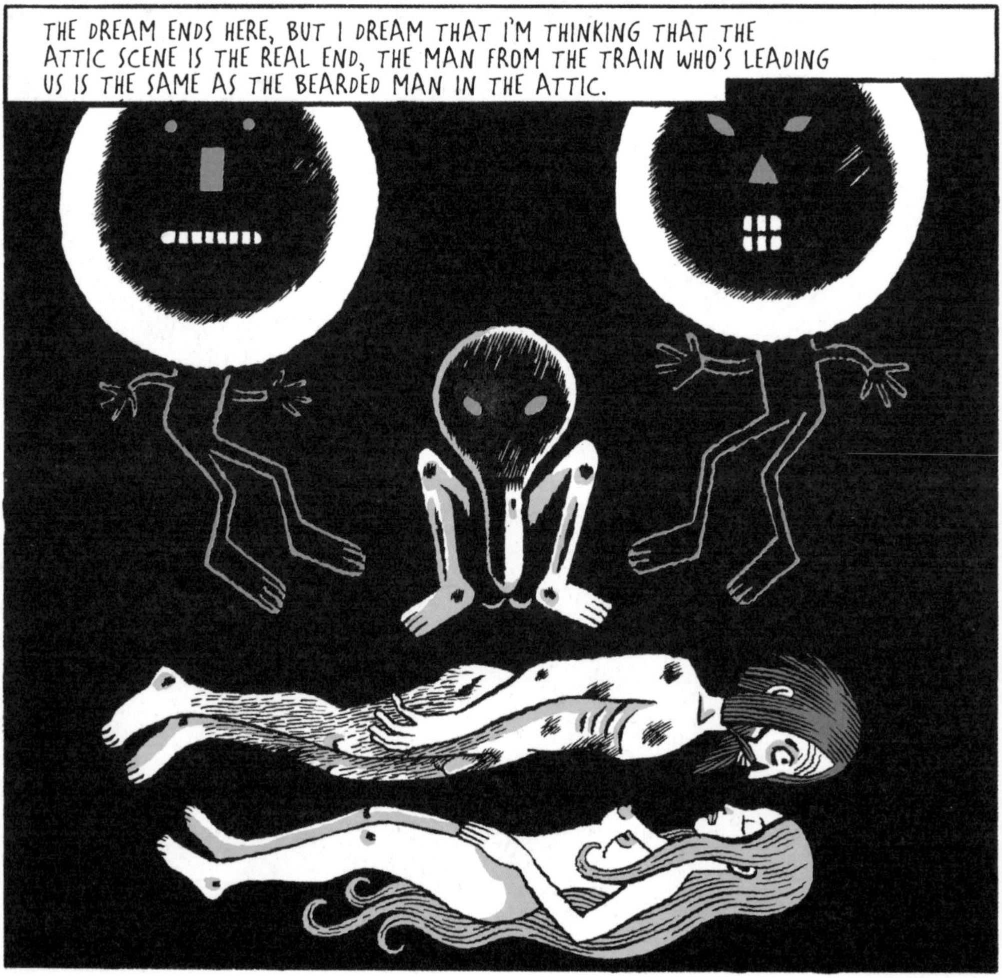
THE DREAM ENDS HERE, BUT I DREAM THAT I'M THINKING THAT THE ATTIC SCENE IS THE REAL END, THE MAN FROM THE TRAIN WHO'S LEADING US IS THE SAME AS THE BEARDED MAN IN THE ATTIC.

7 • The Shaft

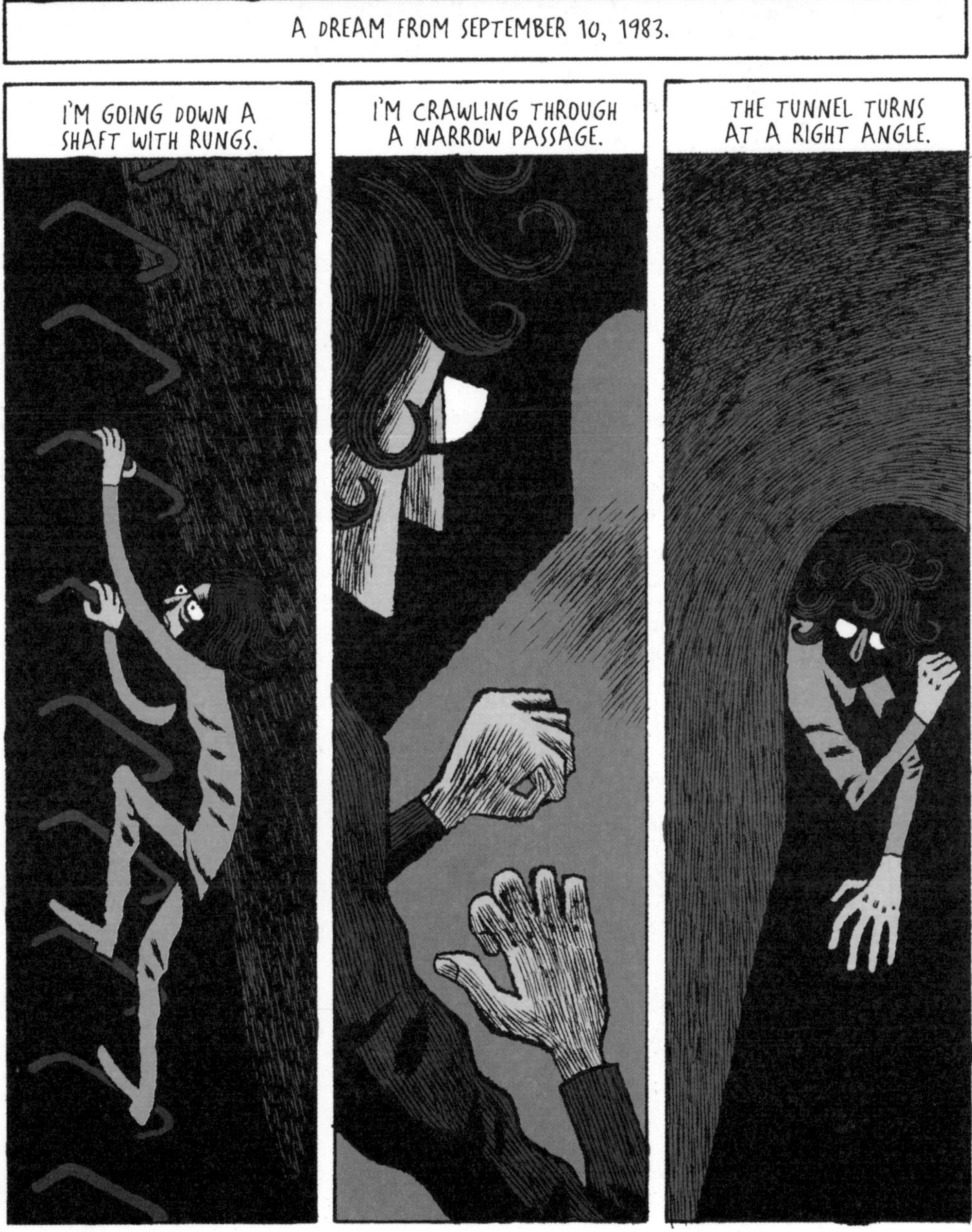
A DREAM FROM SEPTEMBER 10, 1983.
I'M GOING DOWN A SHAFT WITH RUNGS.
I'M CRAWLING THROUGH A NARROW PASSAGE.
THE TUNNEL TURNS AT A RIGHT ANGLE.

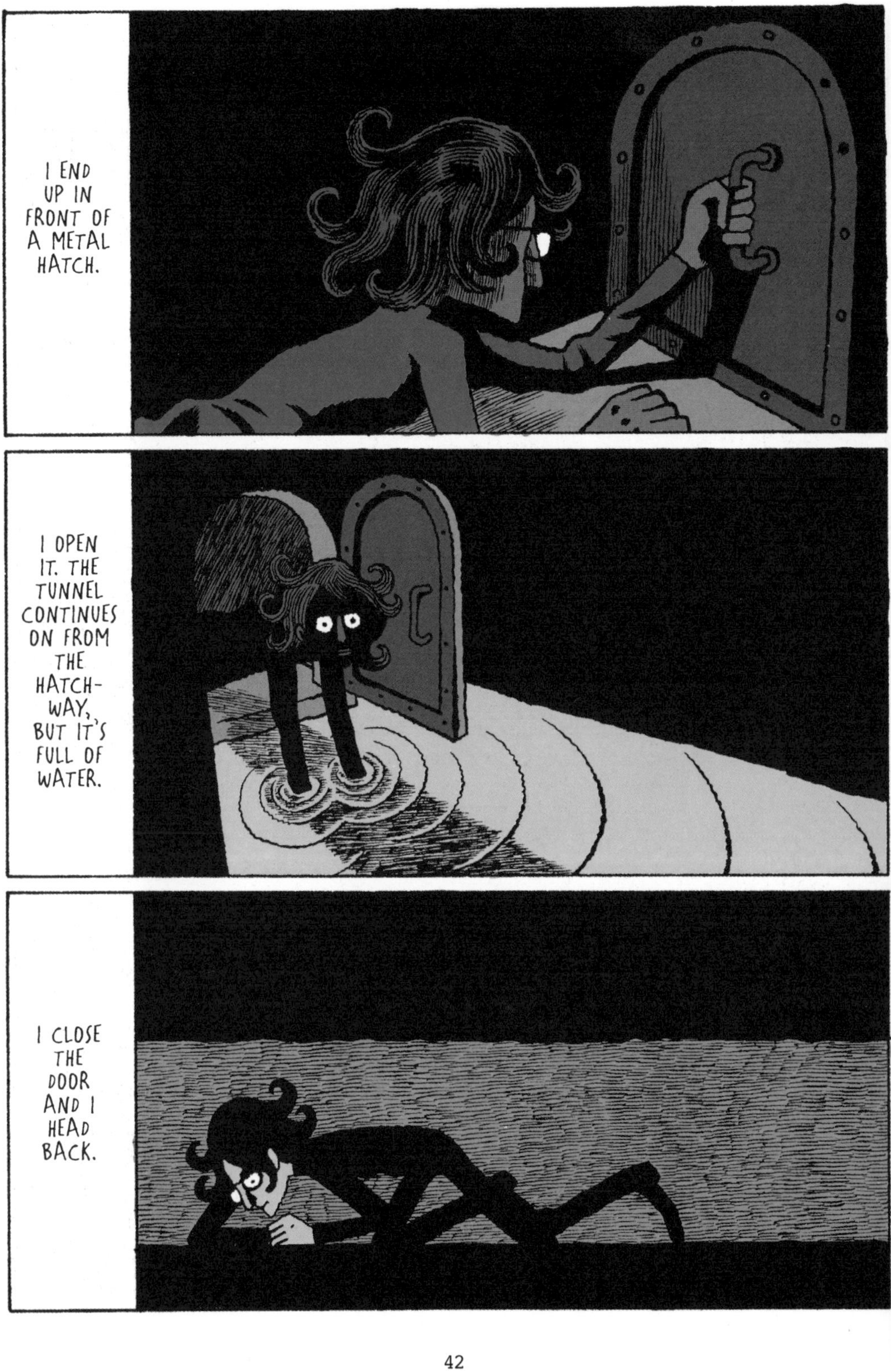
I END UP IN FRONT OF A METAL HATCH.
I OPEN IT. THE TUNNEL CONTINUES ON FROM THE HATCH-WAY, BUT IT'S FULL OF WATER.
I CLOSE THE DOOR AND I HEAD BACK.

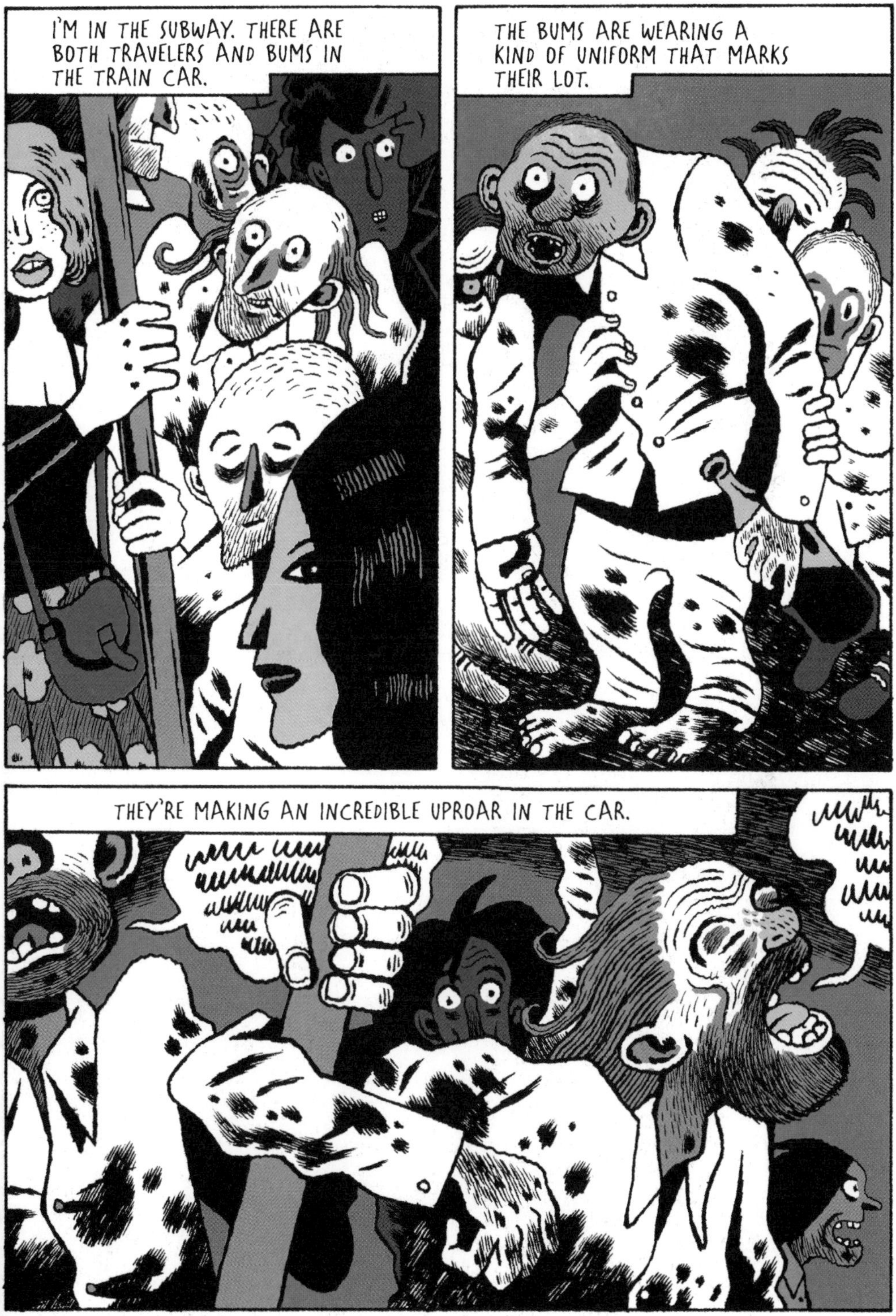
I'M IN THE SUBWAY. THERE ARE BOTH TRAVELERS AND BUMS IN THE TRAIN CAR.
THE BUMS ARE WEARING A KIND OF UNIFORM THAT MARKS THEIR LOT.
THEY'RE MAKING AN INCREDIBLE UPROAR IN THE CAR.

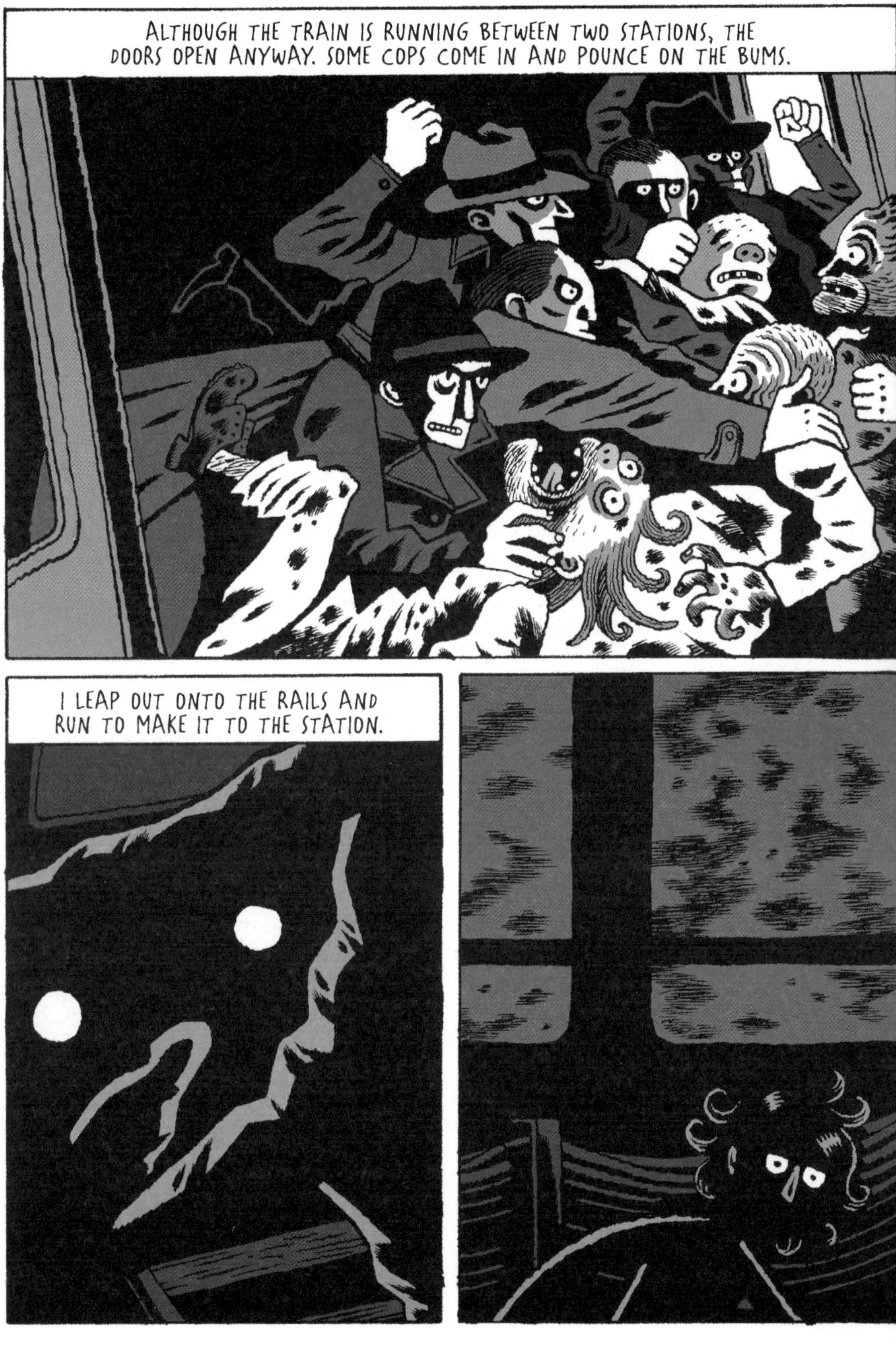
ALTHOUGH THE TRAIN IS RUNNING BETWEEN TWO STATIONS, THE DOORS OPEN ANYWAY. SOME COPS COME IN AND POUNCE ON THE BUMS.
I LEAP OUT ONTO THE RAILS AND RUN TO MAKE IT TO THE STATION.

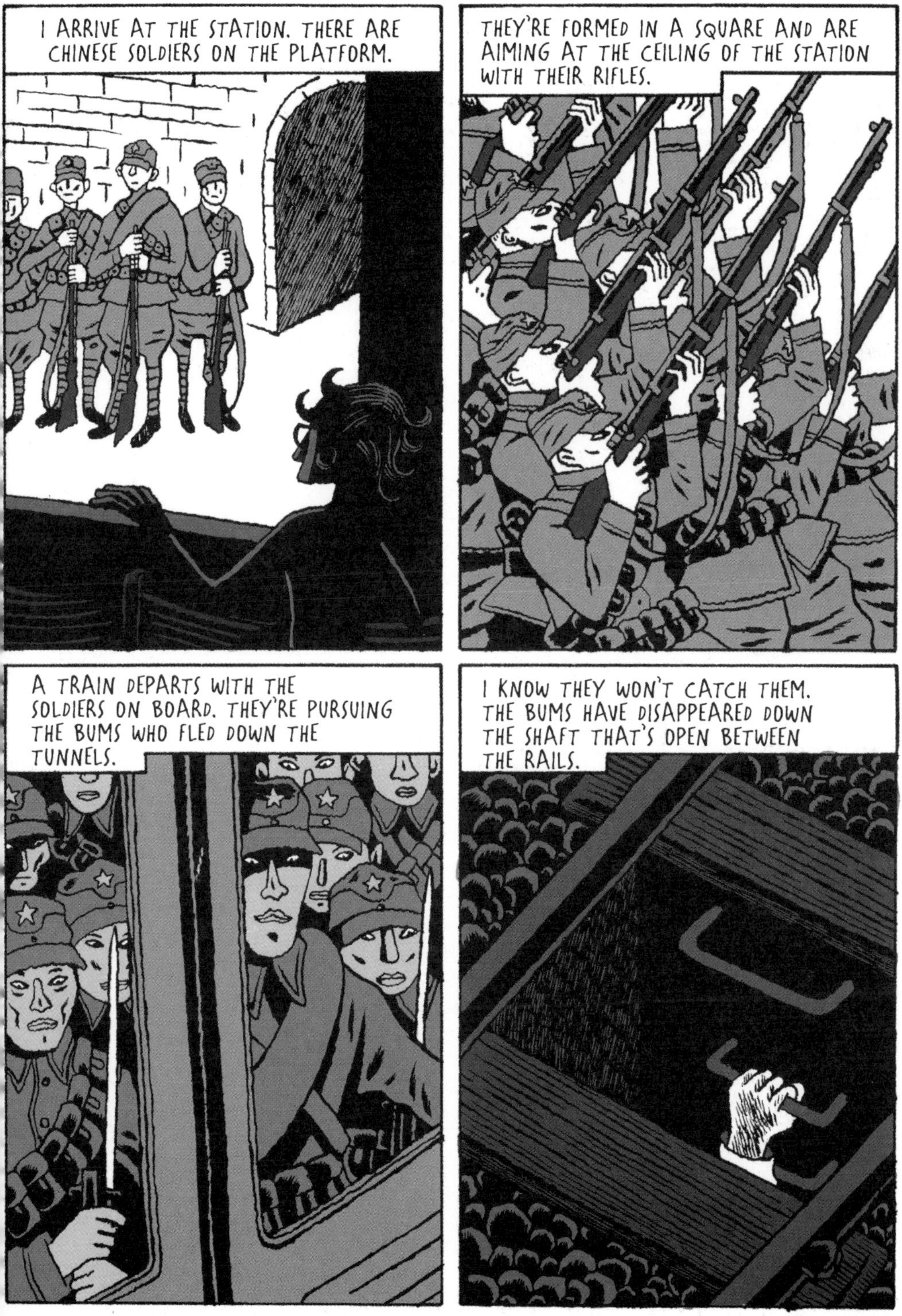
I ARRIVE AT THE STATION. THERE ARE CHINESE SOLDIERS ON THE PLATFORM.
THEY'RE FORMED IN A SQUARE AND ARE AIMING AT THE CEILING OF THE STATION WITH THEIR RIFLES.
A TRAIN DEPARTS WITH THE SOLDIERS ON BOARD. THEY'RE PURSUING THE BUMS WHO FLED DOWN THE TUNNELS.
I KNOW THEY WON'T CATCH THEM. THE BUMS HAVE DISAPPEARED DOWN THE SHAFT THAT'S OPEN BETWEEN THE RAILS.

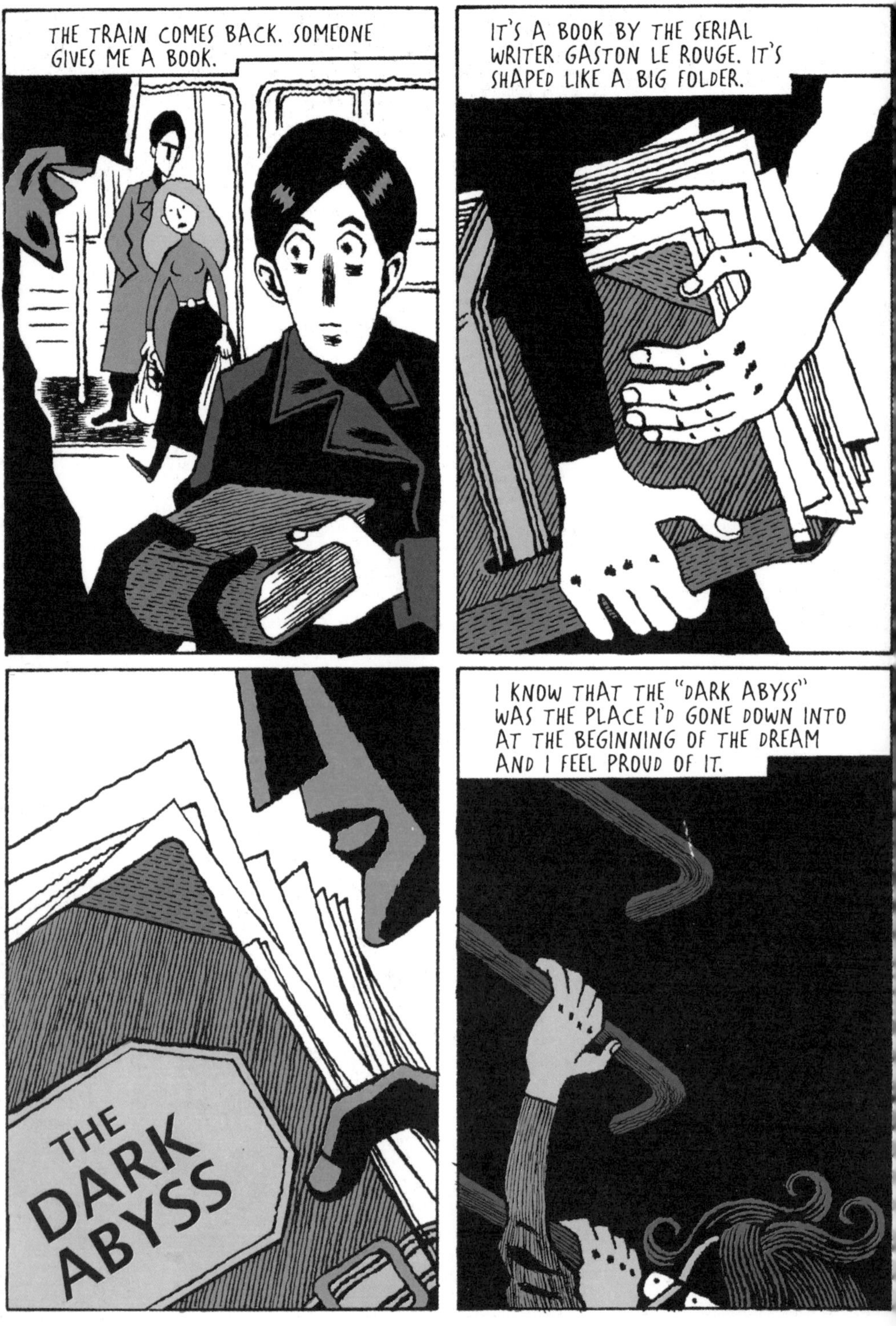
THE TRAIN COMES BACK. SOMEONE GIVES ME A BOOK.
IT'S A BOOK BY THE SERIAL WRITER GASTON LE ROUGE. IT'S SHAPED LIKE A BIG FOLDER.
THE DARK ABYSS
I KNOW THAT THE "DARK ABYSS" WAS THE PLACE I'D GONE DOWN INTO AT THE BEGINNING OF THE DREAM AND I FEEL PROUD OF IT.

8 • Massacre

A DREAM FROM AUGUST 18, 1991.

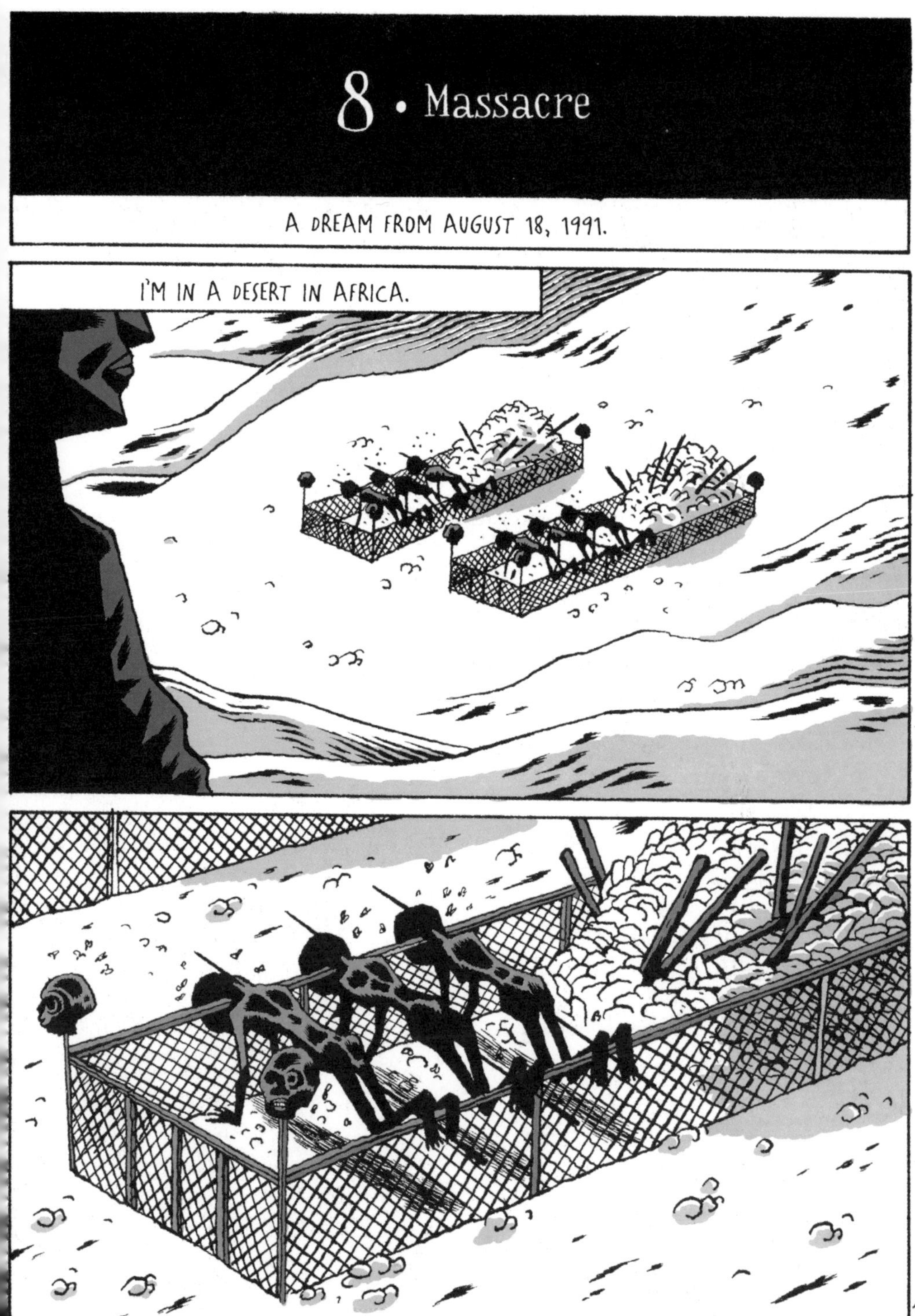
I'M IN A DESERT IN AFRICA.

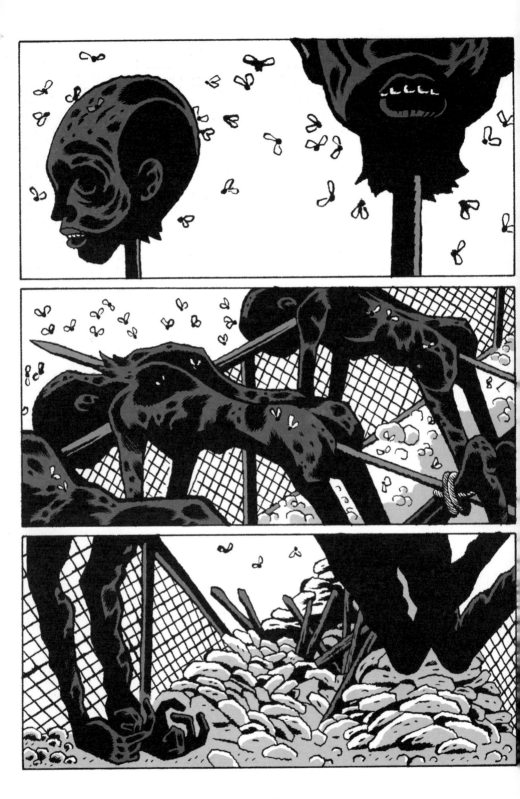

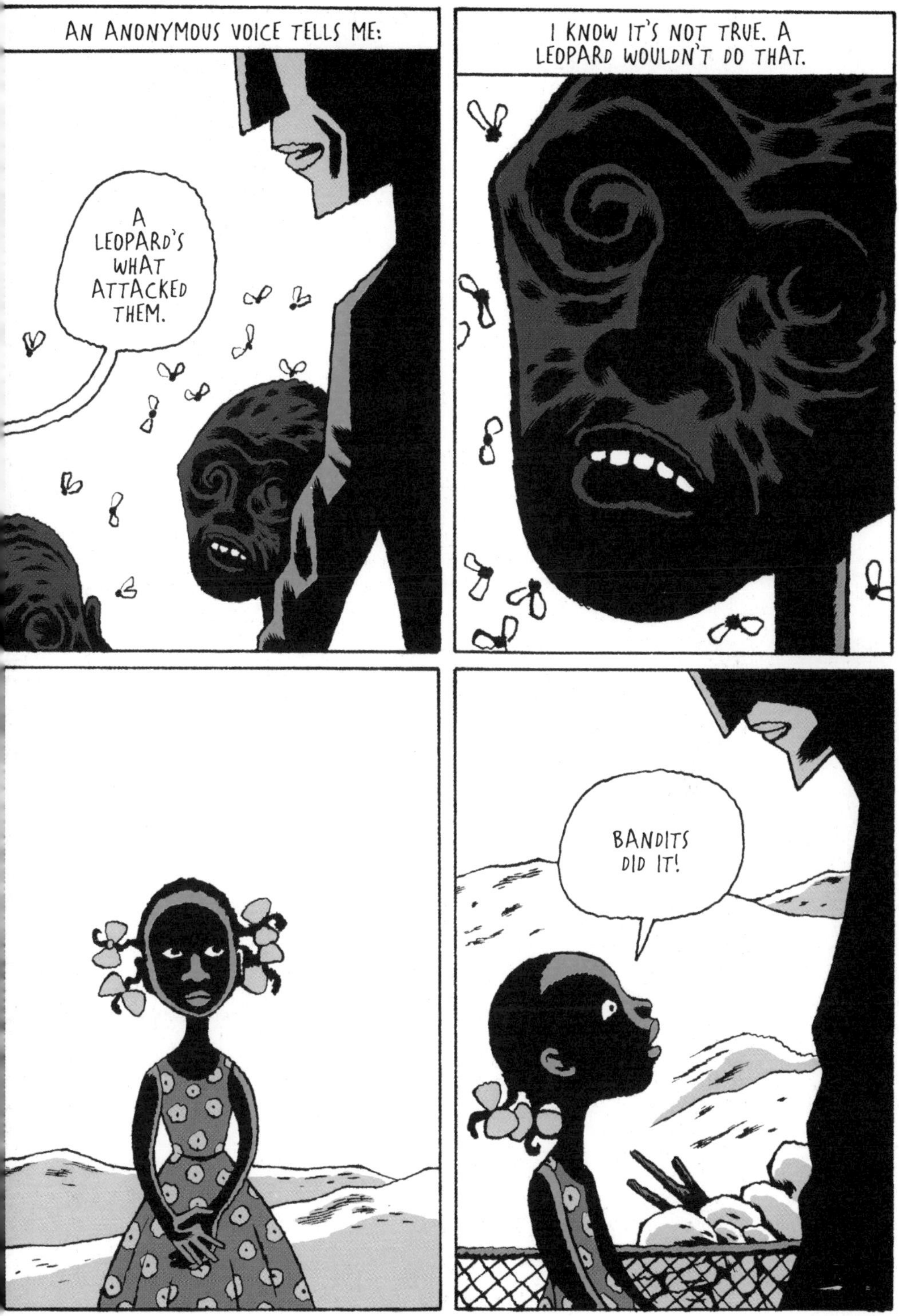
AN ANONYMOUS VOICE TELLS ME:
A LEOPARD'S WHAT ATTACKED THEM.
I KNOW IT'S NOT TRUE. A LEOPARD WOULDN'T DO THAT.
BANDITS DID IT!

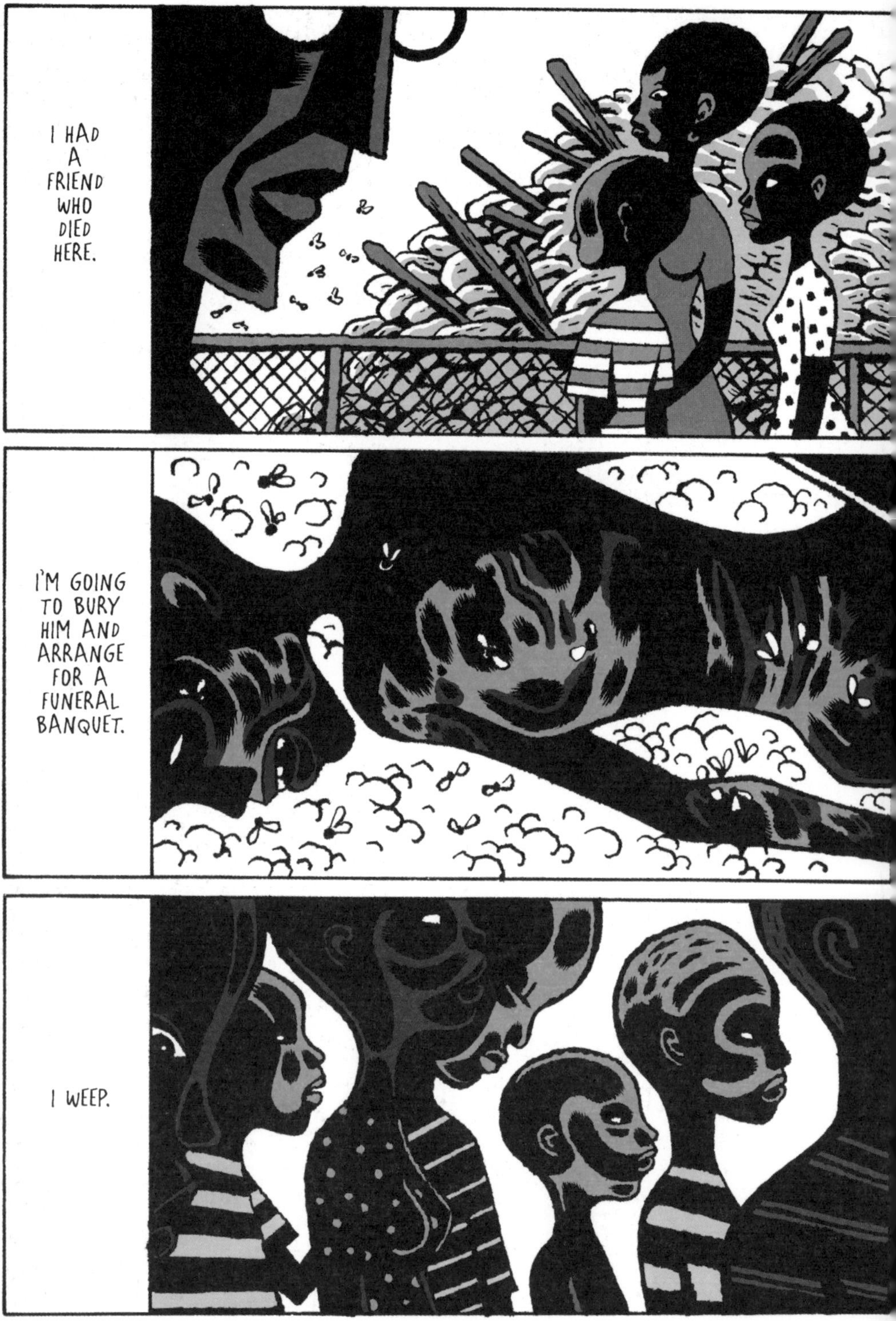
I HAD A FRIEND WHO DIED HERE.
I'M GOING TO BURY HIM AND ARRANGE FOR A FUNERAL BANQUET.
I WEEP.

9 • The eye

A DREAM FROM SEPTEMBER 2, 1991.

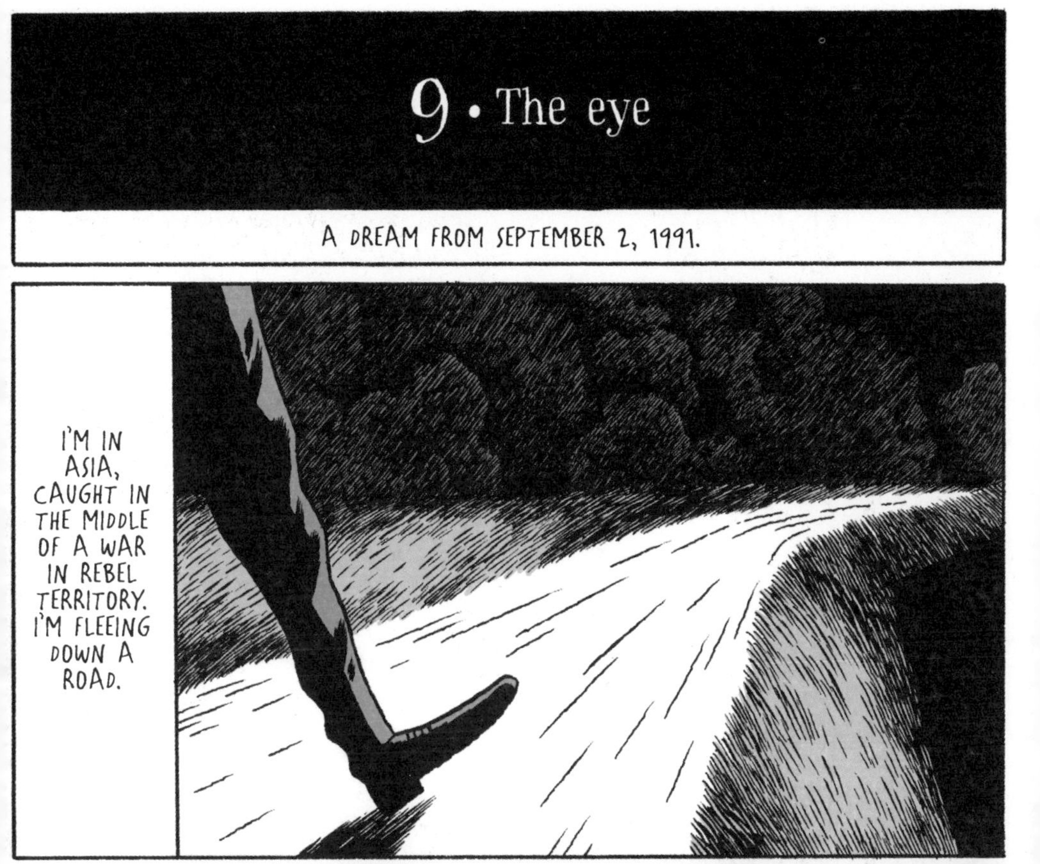
I'M IN ASIA, CAUGHT IN THE MIDDLE OF A WAR IN REBEL TERRITORY. I'M FLEEING DOWN A ROAD.

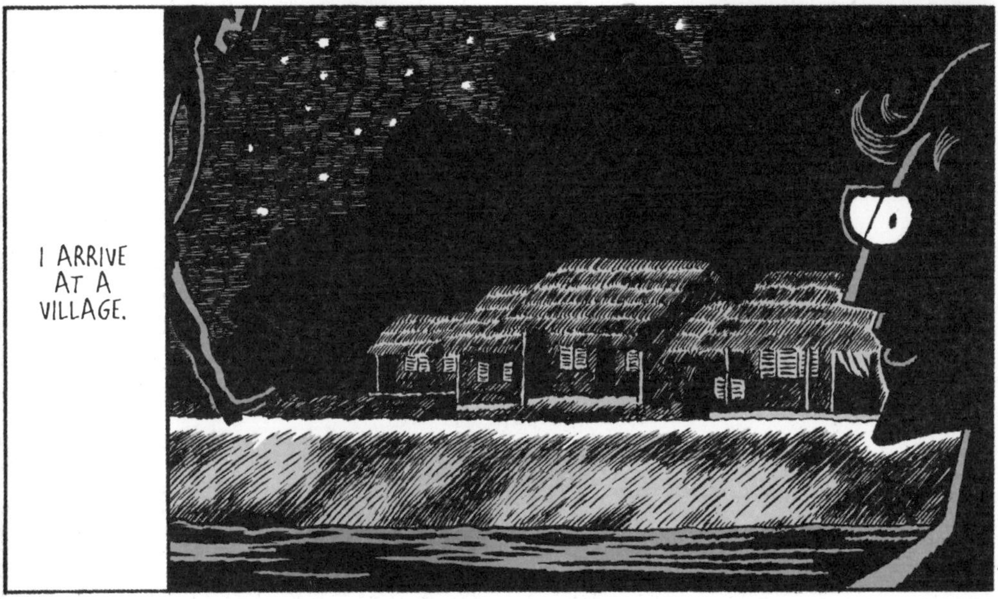
I ARRIVE AT A VILLAGE.

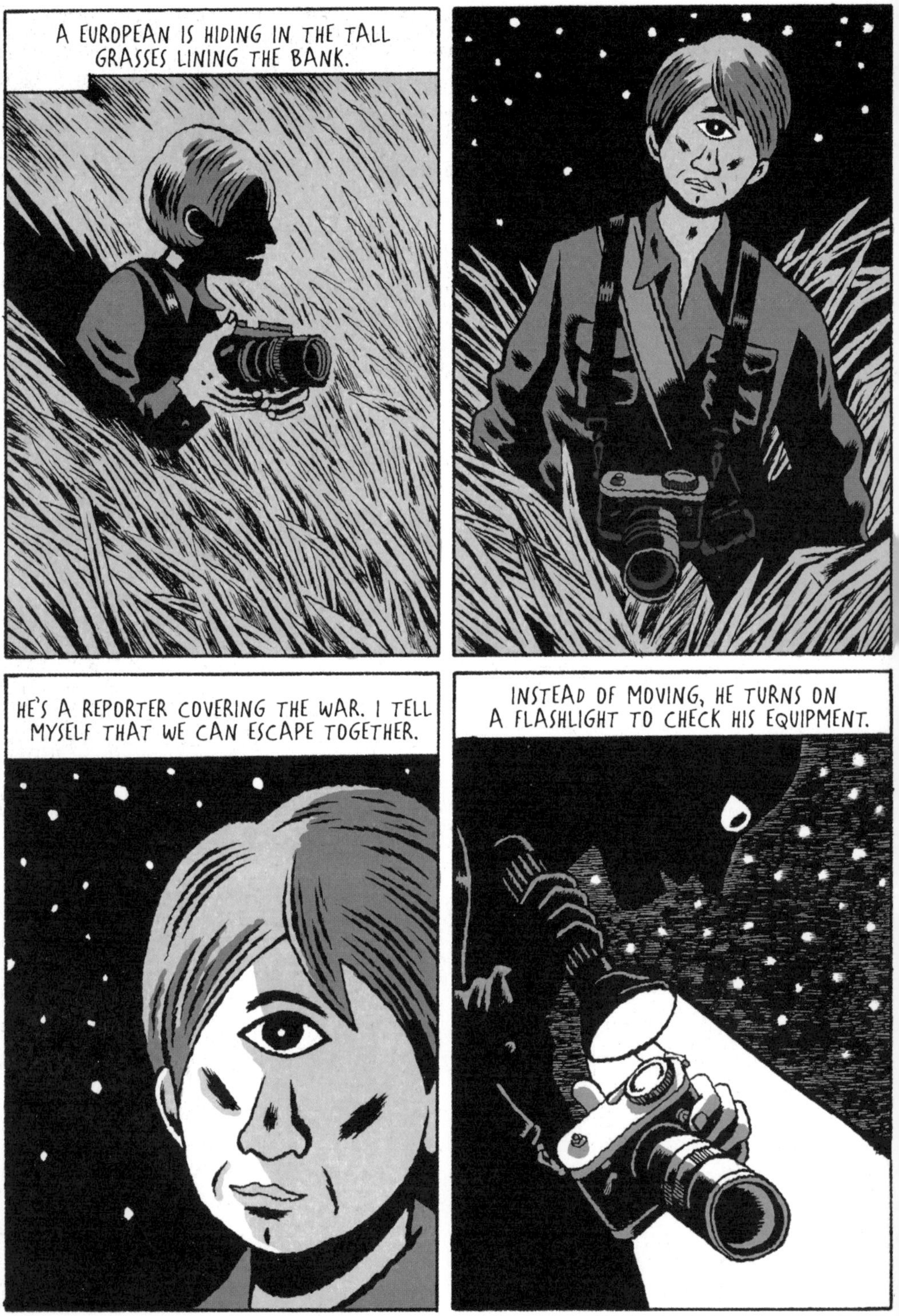
A EUROPEAN IS HIDING IN THE TALL GRASSES LINING THE BANK.
HE'S A REPORTER COVERING THE WAR. I TELL MYSELF THAT WE CAN ESCAPE TOGETHER.
INSTEAD OF MOVING, HE TURNS ON A FLASHLIGHT TO CHECK HIS EQUIPMENT.

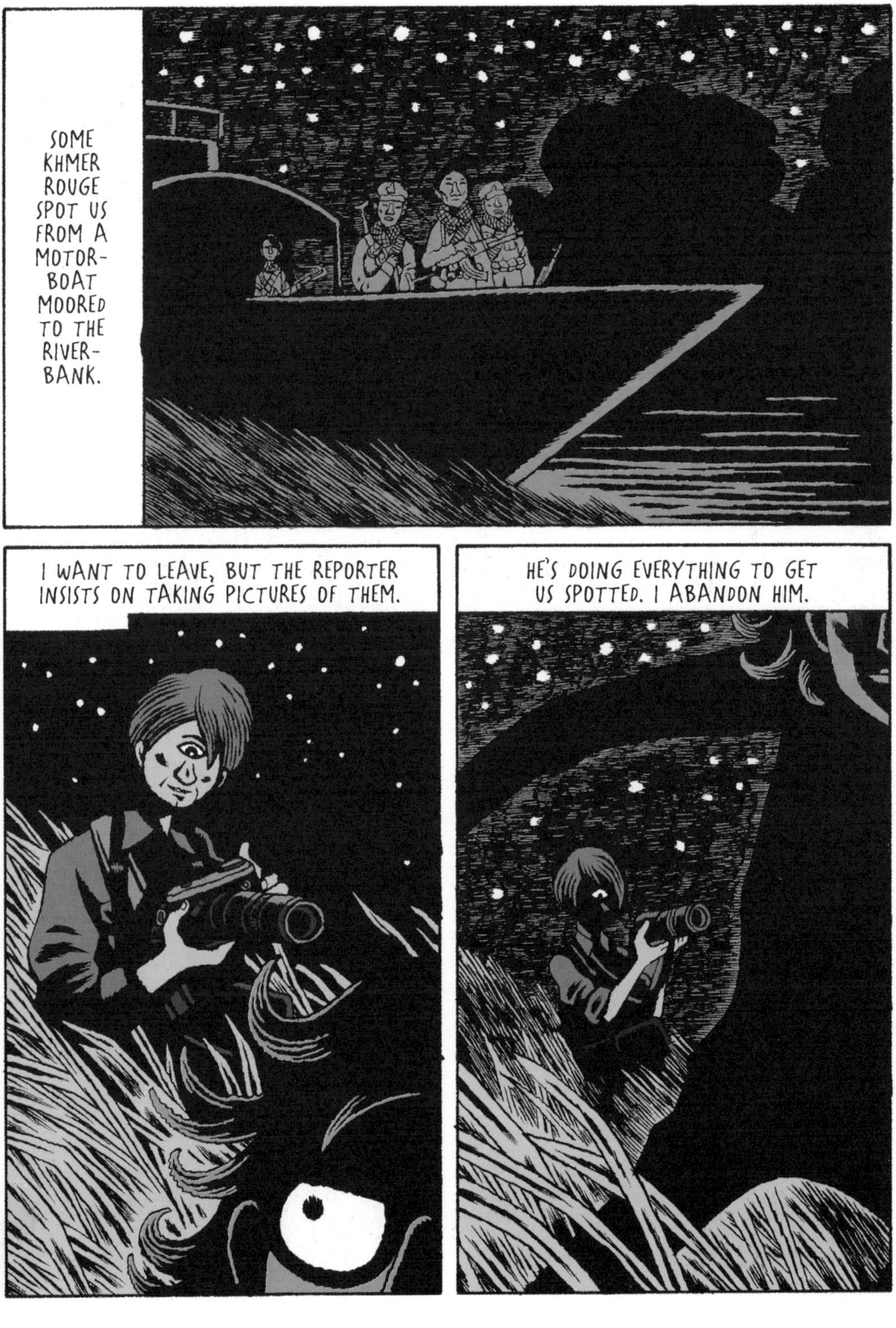
SOME KHMER ROUGE SPOT US FROM A MOTOR-BOAT MOORED TO THE RIVER-BANK.
I WANT TO LEAVE, BUT THE REPORTER INSISTS ON TAKING PICTURES OF THEM.
HE'S DOING EVERYTHING TO GET US SPOTTED. I ABANDON HIM.

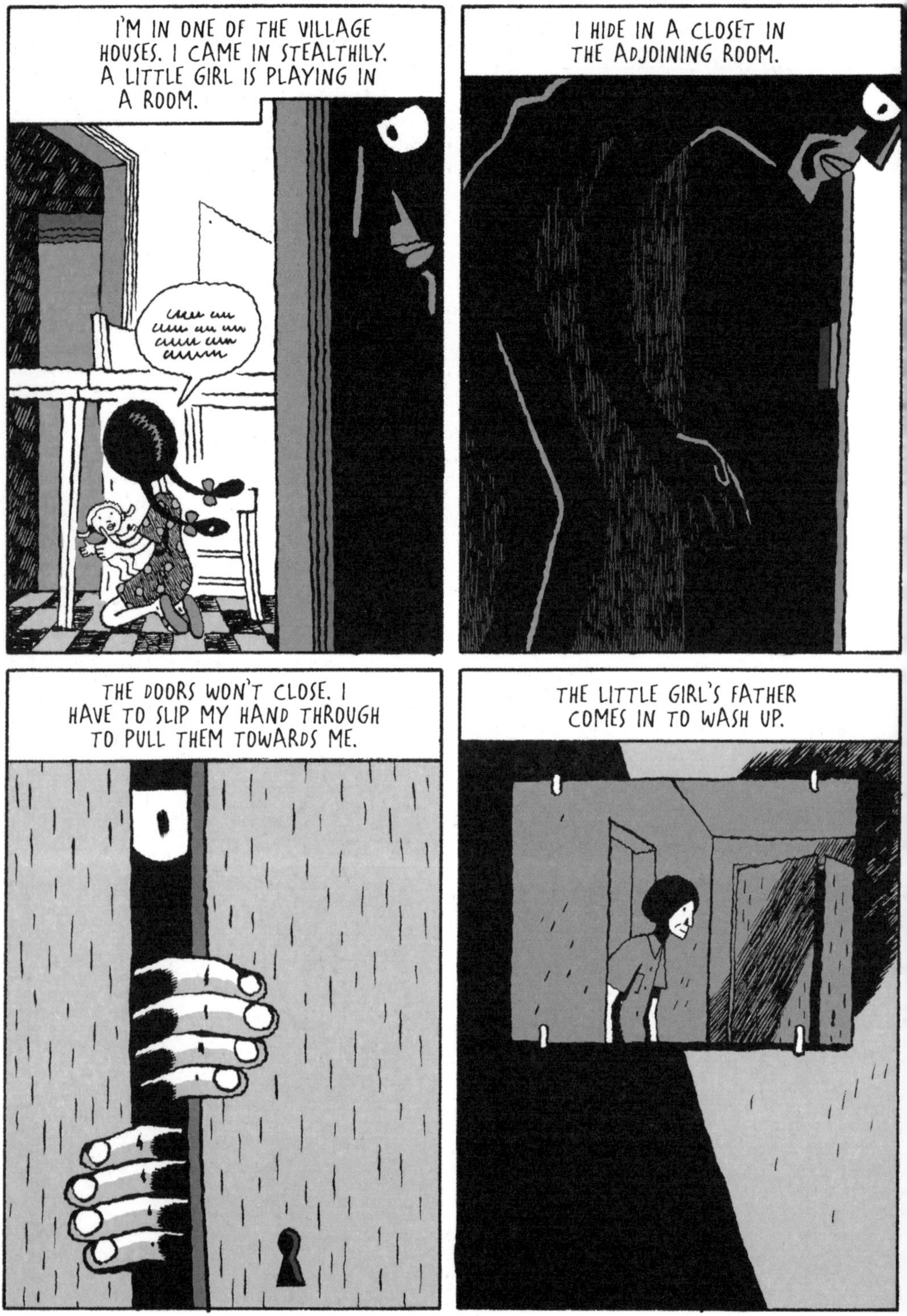
I'M IN ONE OF THE VILLAGE HOUSES. I CAME IN STEALTHILY. A LITTLE GIRL IS PLAYING IN A ROOM.
I HIDE IN A CLOSET IN THE ADJOINING ROOM.
THE DOORS WON'T CLOSE. I HAVE TO SLIP MY HAND THROUGH TO PULL THEM TOWARDS ME.
THE LITTLE GIRL'S FATHER COMES IN TO WASH UP.

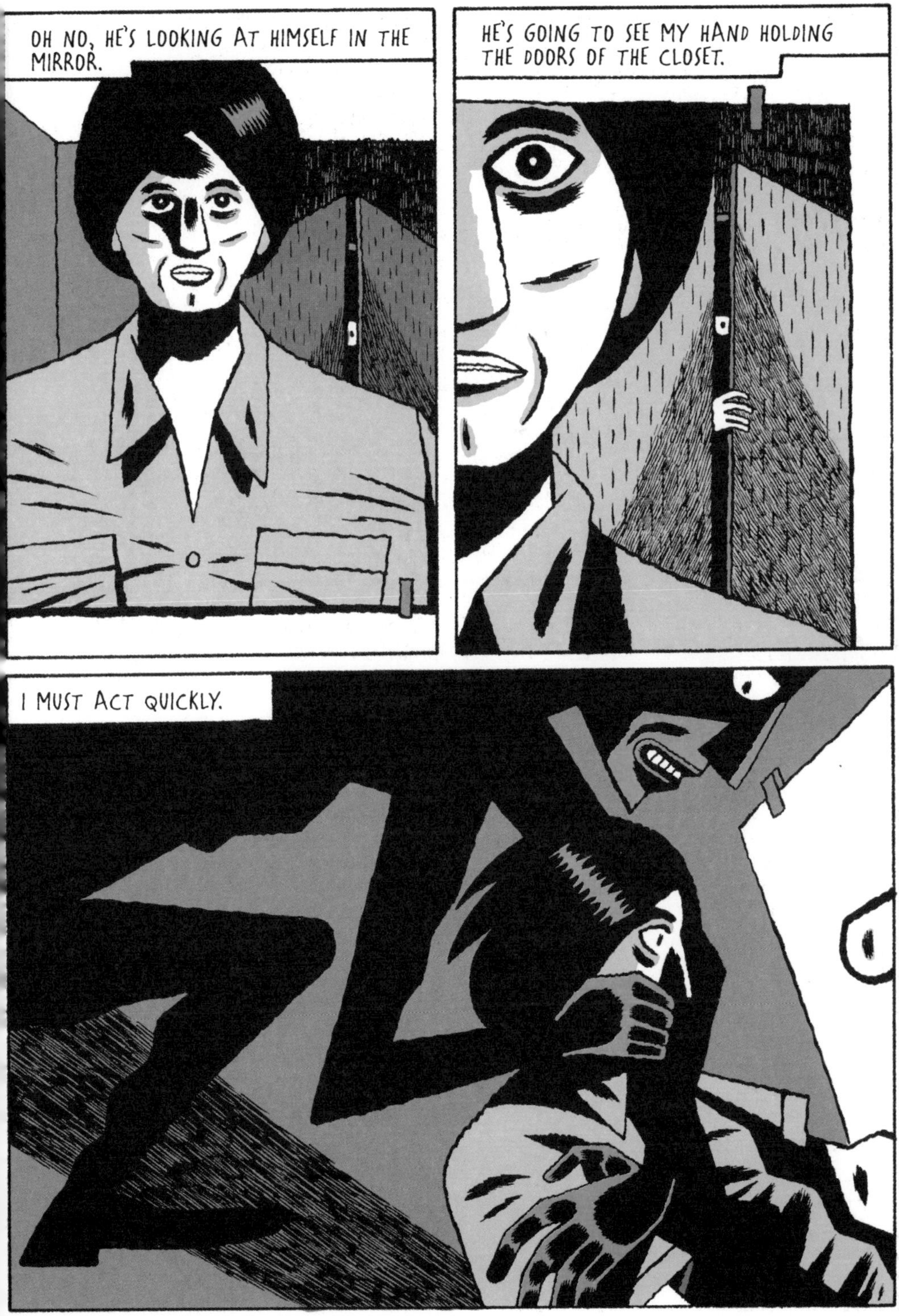
OH NO, HE'S LOOKING AT HIMSELF IN THE MIRROR.
HE'S GOING TO SEE MY HAND HOLDING THE DOORS OF THE CLOSET.
I MUST ACT QUICKLY.

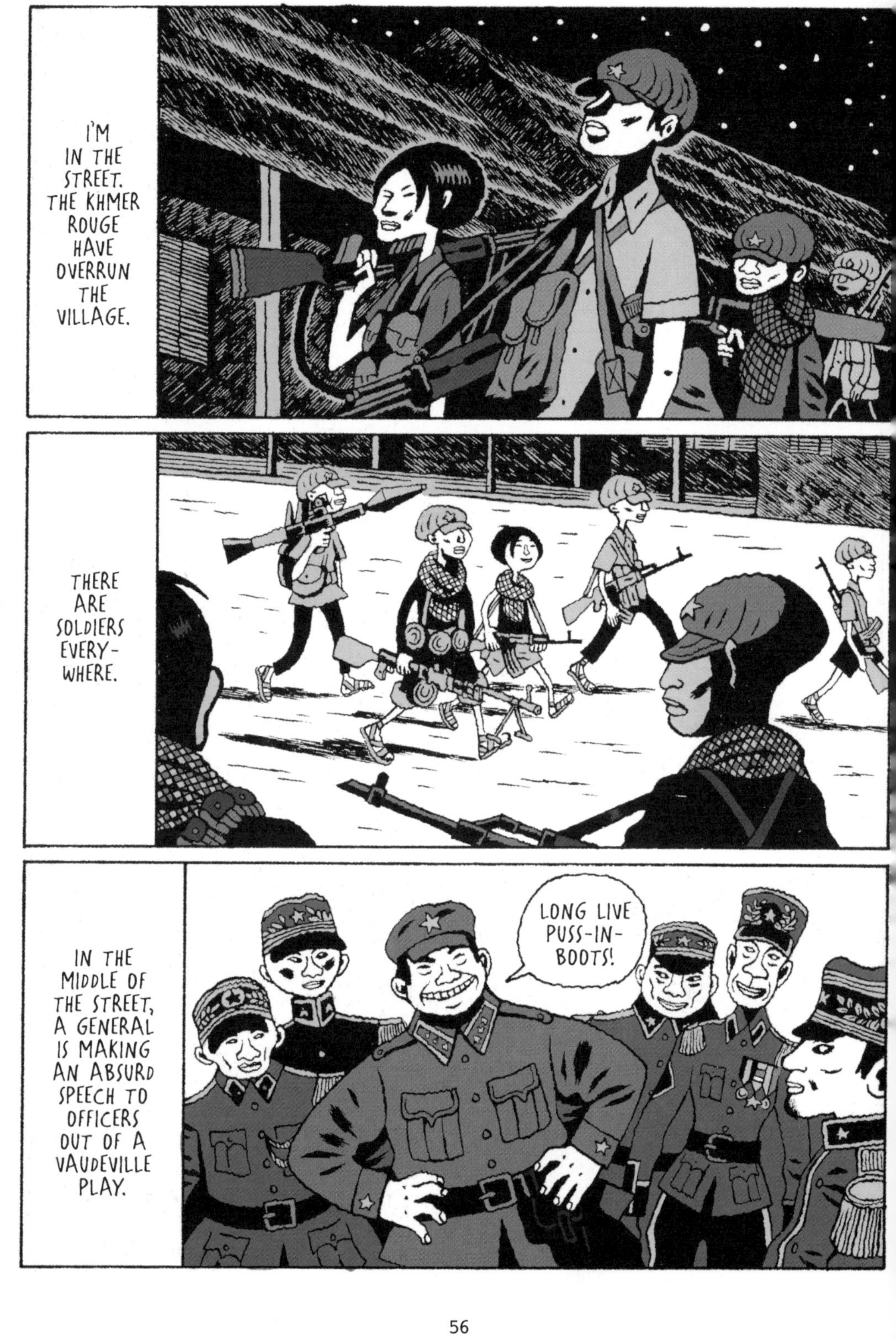
I'M IN THE STREET. THE KHMER ROUGE HAVE OVERRUN THE VILLAGE.
THERE ARE SOLDIERS EVERY-WHERE.
IN THE MIDDLE OF THE STREET, A GENERAL IS MAKING AN ABSURD SPEECH TO OFFICERS OUT OF A VAUDEVILLE PLAY.
LONG LIVE PUSS-IN-BOOTS!

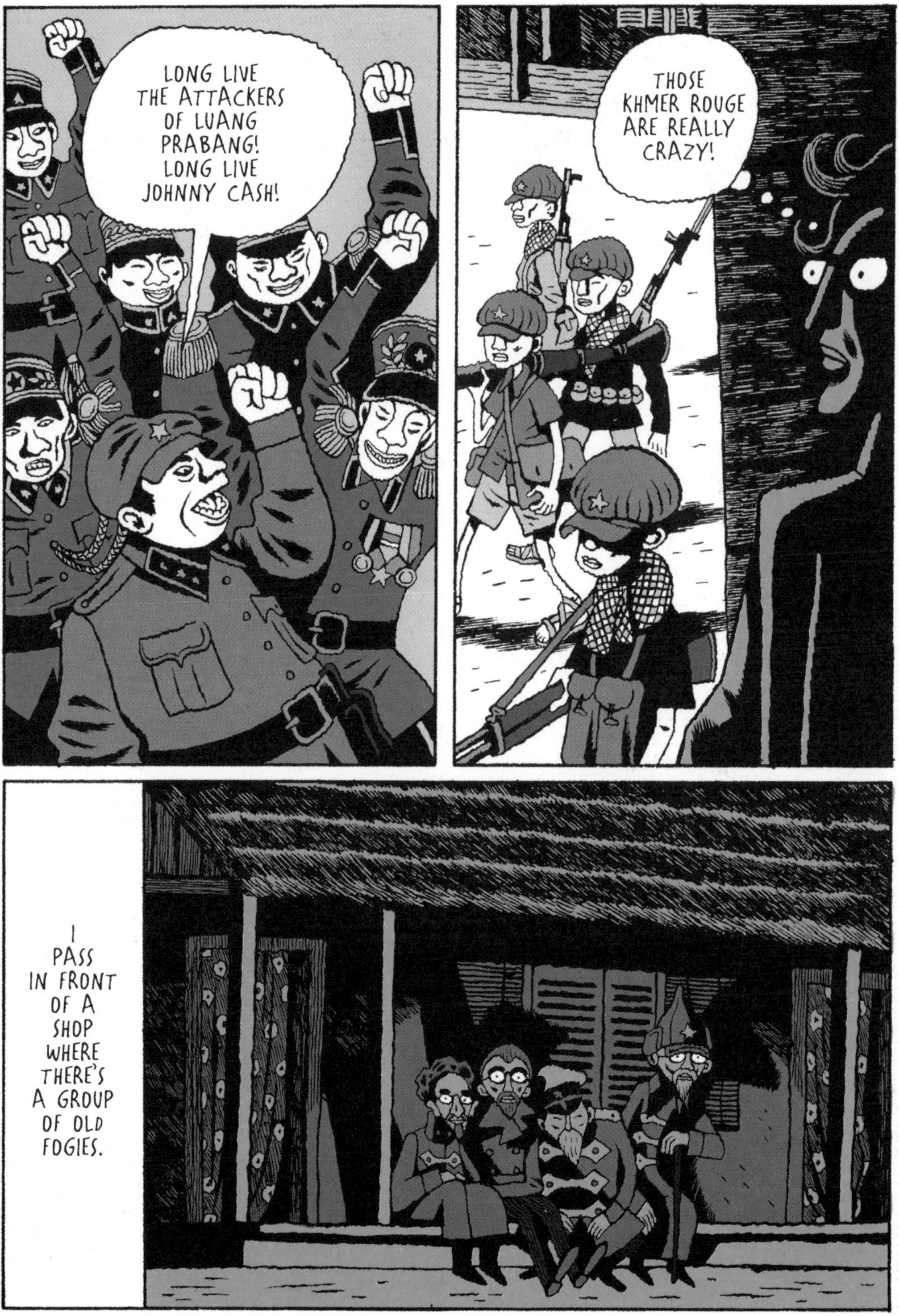
LONG LIVE THE ATTACKERS OF LUANG PRABANG! LONG LIVE JOHNNY CASH!
THOSE KHMER ROUGE ARE REALLY CRAZY!
I PASS IN FRONT OF A SHOP WHERE THERE'S A GROUP OF OLD FOGIES.

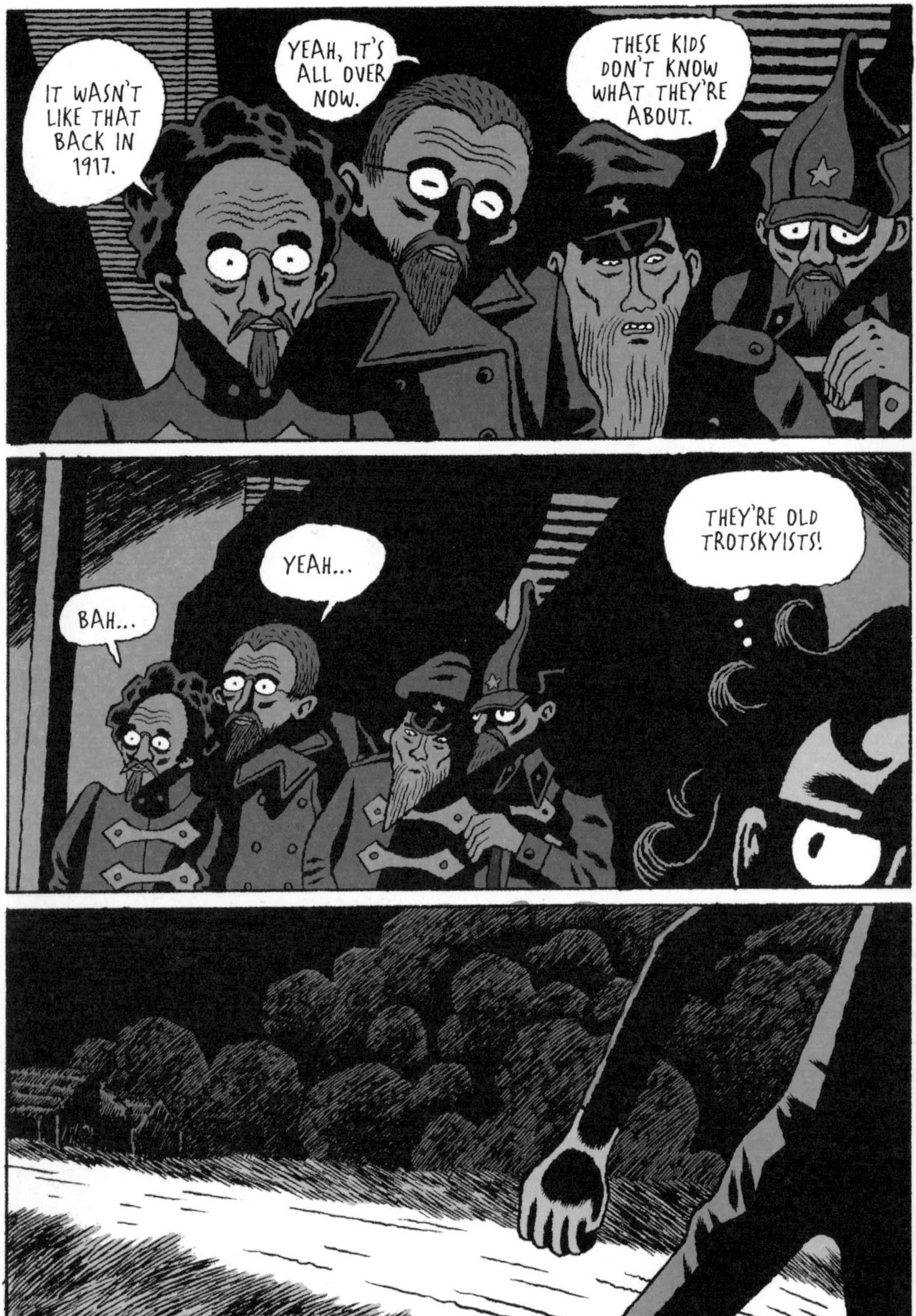
IT WASN'T LIKE THAT BACK IN 1917.
YEAH, IT'S ALL OVER NOW.
THESE KIDS DON'T KNOW WHAT THEY'RE ABOUT.
BAH...
YEAH...
THEY'RE OLD TROTSKYISTS!

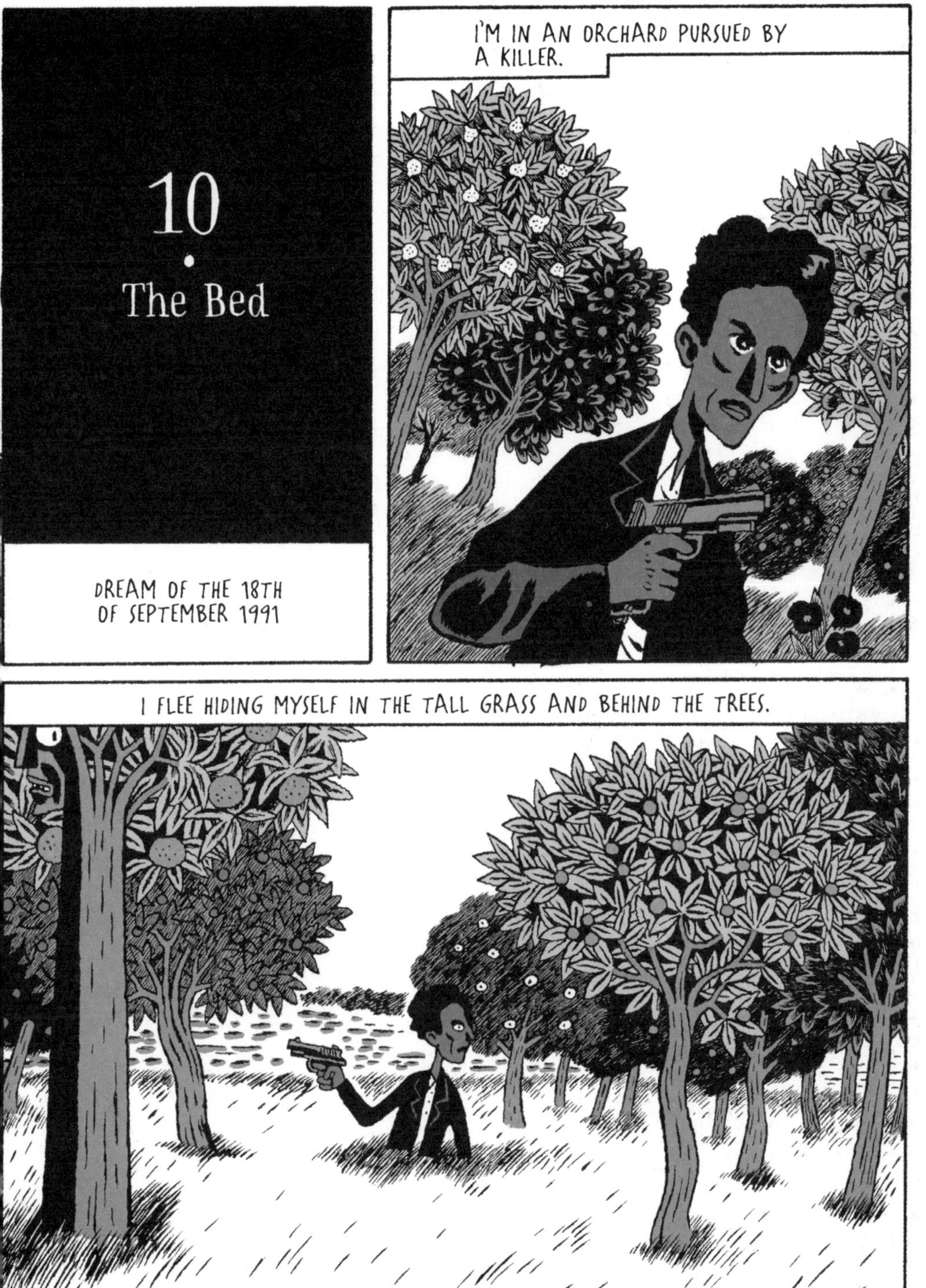
10
The Bed
DREAM OF THE 18TH OF SEPTEMBER 1991
I'M IN AN ORCHARD PURSUED BY A KILLER.
I FLEE HIDING MYSELF IN THE TALL GRASS AND BEHIND THE TREES.
1

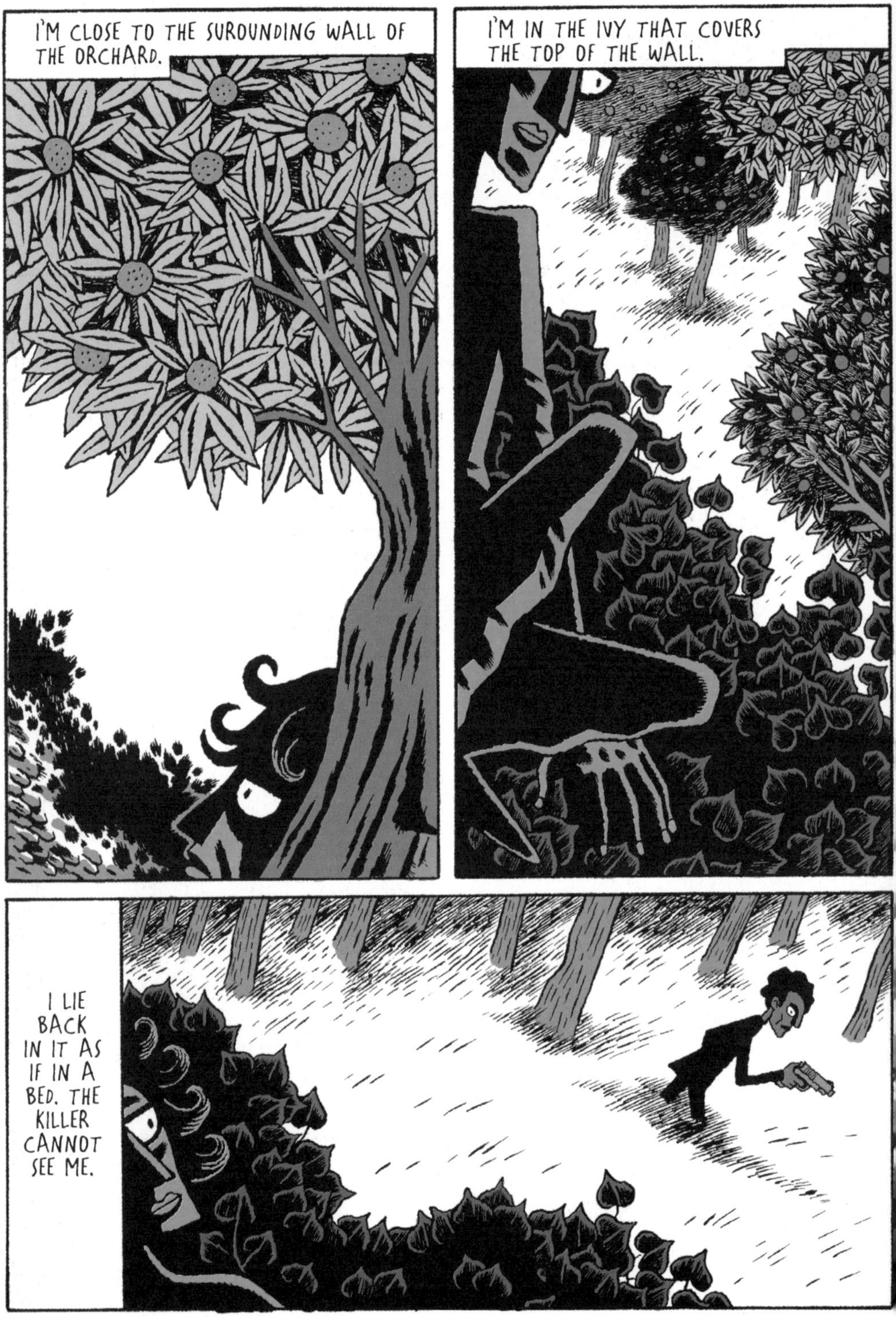
I'M CLOSE TO THE SUROUNDING WALL OF THE ORCHARD.
I'M IN THE IVY THAT COVERS THE TOP OF THE WALL.
I LIE BACK IN IT AS IF IN A BED. THE KILLER CANNOT SEE ME.

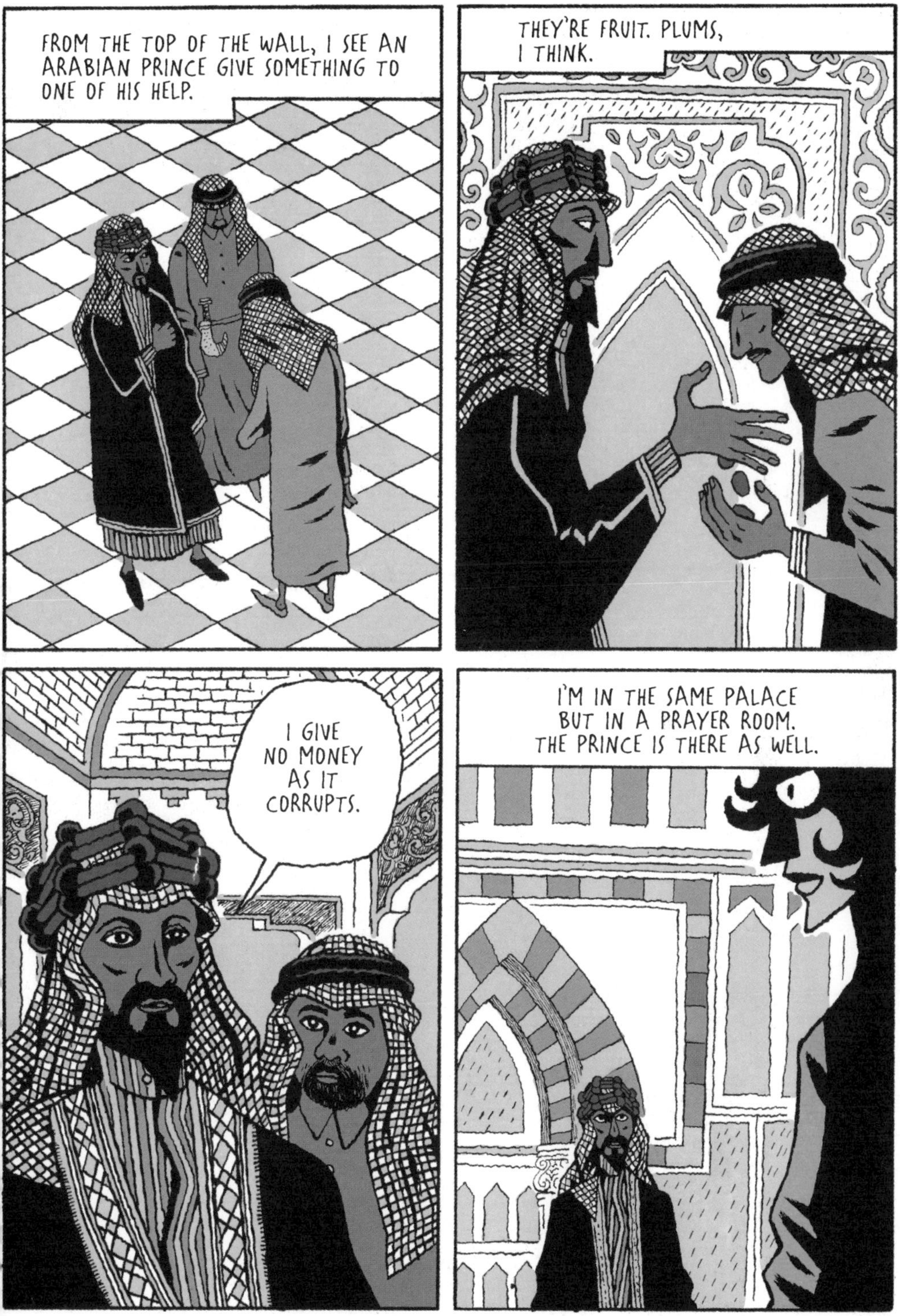
FROM THE TOP OF THE WALL, I SEE AN ARABIAN PRINCE GIVE SOMETHING TO ONE OF HIS HELP.
THEY'RE FRUIT. PLUMS, I THINK.
I GIVE NO MONEY AS IT CORRUPTS.
I'M IN THE SAME PALACE BUT IN A PRAYER ROOM. THE PRINCE IS THERE AS WELL.

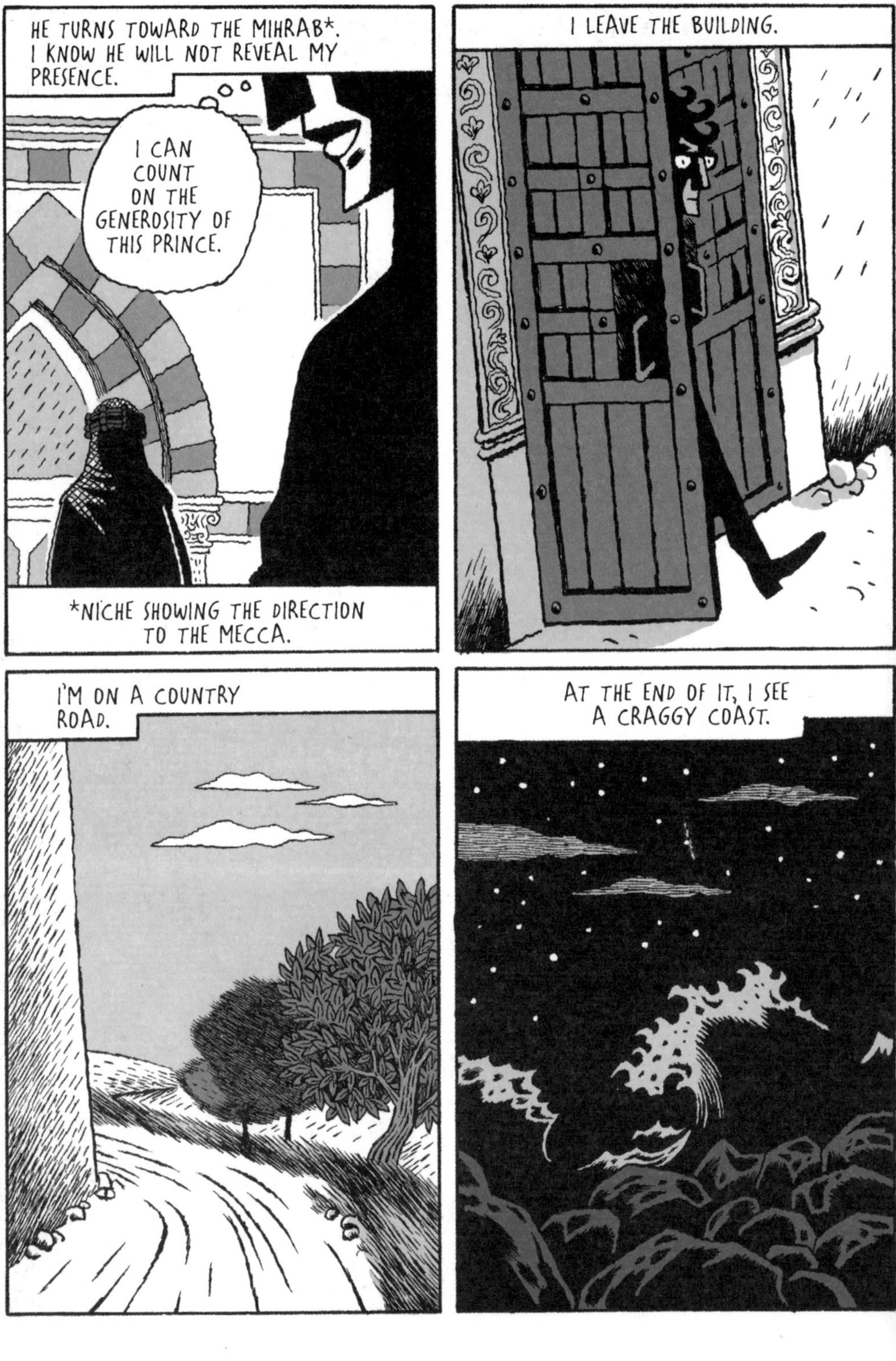
HE TURNS TOWARD THE MIHRAB*. I KNOW HE WILL NOT REVEAL MY PRESENCE.
I CAN COUNT ON THE GENEROSITY OF THIS PRINCE.
*NICHE SHOWING THE DIRECTION TO THE MECCA.
I LEAVE THE BUILDING.
I'M ON A COUNTRY ROAD.
AT THE END OF IT, I SEE A CRAGGY COAST.

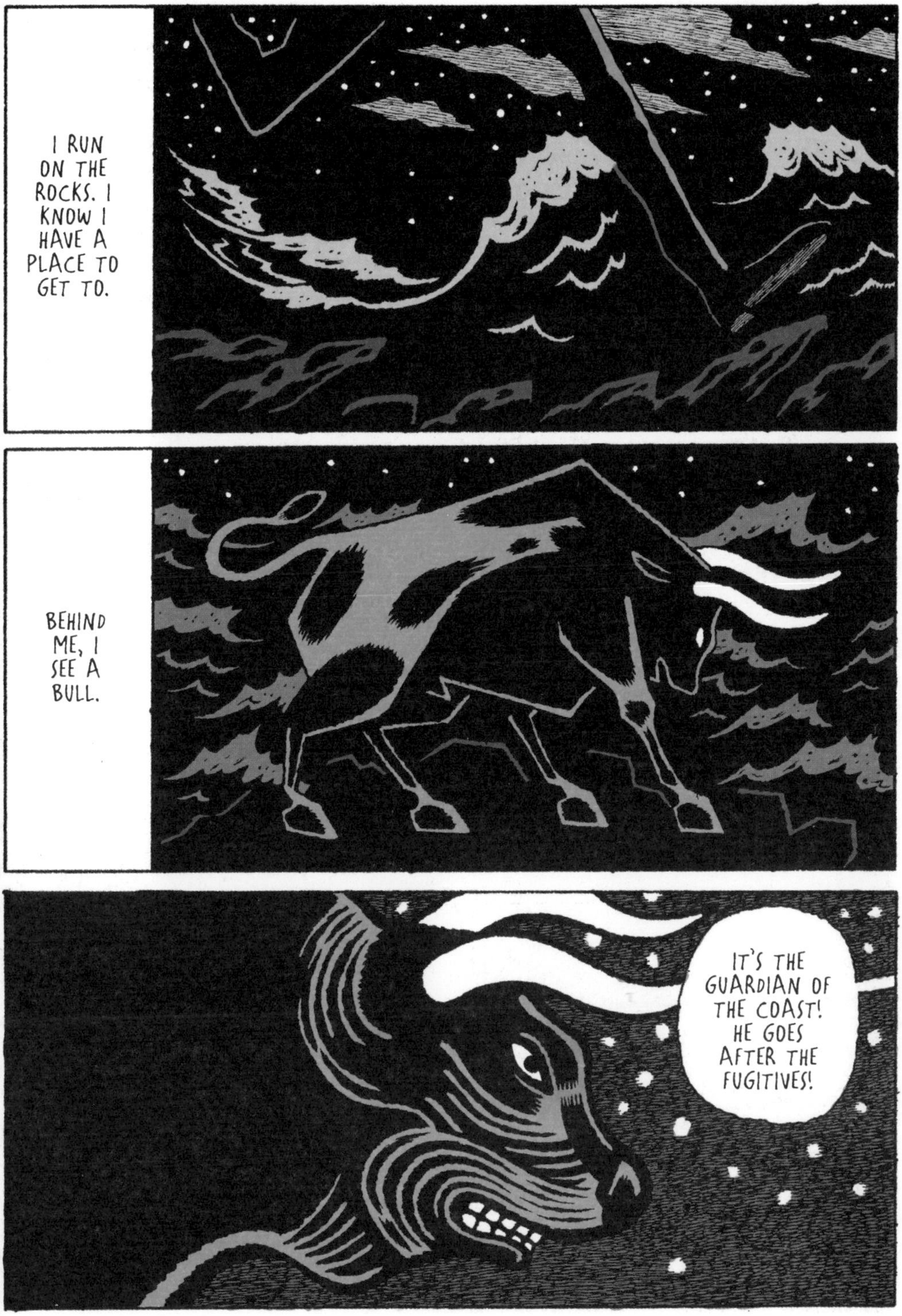
I RUN ON THE ROCKS. I KNOW I HAVE A PLACE TO GET TO.
BEHIND ME, I SEE A BULL.
IT'S THE GUARDIAN OF THE COAST! HE GOES AFTER THE FUGITIVES!

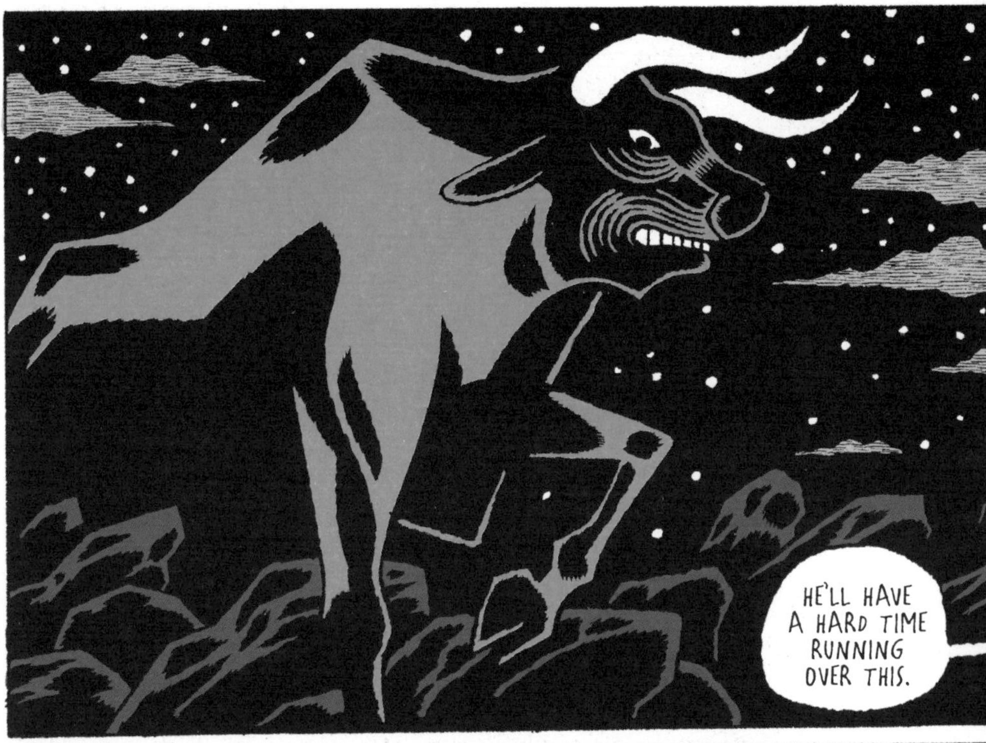

HE'LL HAVE A HARD TIME RUNNING OVER THIS.

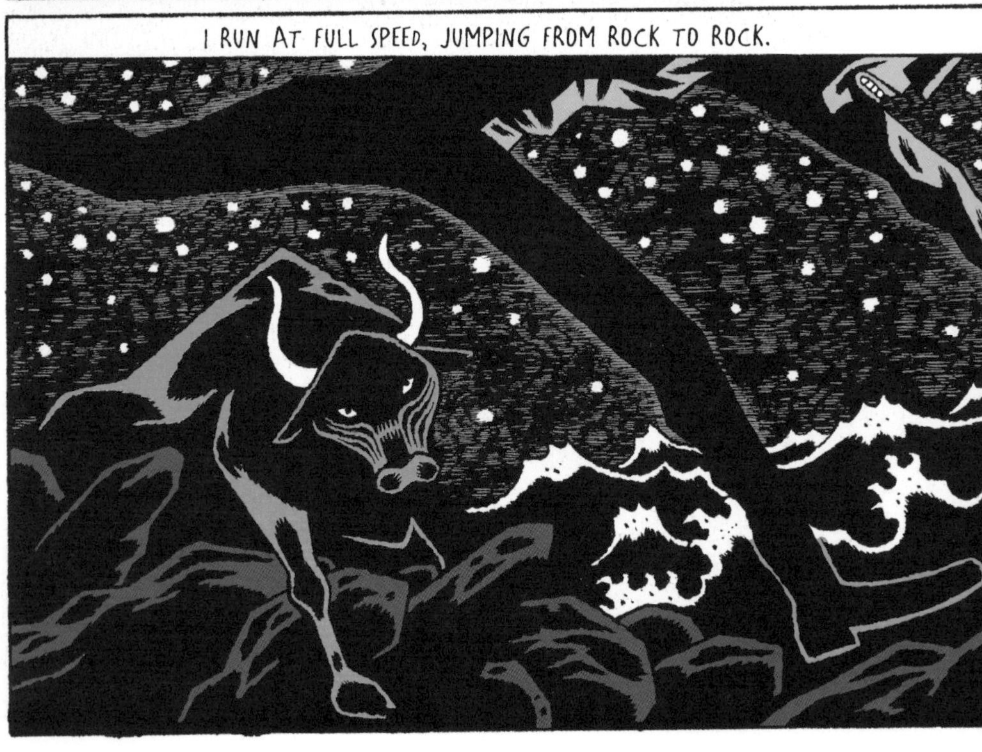

I RUN AT FULL SPEED, JUMPING FROM ROCK TO ROCK.

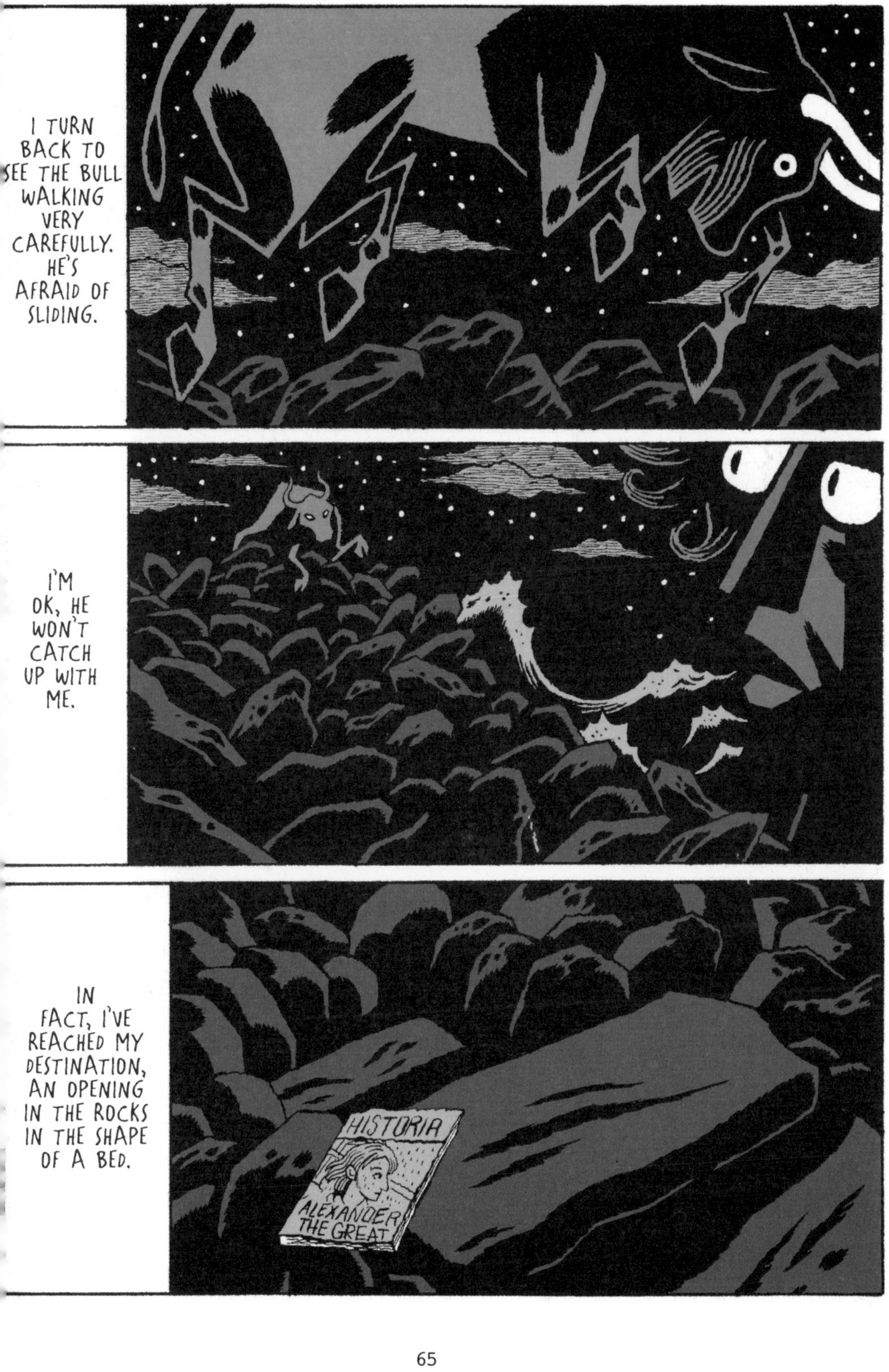
I TURN BACK TO SEE THE BULL WALKING VERY CAREFULLY. HE'S AFRAID OF SLIDING.
I'M OK, HE WON'T CATCH UP WITH ME.
IN FACT, I'VE REACHED MY DESTINATION, AN OPENING IN THE ROCKS IN THE SHAPE OF A BED.
HISTORIA
ALEXANDER THE GREAT

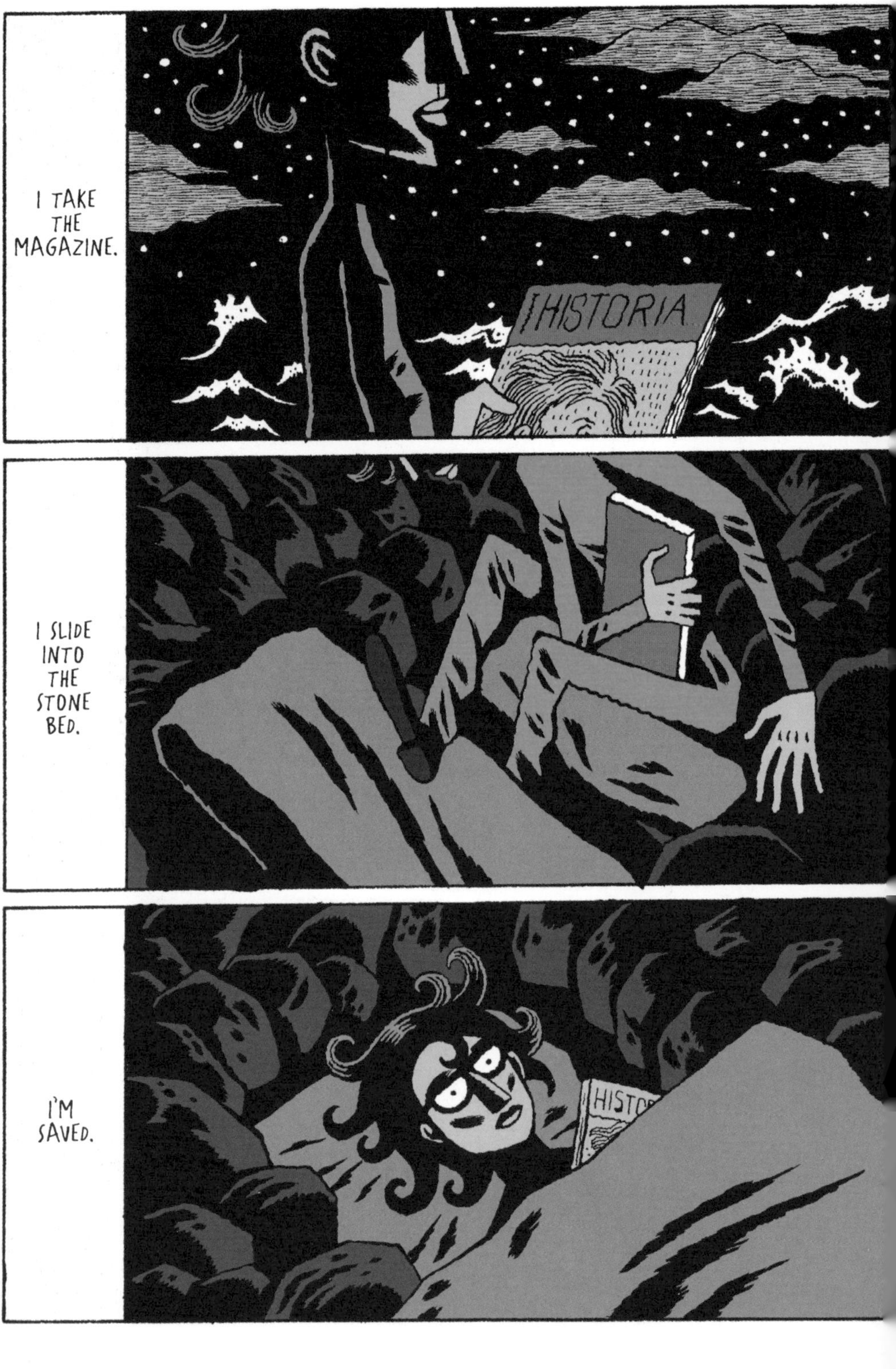
I TAKE THE MAGAZINE.
HISTORIA
I SLIDE INTO THE STONE BED.
HISTO
I'M SAVED.

11 • The Cat

A DREAM FROM SEPTEMBER 24, 1991

I'M WALKING THROUGH THE MAEGHT FOUNDATION'S* PINEWOODS. I FEEL LIKE I'M BEING FOL-LOWED.

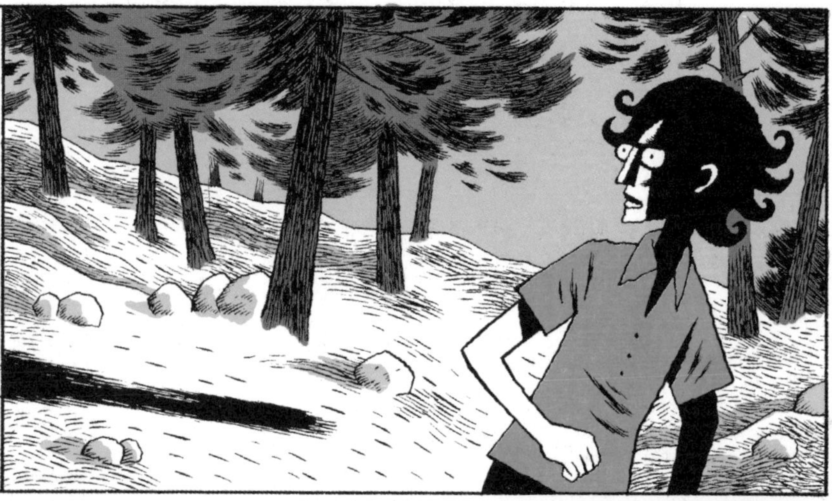

IT'S GIACOMETTI'S CAT THAT'S FOLLOWING ME. IT'S THE GUARDIAN OF THE WOODS.

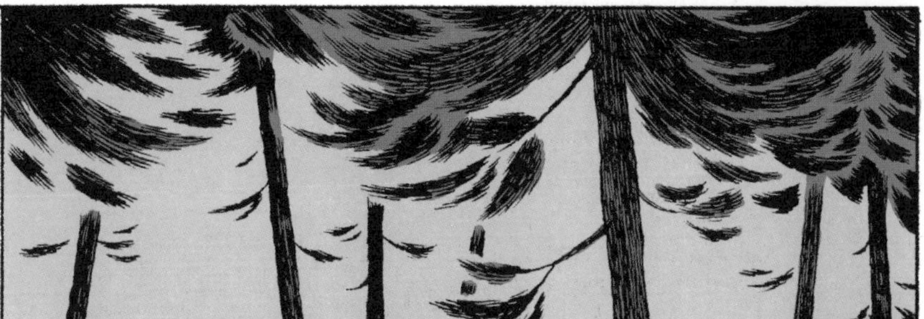

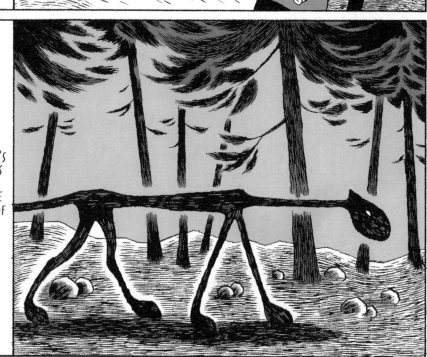

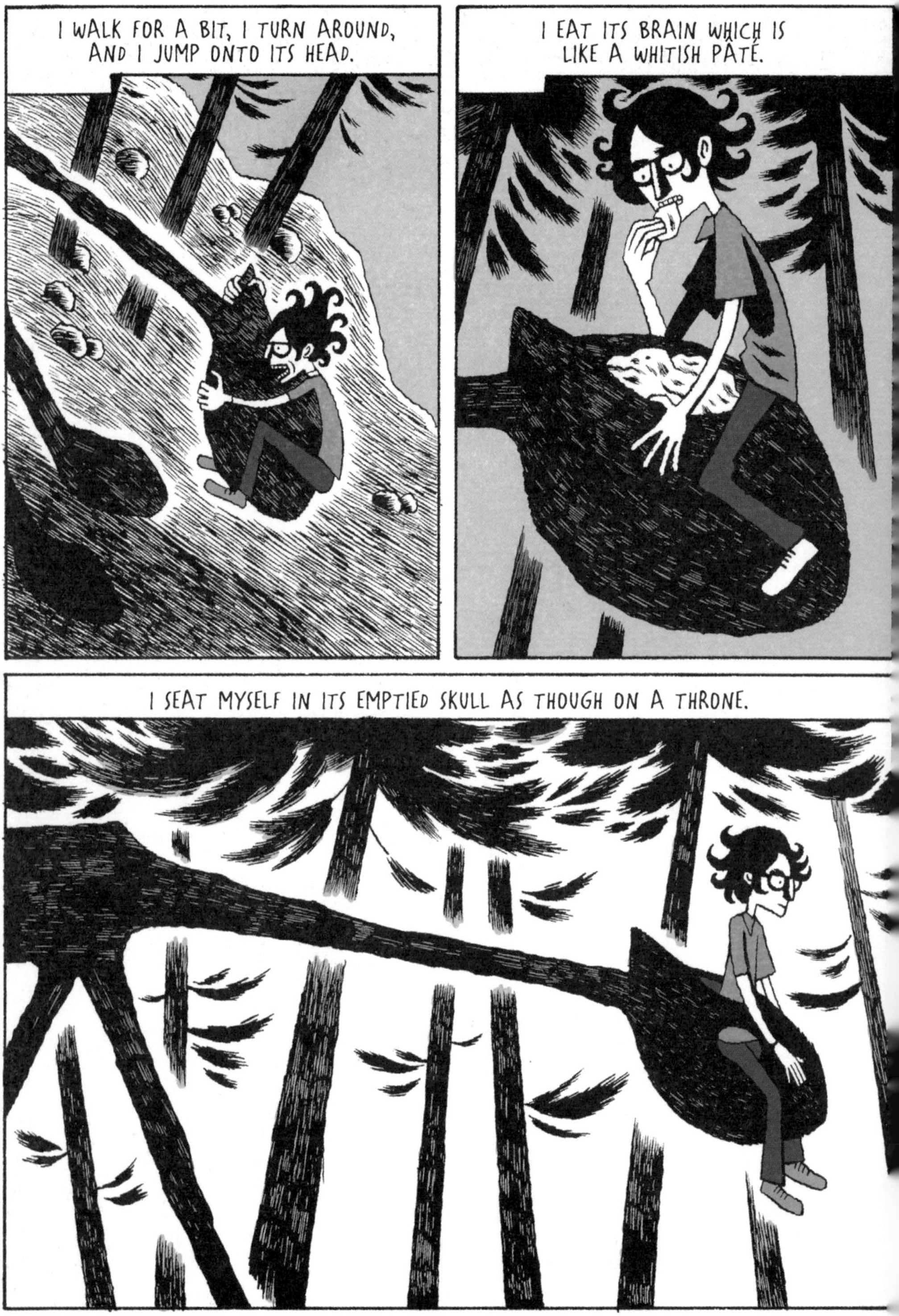
I WALK FOR A BIT, I TURN AROUND, AND I JUMP ONTO ITS HEAD.
I EAT ITS BRAIN WHICH IS LIKE A WHITISH PÂTÉ.
I SEAT MYSELF IN ITS EMPTIED SKULL AS THOUGH ON A THRONE.

12 • The Serials

A DREAM FROM OCTOBER 27, 1991.

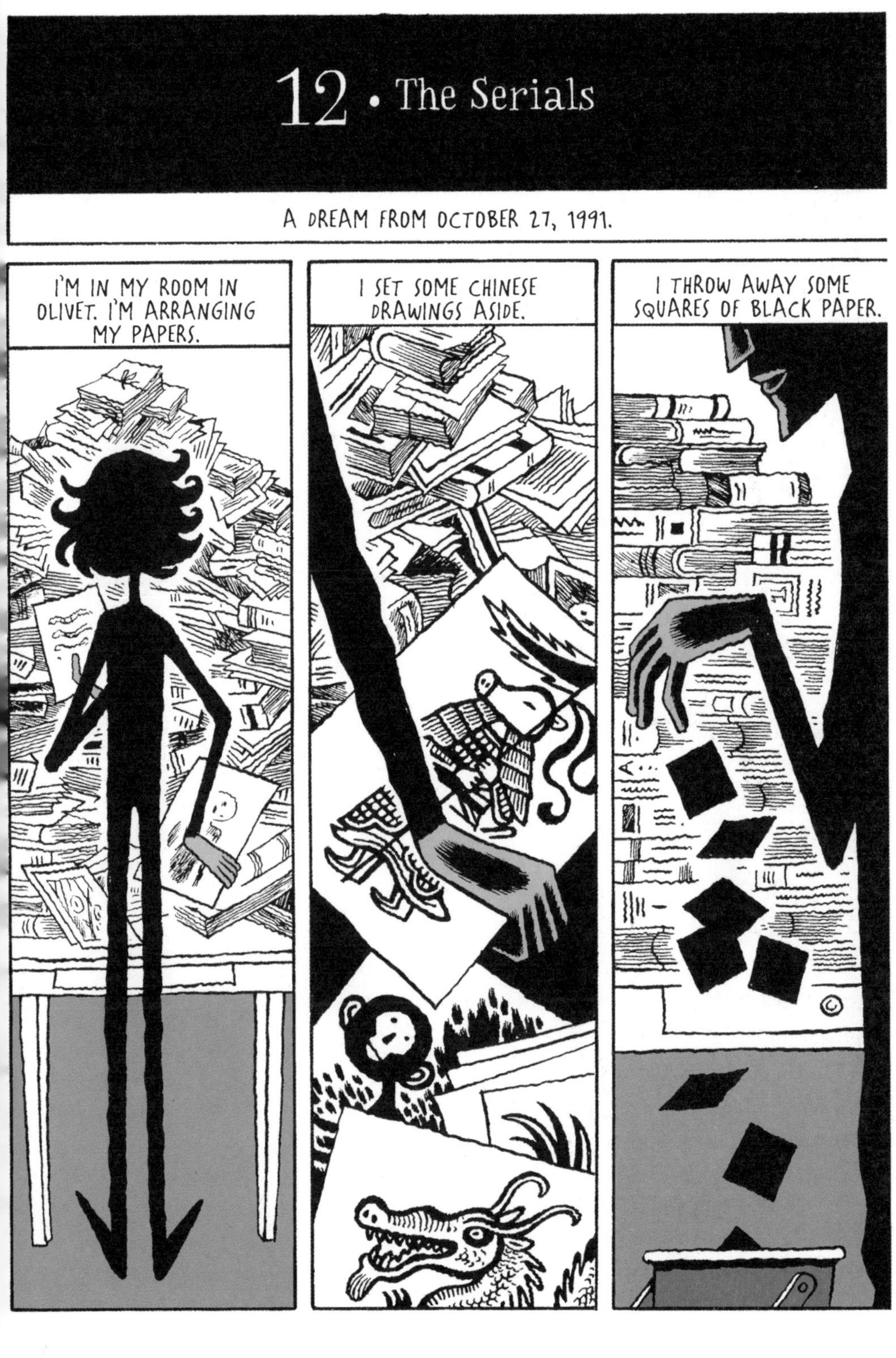
I'M IN MY ROOM IN OLIVET. I'M ARRANGING MY PAPERS.
I SET SOME CHINESE DRAWINGS ASIDE.
I THROW AWAY SOME SQUARES OF BLACK PAPER.

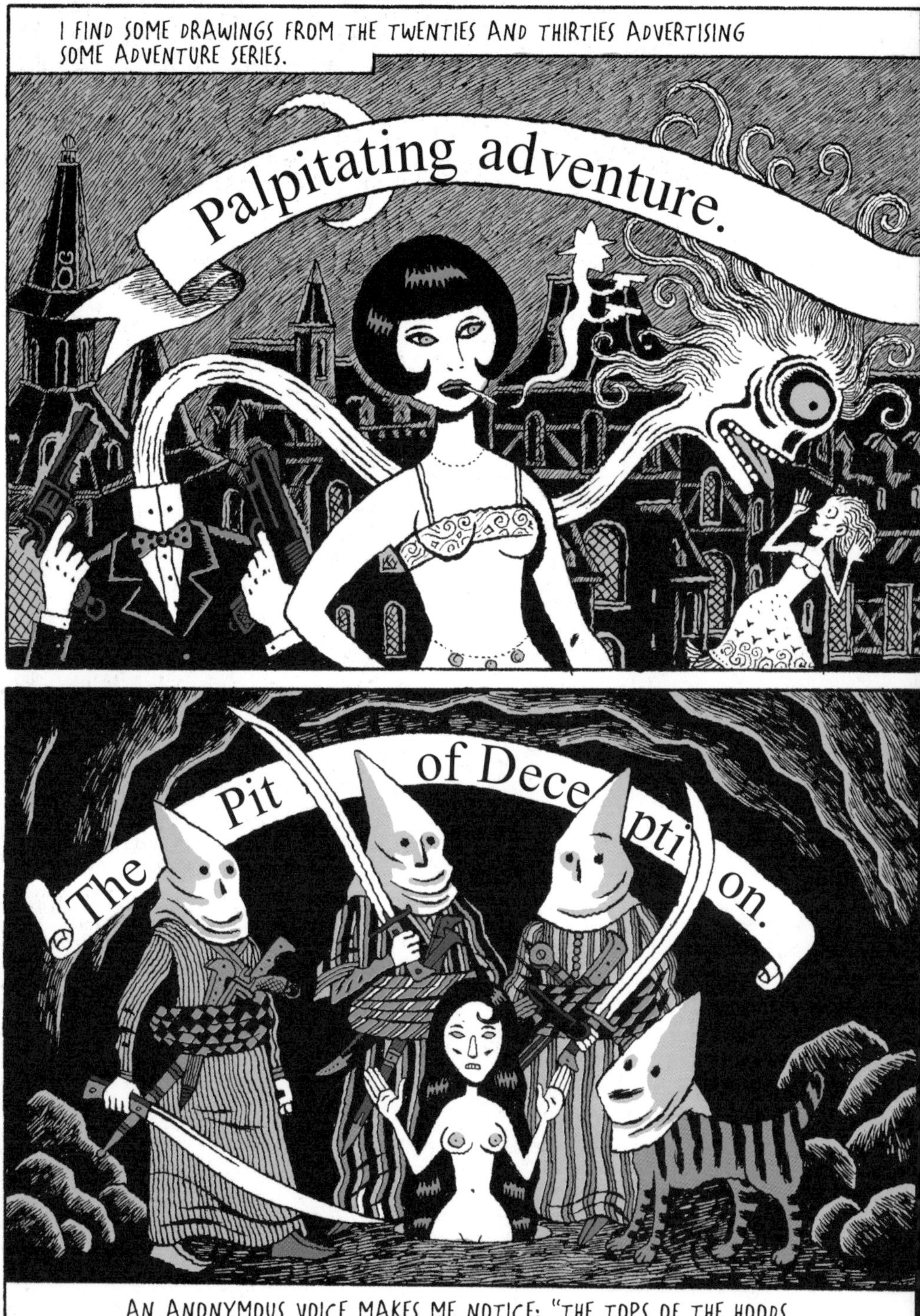
I FIND SOME DRAWINGS FROM THE TWENTIES AND THIRTIES ADVERTISING SOME ADVENTURE SERIES.
Palpitating adventure.
The Pit of Deception.
AN ANONYMOUS VOICE MAKES ME NOTICE: "THE TOPS OF THE HOODS ARE DRAWN IN THE STYLE OF..." THE END OF THE SENTENCE IS LOST.

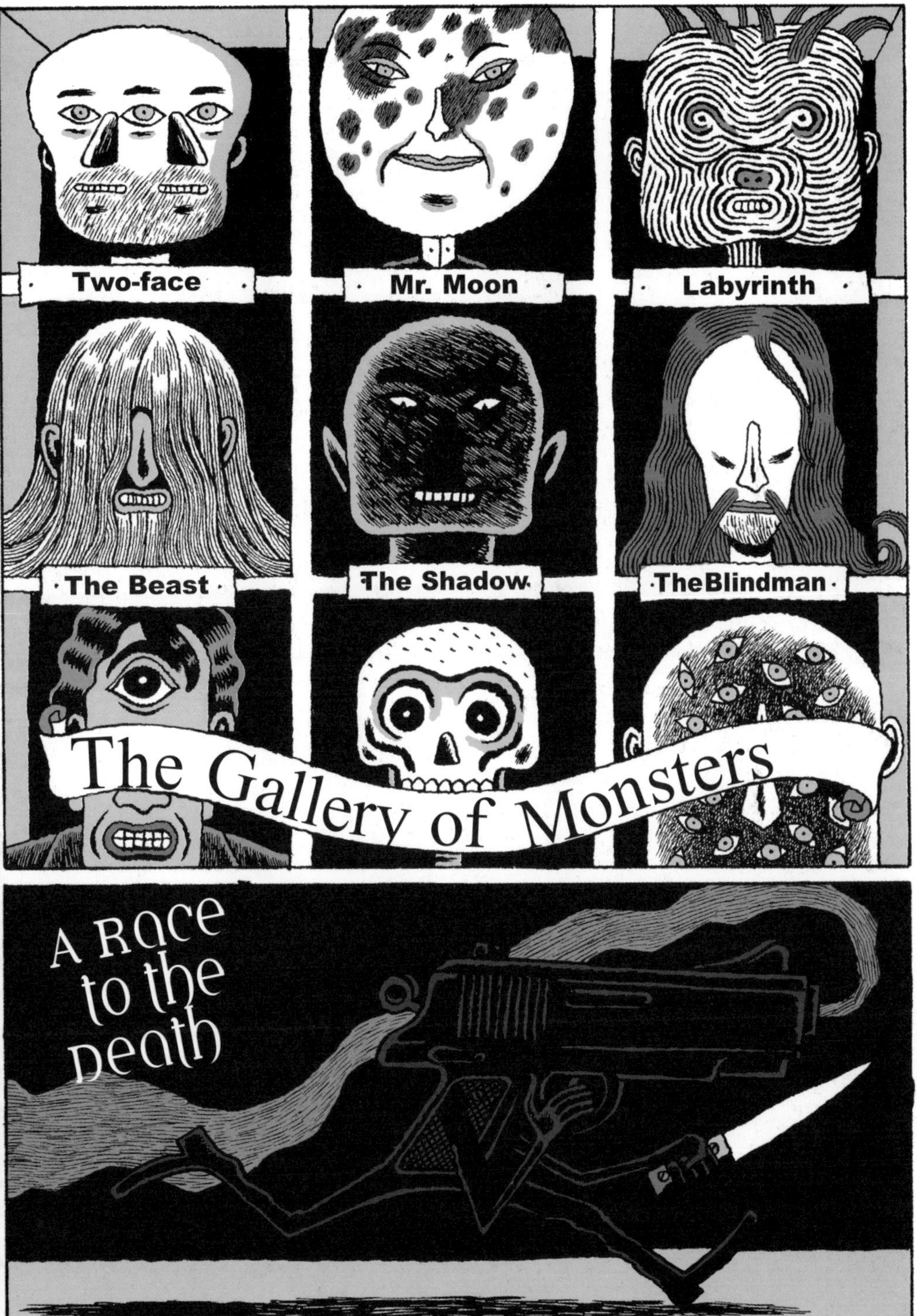
Two-face
Mr. Moon
Labyrinth
The Beast
The Shadow
TheBlindman
The Gallery of Monsters
A Race to the Death

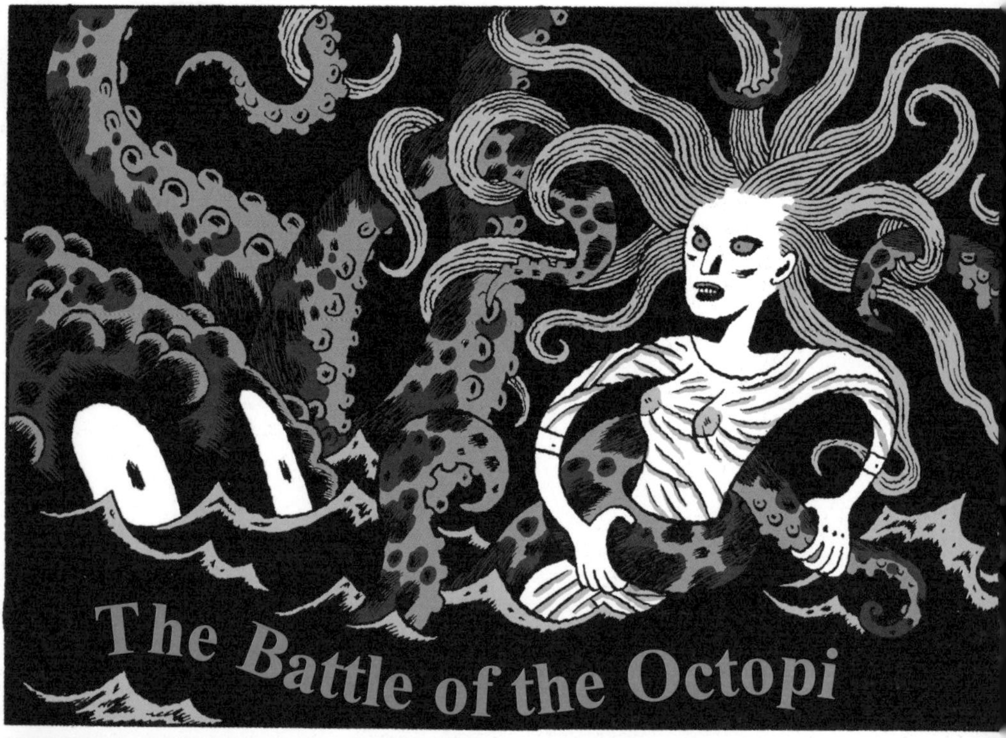
The Battle of the Octopi

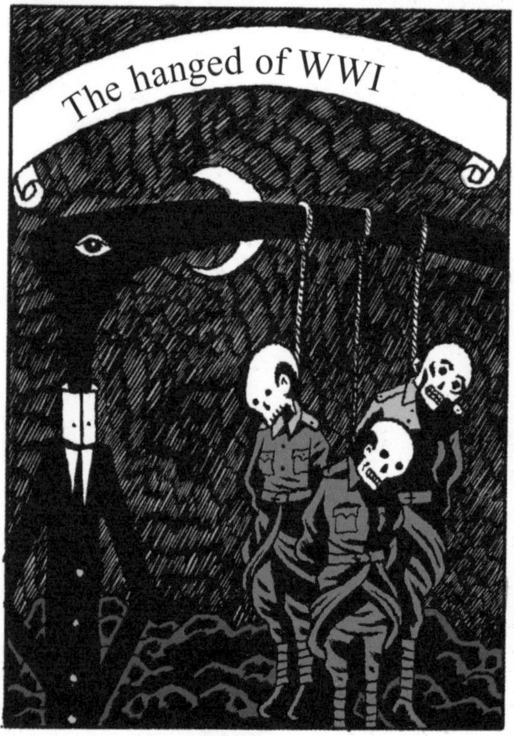
The hanged of WWI

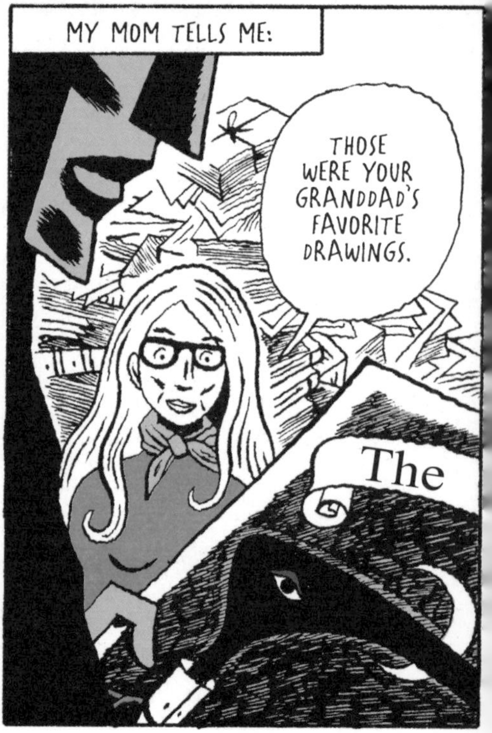
MY MOM TELLS ME:
THOSE WERE YOUR GRANDDAD'S FAVORITE DRAWINGS.
The

13 • Cats and Tigers

MIXED UP DREAMS FROM JANUARY 19, 1992 AND MARCH 20, 2005

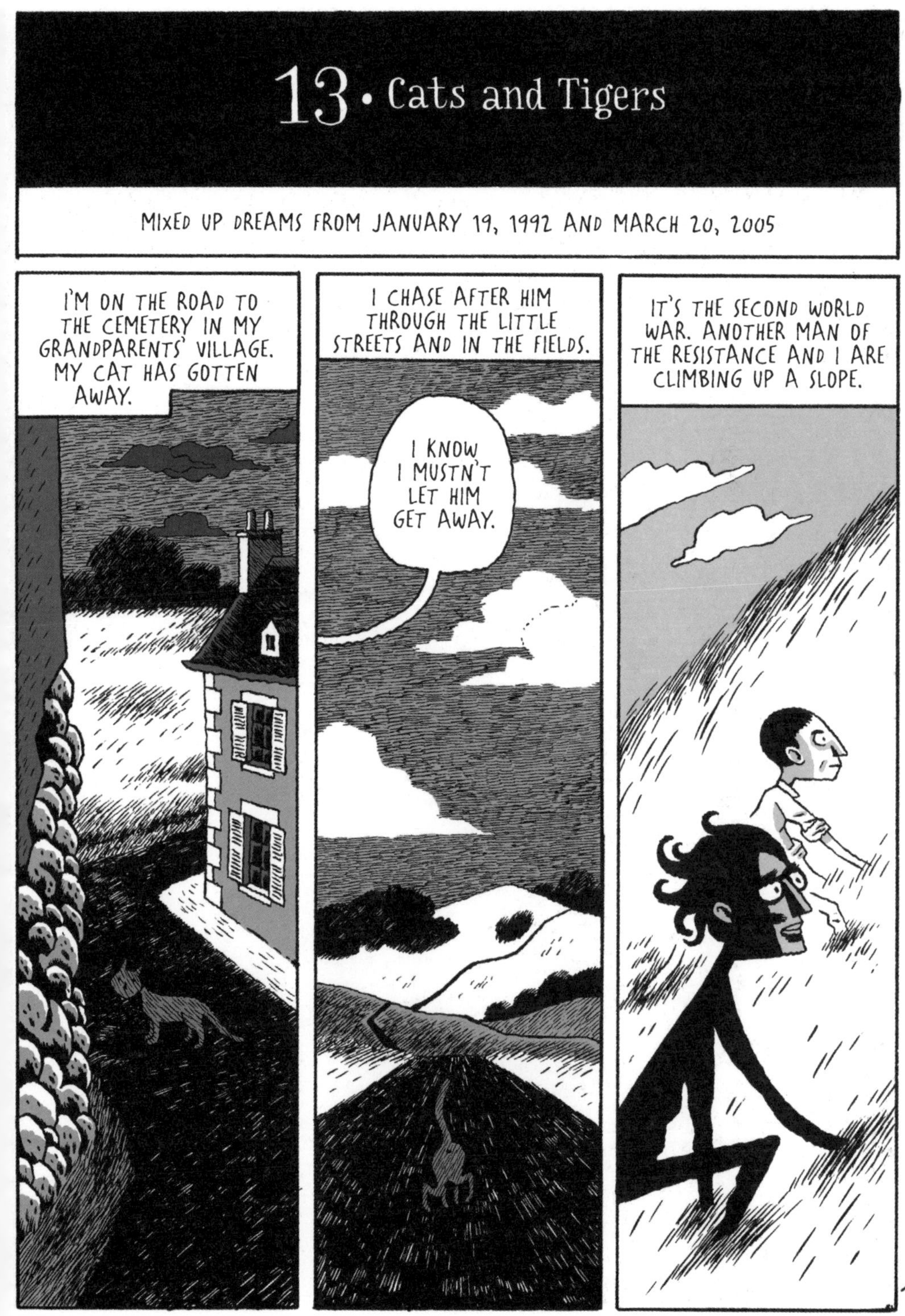

I'M ON THE ROAD TO THE CEMETERY IN MY GRANDPARENTS' VILLAGE. MY CAT HAS GOTTEN AWAY.
I CHASE AFTER HIM THROUGH THE LITTLE STREETS AND IN THE FIELDS.
I KNOW I MUSTN'T LET HIM GET AWAY.
IT'S THE SECOND WORLD WAR. ANOTHER MAN OF THE RESISTANCE AND I ARE CLIMBING UP A SLOPE.

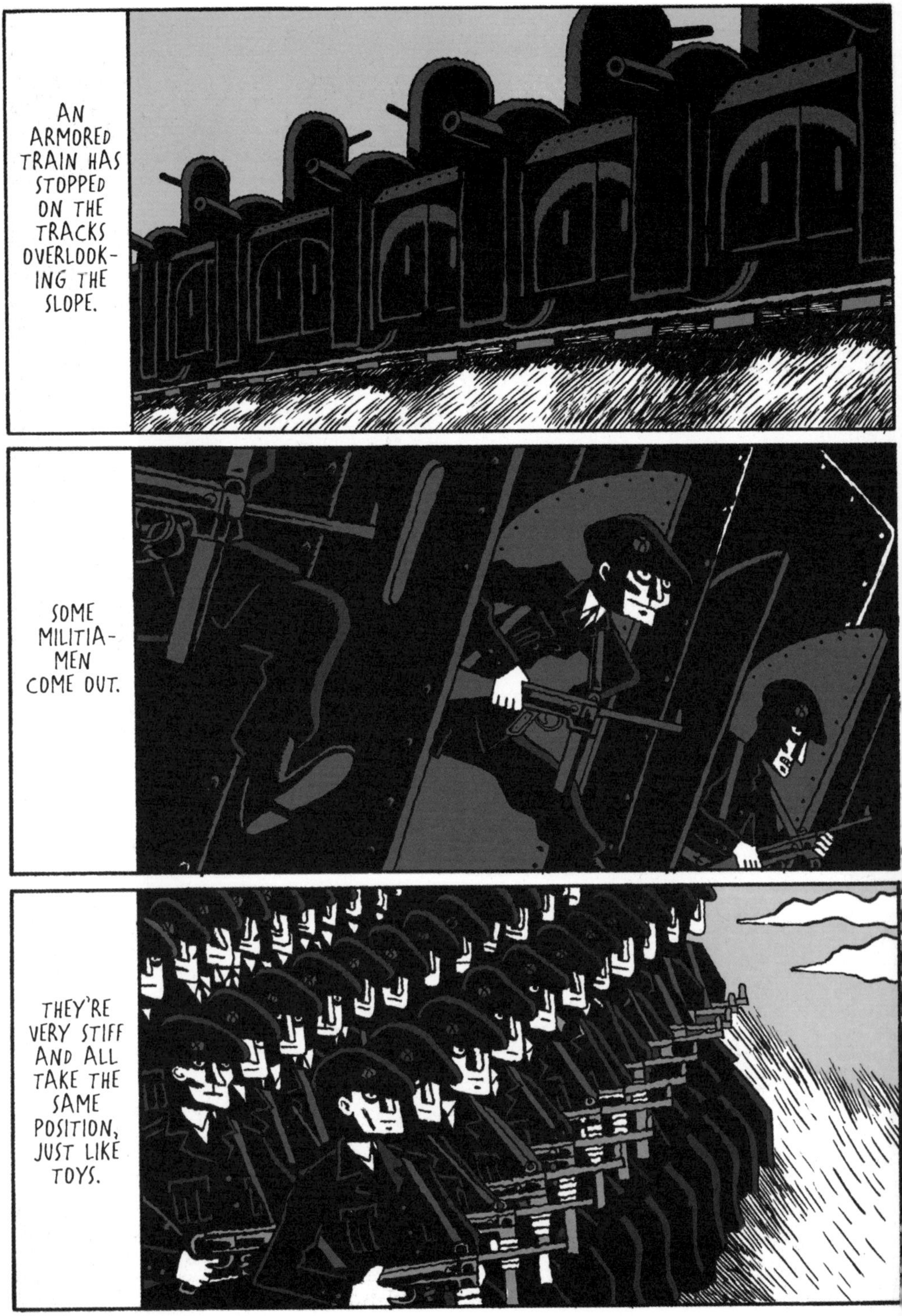
AN ARMORED TRAIN HAS STOPPED ON THE TRACKS OVERLOOK-ING THE SLOPE.
SOME MILITIA-MEN COME OUT.
THEY'RE VERY STIFF AND ALL TAKE THE SAME POSITION, JUST LIKE TOYS.

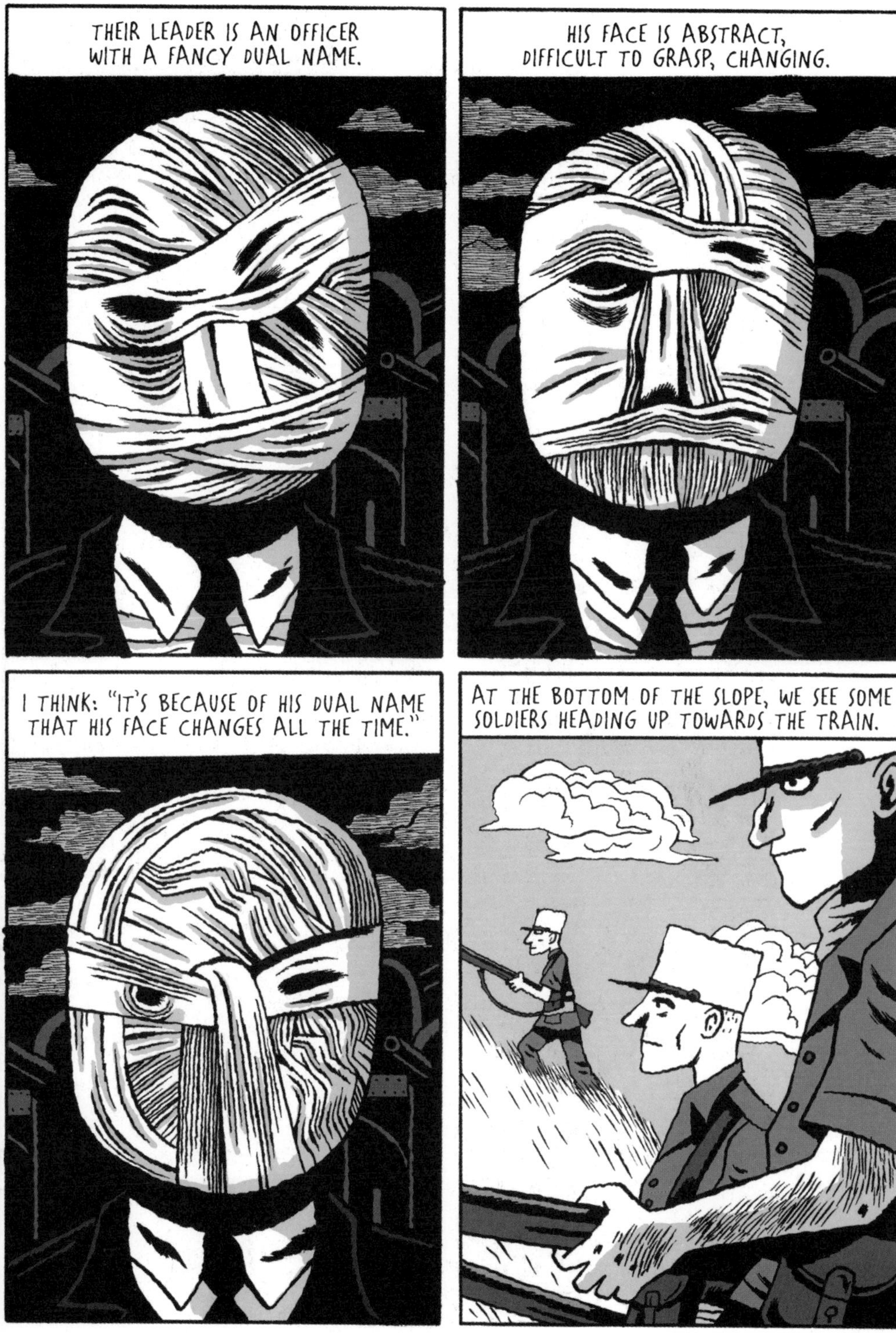
THEIR LEADER IS AN OFFICER WITH A FANCY DUAL NAME.
HIS FACE IS ABSTRACT, DIFFICULT TO GRASP, CHANGING.
I THINK: "IT'S BECAUSE OF HIS DUAL NAME THAT HIS FACE CHANGES ALL THE TIME."
AT THE BOTTOM OF THE SLOPE, WE SEE SOME SOLDIERS HEADING UP TOWARDS THE TRAIN.

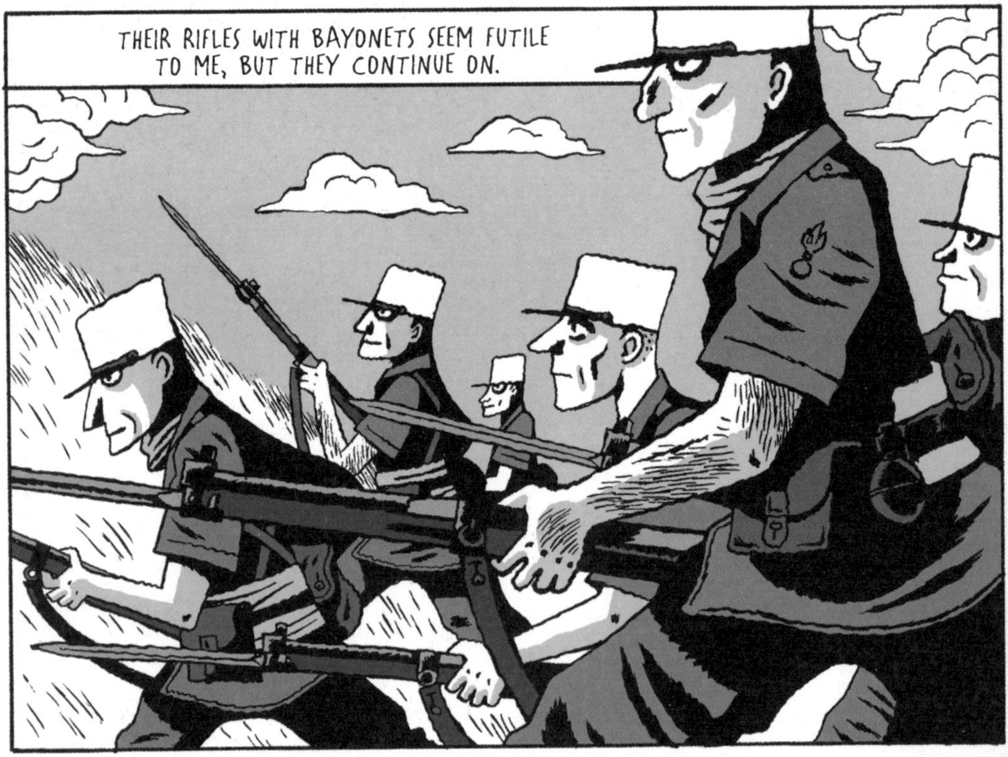
THEIR RIFLES WITH BAYONETS SEEM FUTILE TO ME, BUT THEY CONTINUE ON.

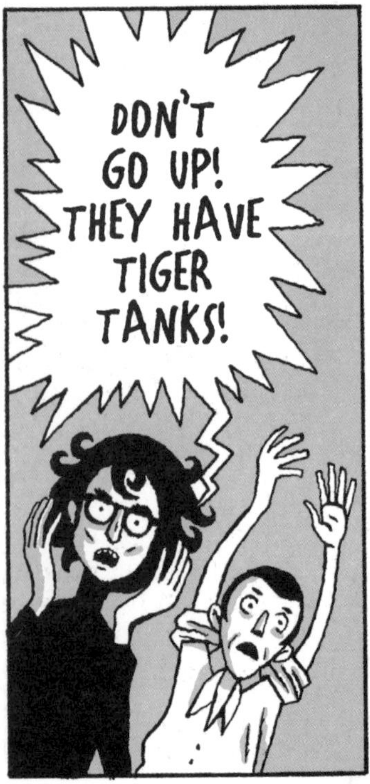
DON'T GO UP! THEY HAVE TIGER TANKS!

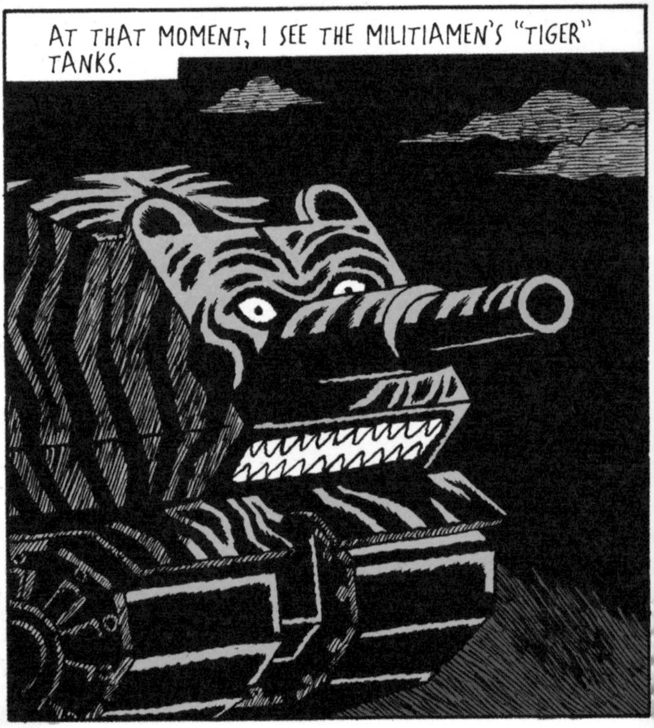
AT THAT MOMENT, I SEE THE MILITIAMEN'S "TIGER" TANKS.

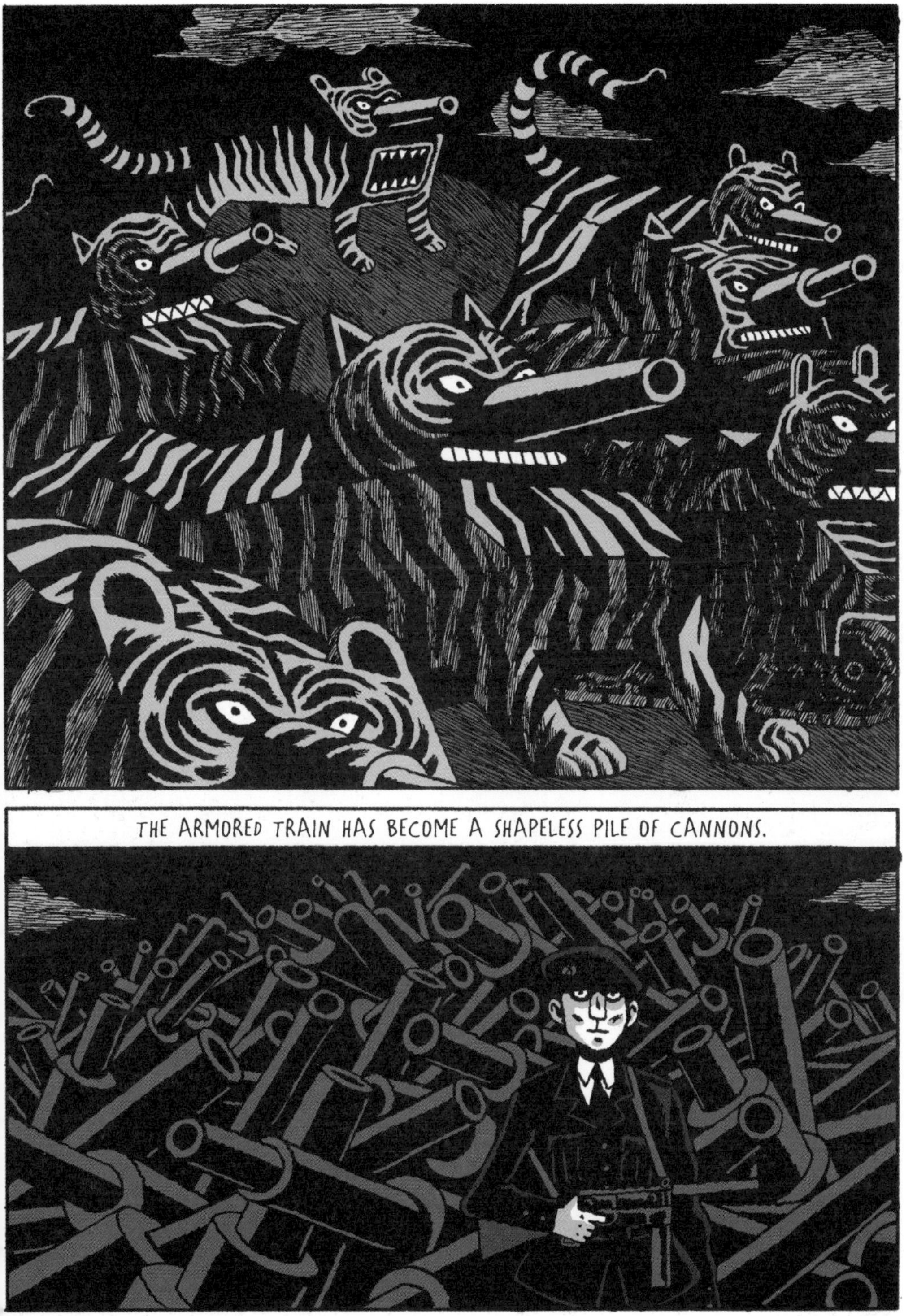
THE ARMORED TRAIN HAS BECOME A SHAPELESS PILE OF CANNONS.

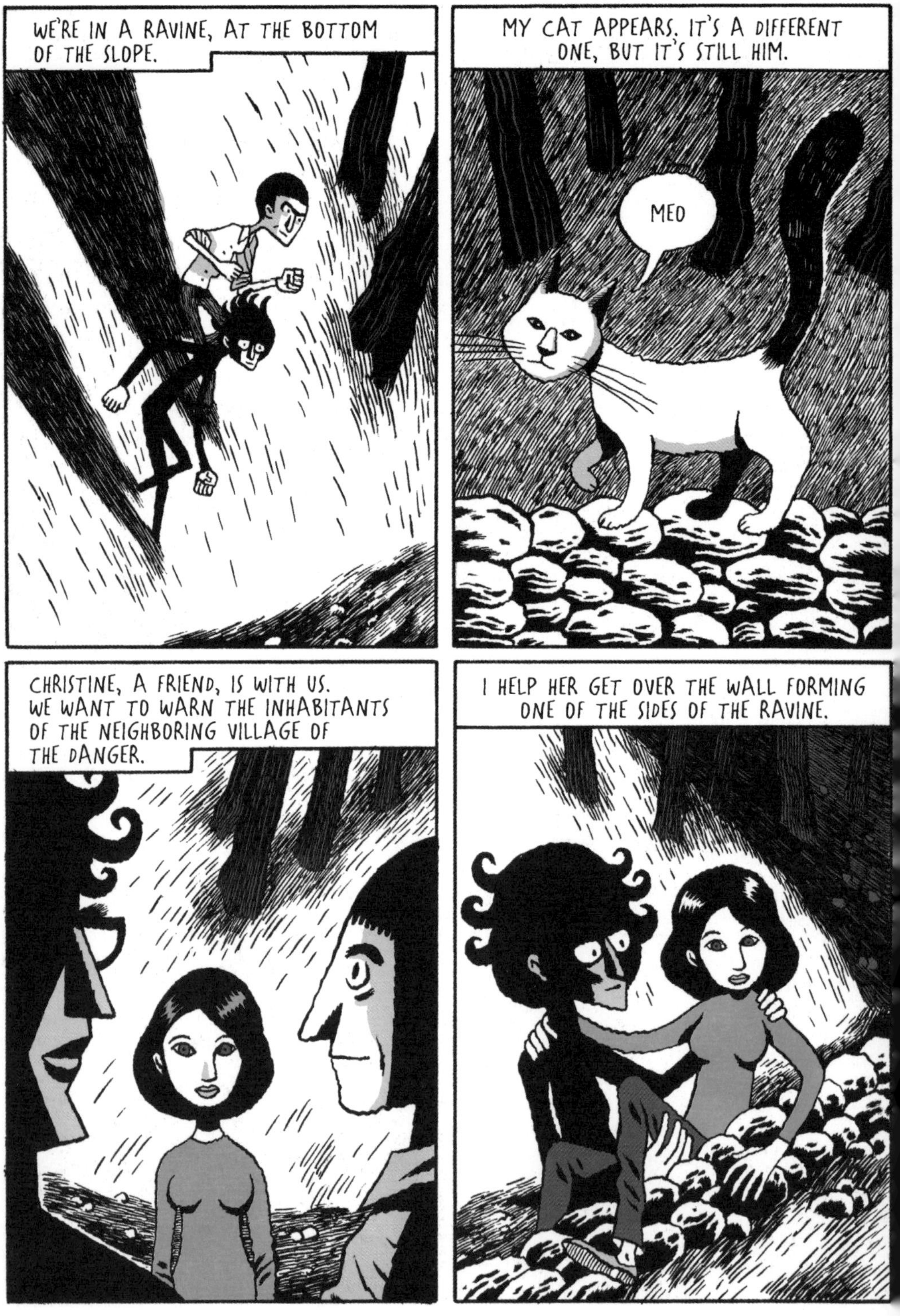
WE'RE IN A RAVINE, AT THE BOTTOM OF THE SLOPE.
MY CAT APPEARS. IT'S A DIFFERENT ONE, BUT IT'S STILL HIM.
MEO
CHRISTINE, A FRIEND, IS WITH US. WE WANT TO WARN THE INHABITANTS OF THE NEIGHBORING VILLAGE OF THE DANGER.
I HELP HER GET OVER THE WALL FORMING ONE OF THE SIDES OF THE RAVINE.

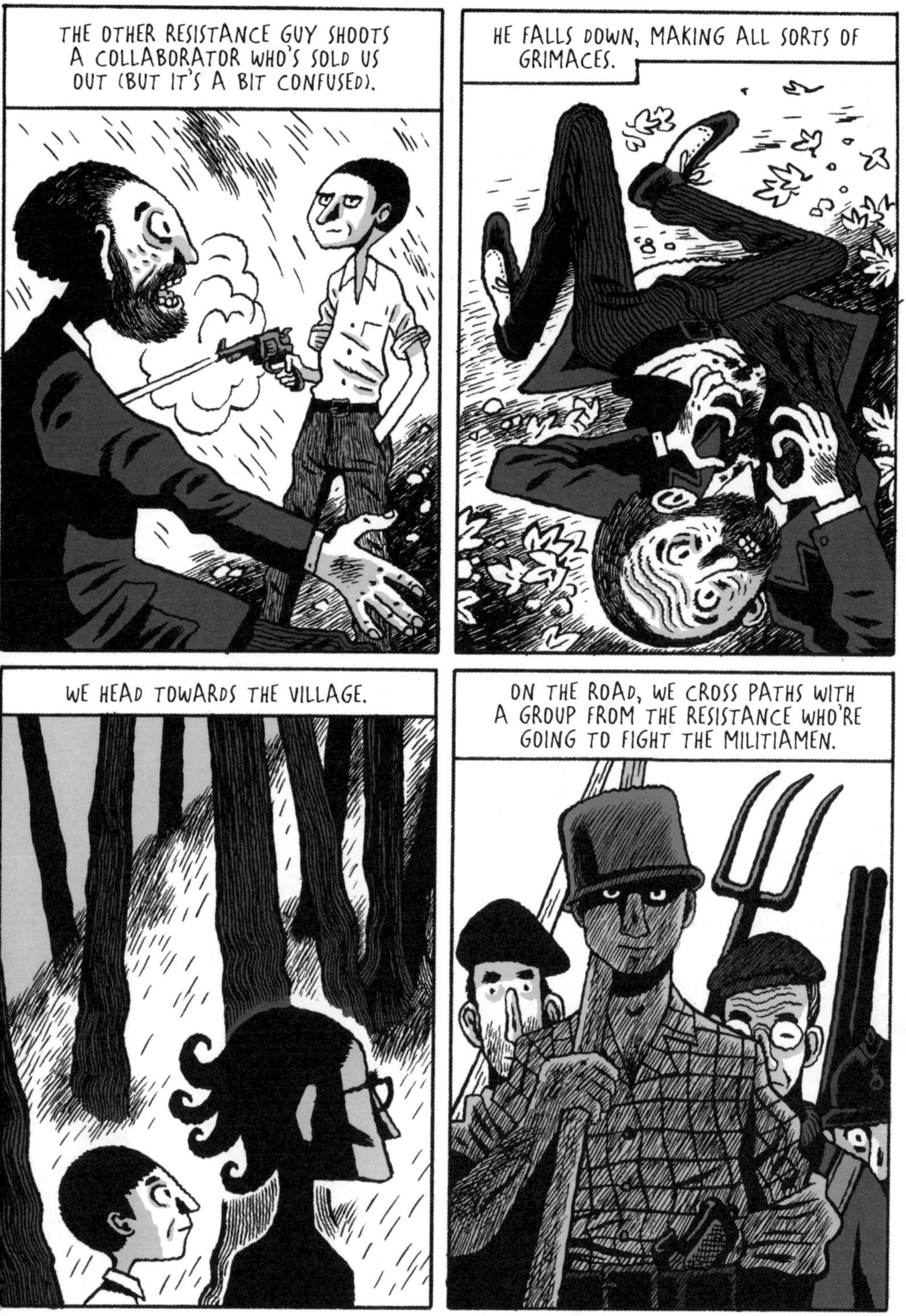
THE OTHER RESISTANCE GUY SHOOTS A COLLABORATOR WHO'S SOLD US OUT (BUT IT'S A BIT CONFUSED).
HE FALLS DOWN, MAKING ALL SORTS OF GRIMACES.
WE HEAD TOWARDS THE VILLAGE.
ON THE ROAD, WE CROSS PATHS WITH A GROUP FROM THE RESISTANCE WHO'RE GOING TO FIGHT THE MILITIAMEN.

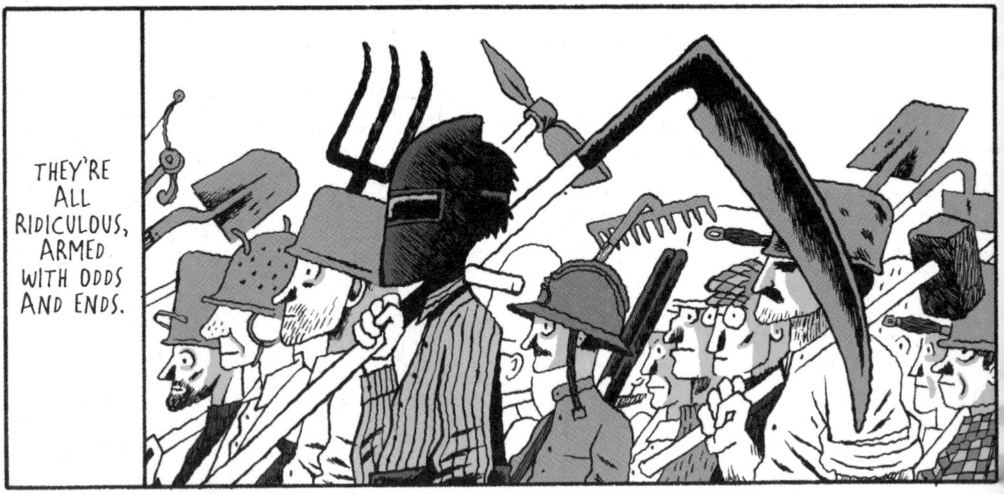
THEY'RE ALL RIDICULOUS, ARMED WITH ODDS AND ENDS.

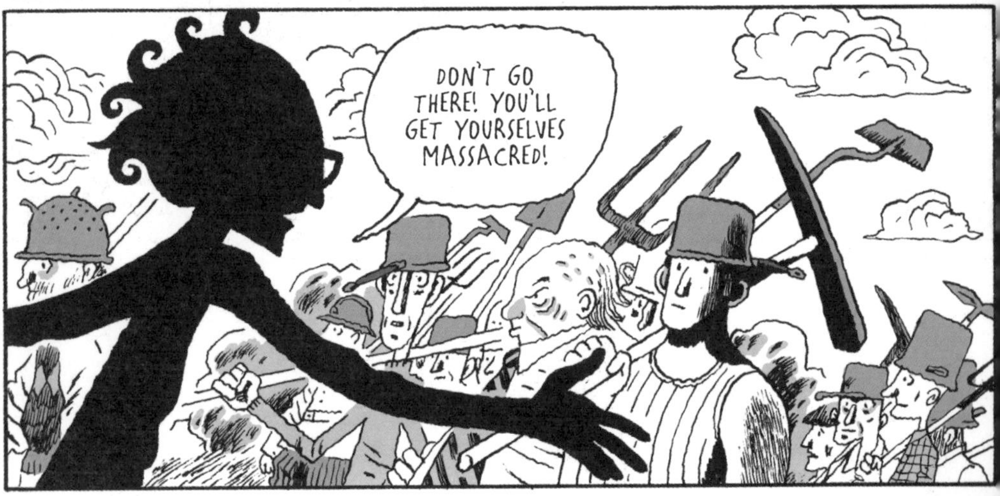
DON'T GO THERE! YOU'LL GET YOURSELVES MASSACRED!

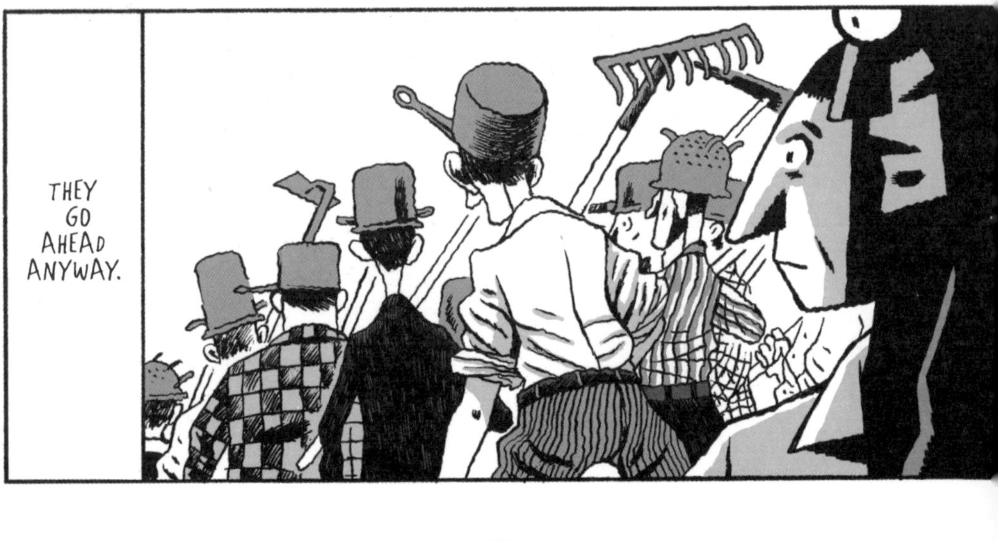
THEY GO AHEAD ANYWAY.

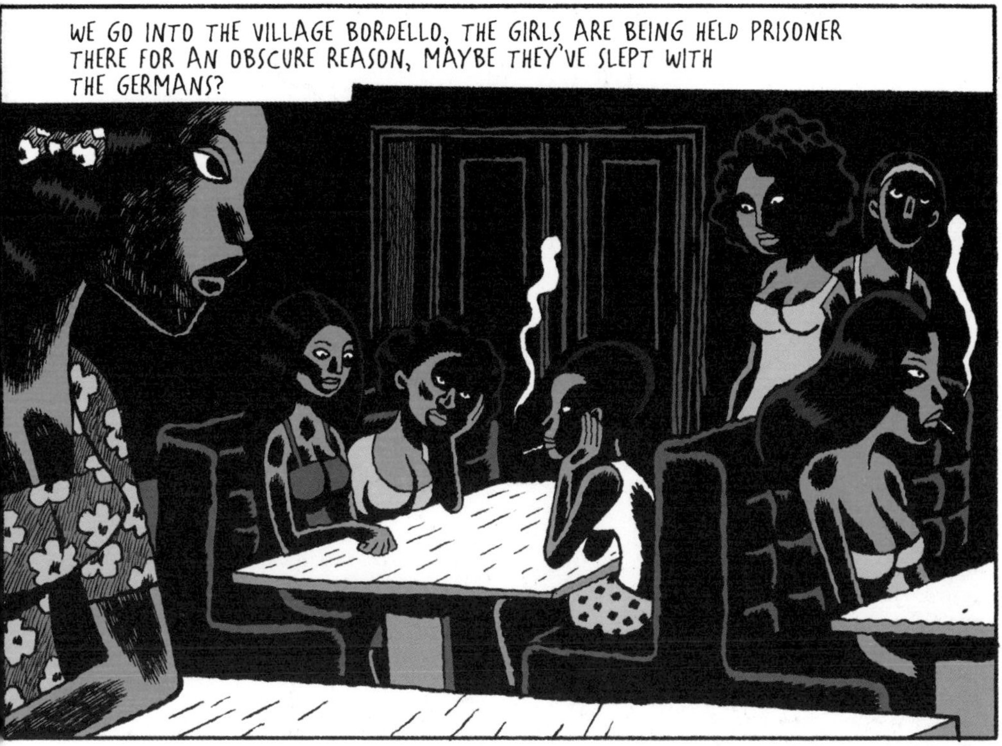
WE GO INTO THE VILLAGE BORDELLO, THE GIRLS ARE BEING HELD PRISONER THERE FOR AN OBSCURE REASON, MAYBE THEY'VE SLEPT WITH THE GERMANS?

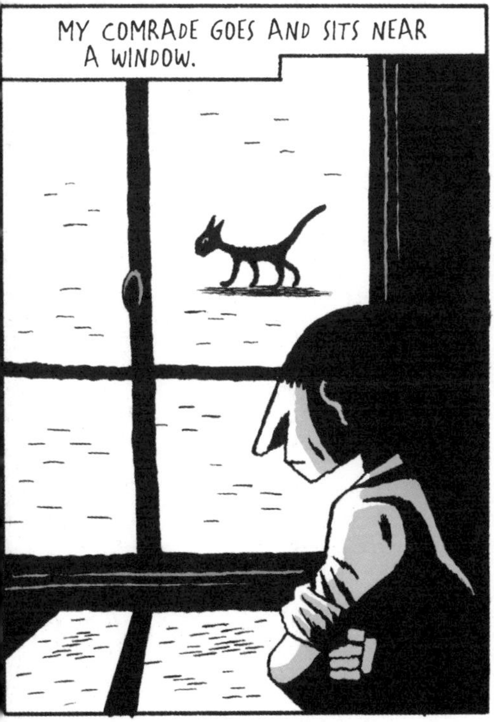
MY COMRADE GOES AND SITS NEAR A WINDOW.

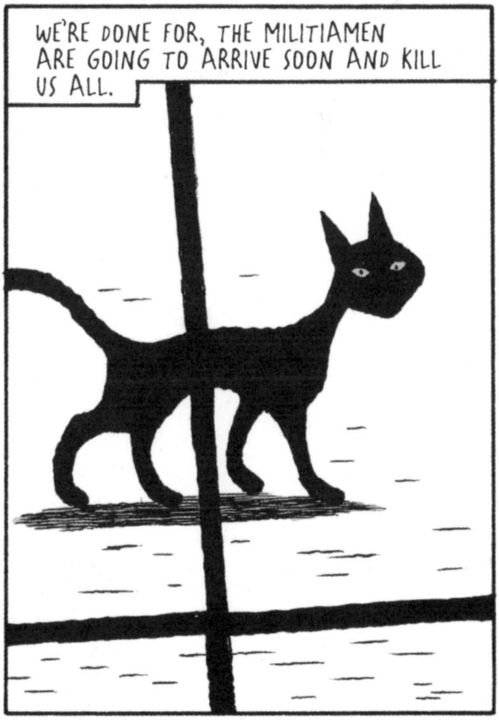
WE'RE DONE FOR, THE MILITIAMEN ARE GOING TO ARRIVE SOON AND KILL US ALL.

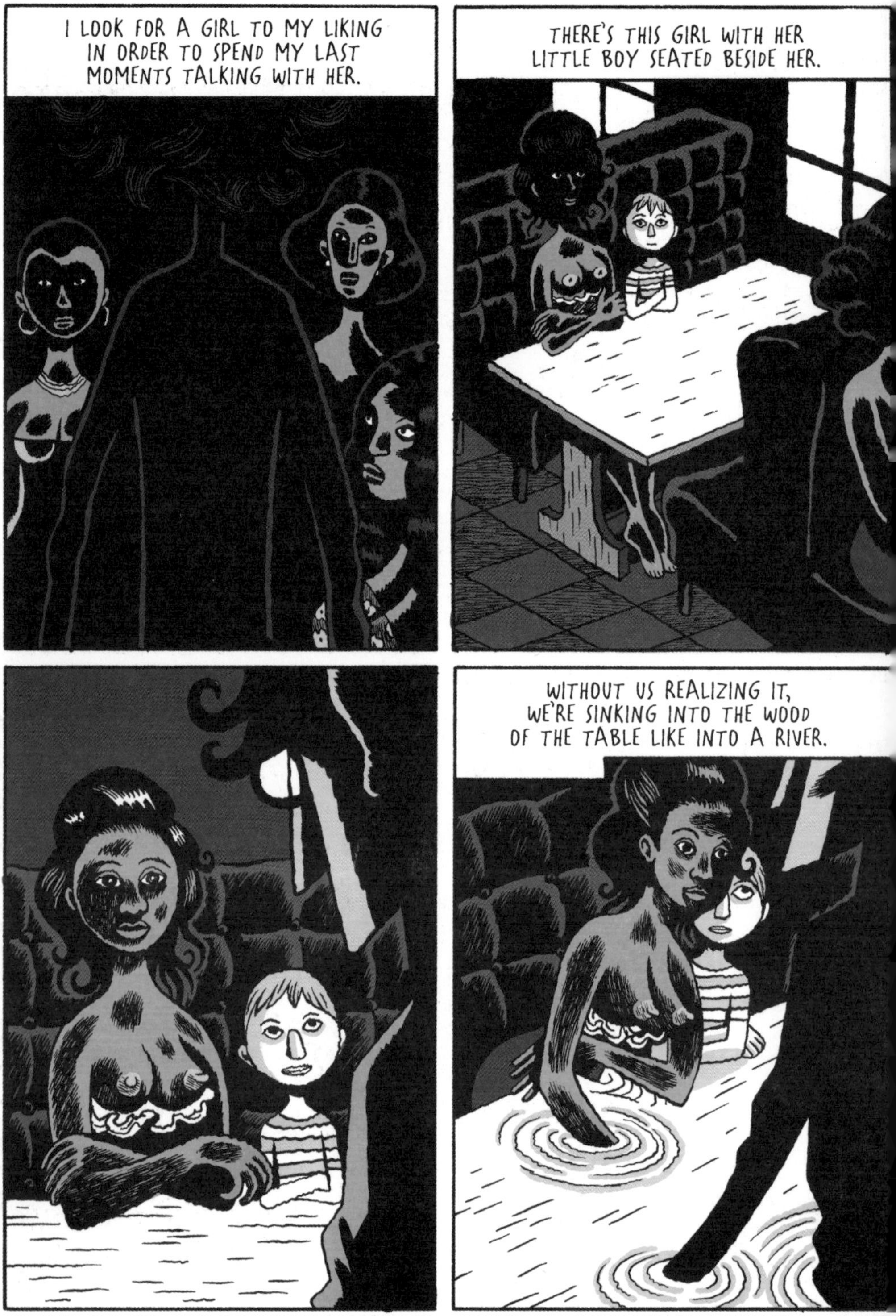
I LOOK FOR A GIRL TO MY LIKING IN ORDER TO SPEND MY LAST MOMENTS TALKING WITH HER.
THERE'S THIS GIRL WITH HER LITTLE BOY SEATED BESIDE HER.
WITHOUT US REALIZING IT, WE'RE SINKING INTO THE WOOD OF THE TABLE LIKE INTO A RIVER.

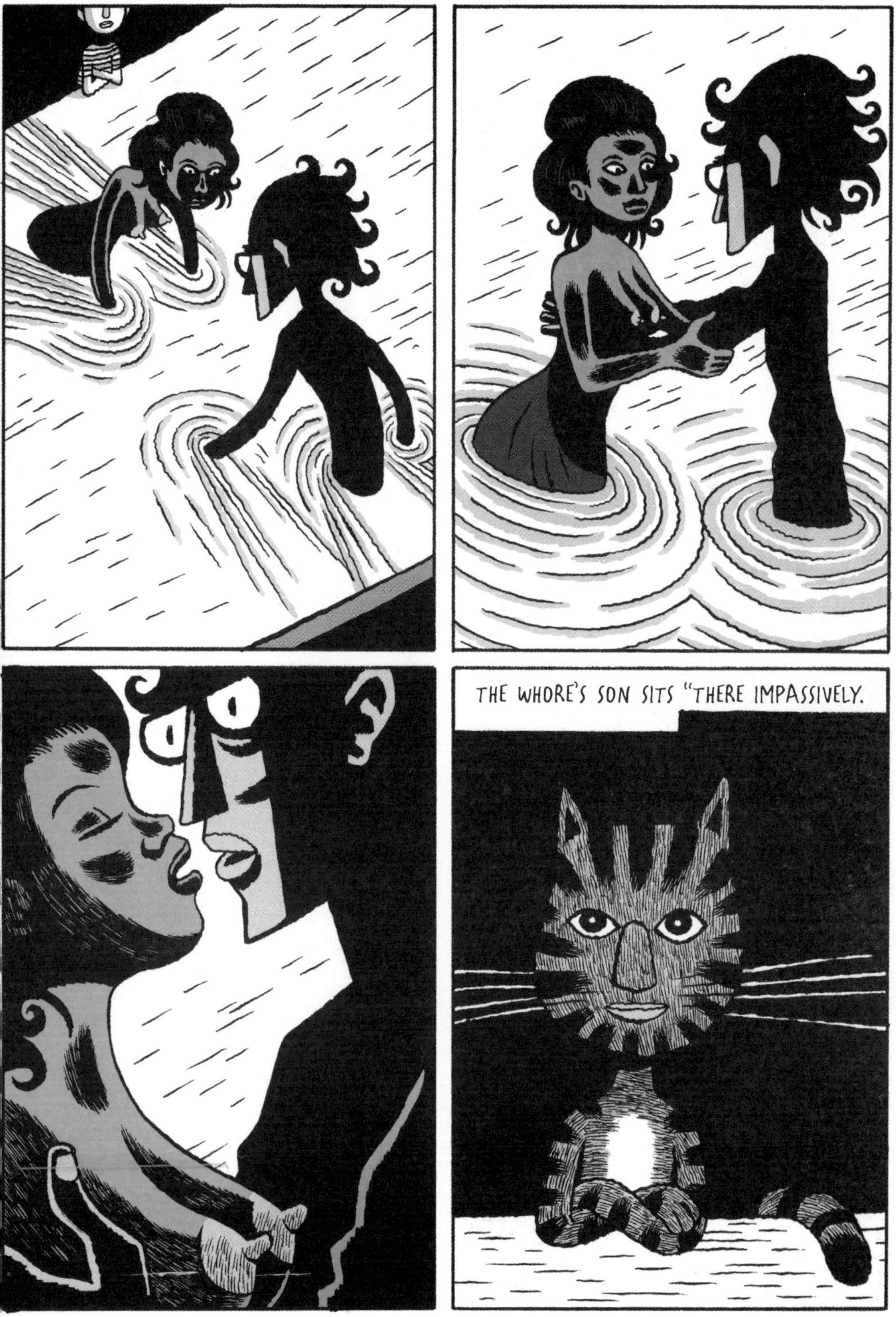
THE WHORE'S SON SITS "THERE IMPASSIVELY.

14 • Blind

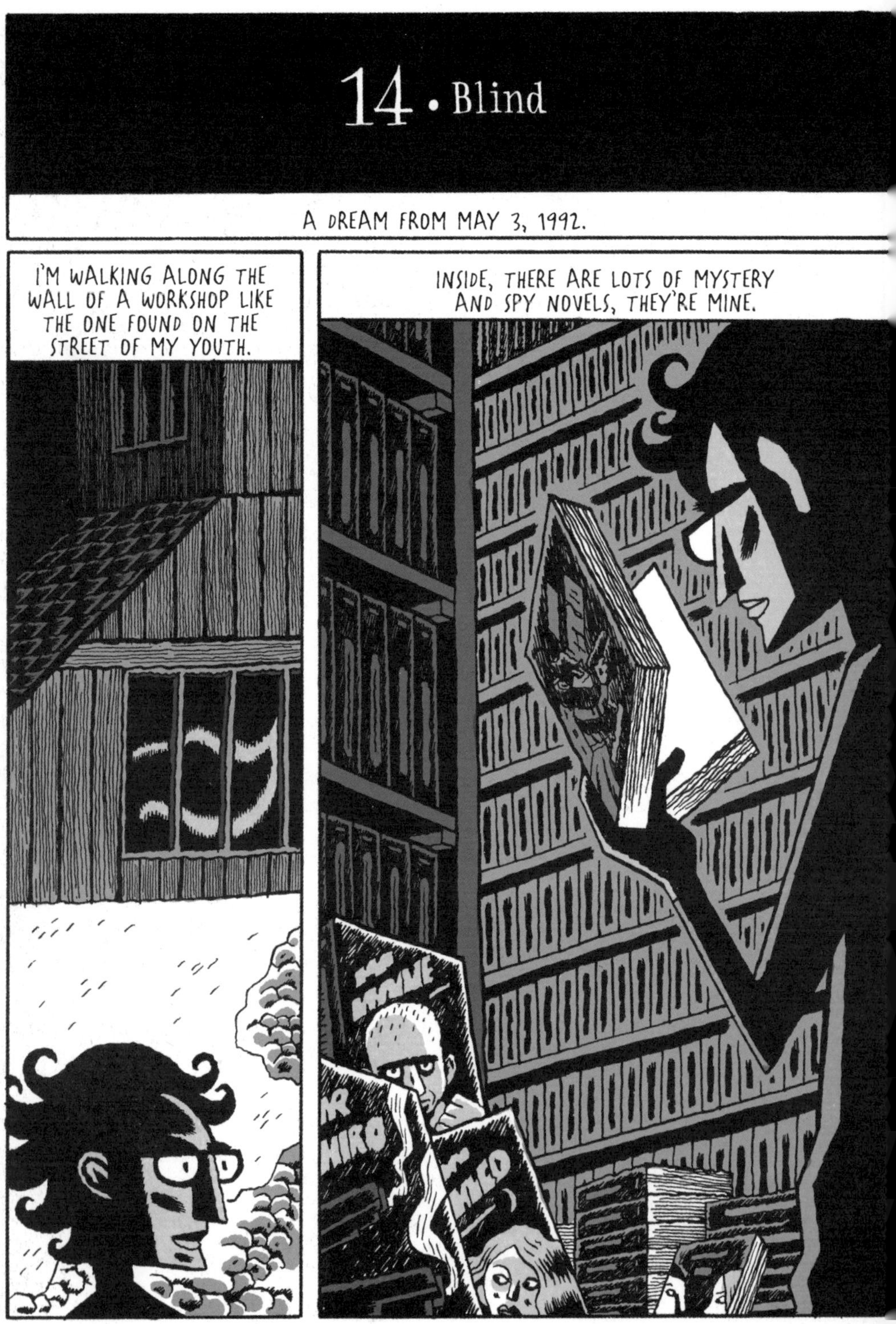
A DREAM FROM MAY 3, 1992.
I'M WALKING ALONG THE WALL OF A WORKSHOP LIKE THE ONE FOUND ON THE STREET OF MY YOUTH.
INSIDE, THERE ARE LOTS OF MYSTERY AND SPY NOVELS, THEY'RE MINE.

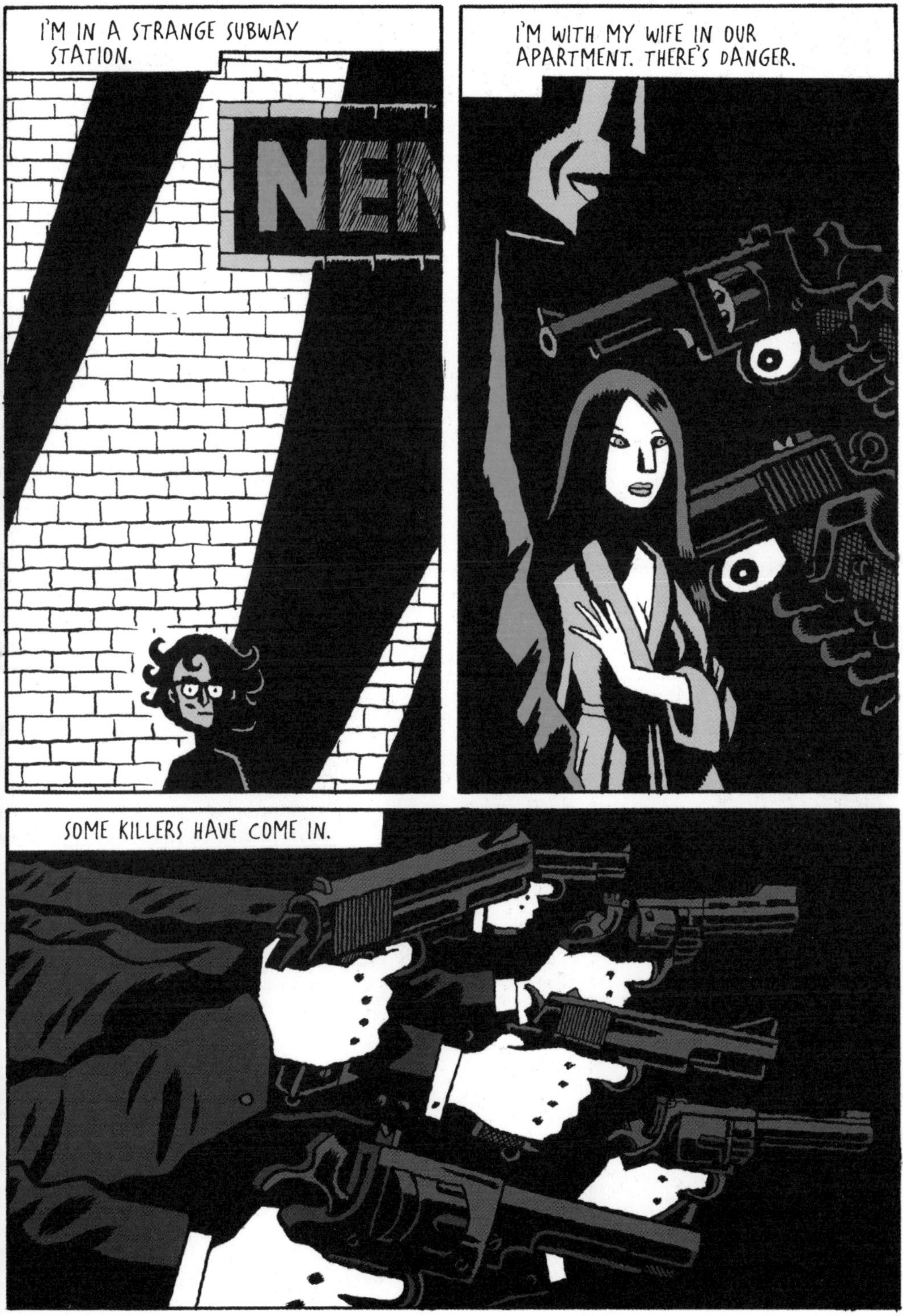
I'M IN A STRANGE SUBWAY STATION.
I'M WITH MY WIFE IN OUR APARTMENT. THERE'S DANGER.
SOME KILLERS HAVE COME IN.

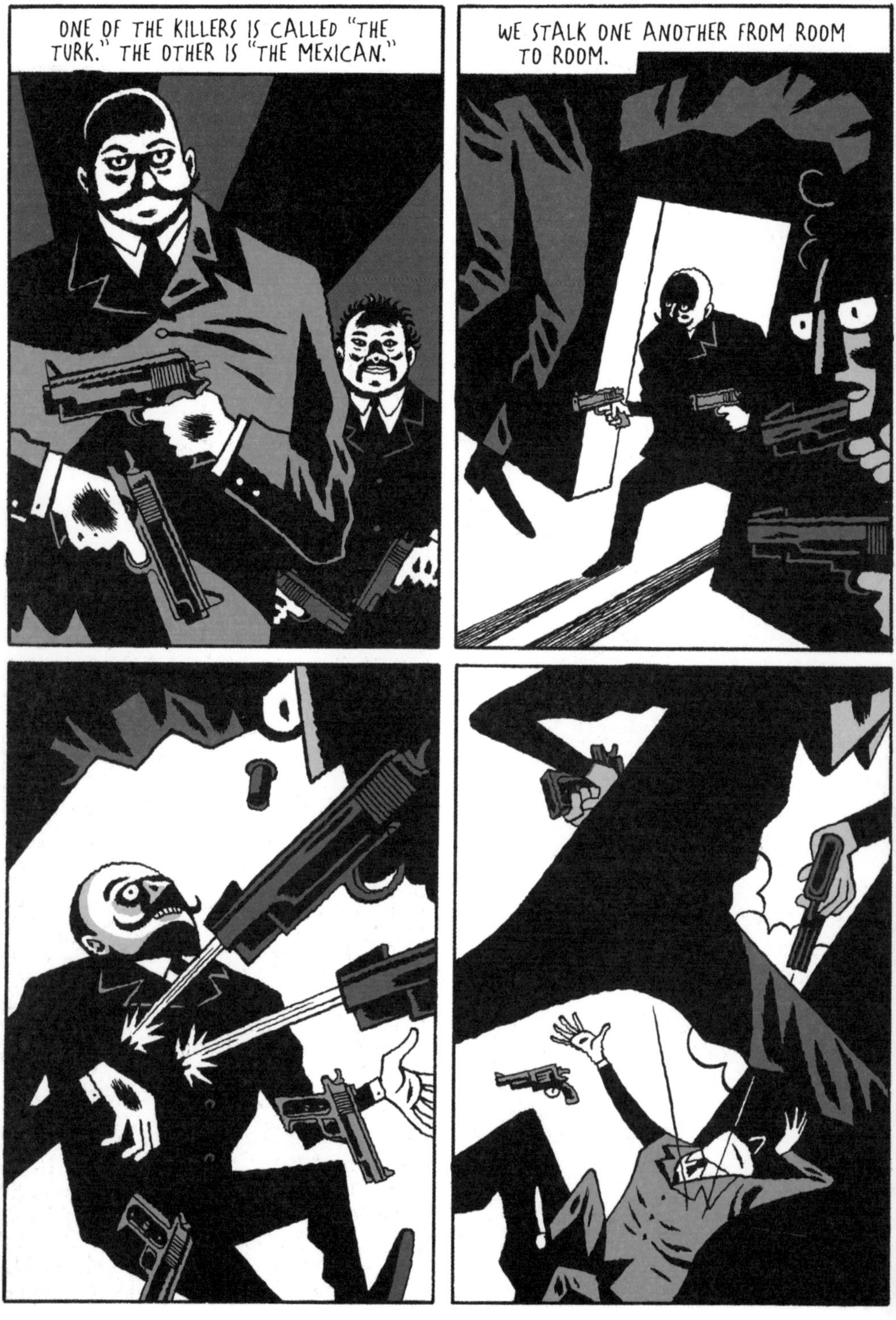
ONE OF THE KILLERS IS CALLED "THE TURK." THE OTHER IS "THE MEXICAN."
WE STALK ONE ANOTHER FROM ROOM TO ROOM.

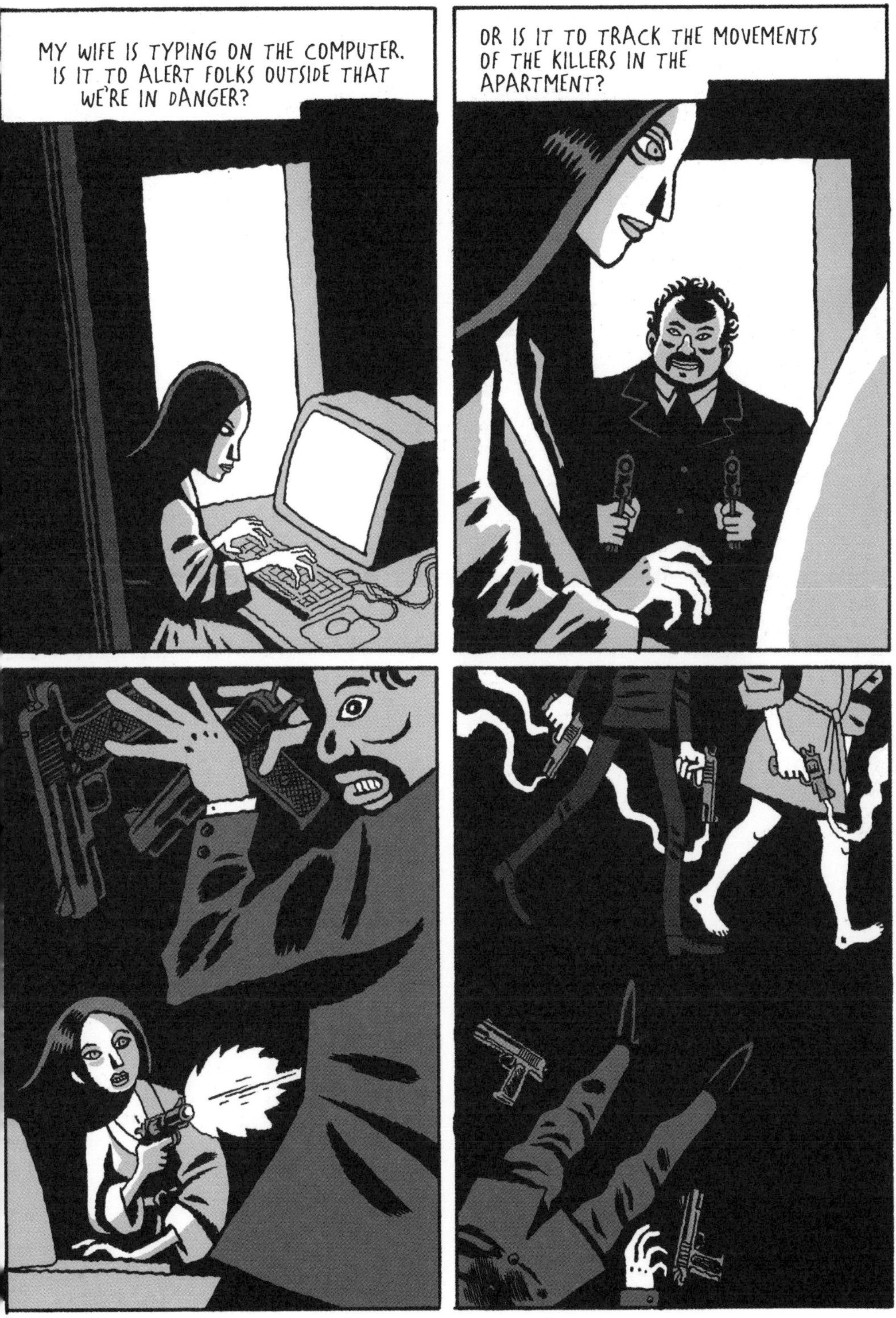
MY WIFE IS TYPING ON THE COMPUTER. IS IT TO ALERT FOLKS OUTSIDE THAT WE'RE IN DANGER?
OR IS IT TO TRACK THE MOVEMENTS OF THE KILLERS IN THE APARTMENT?

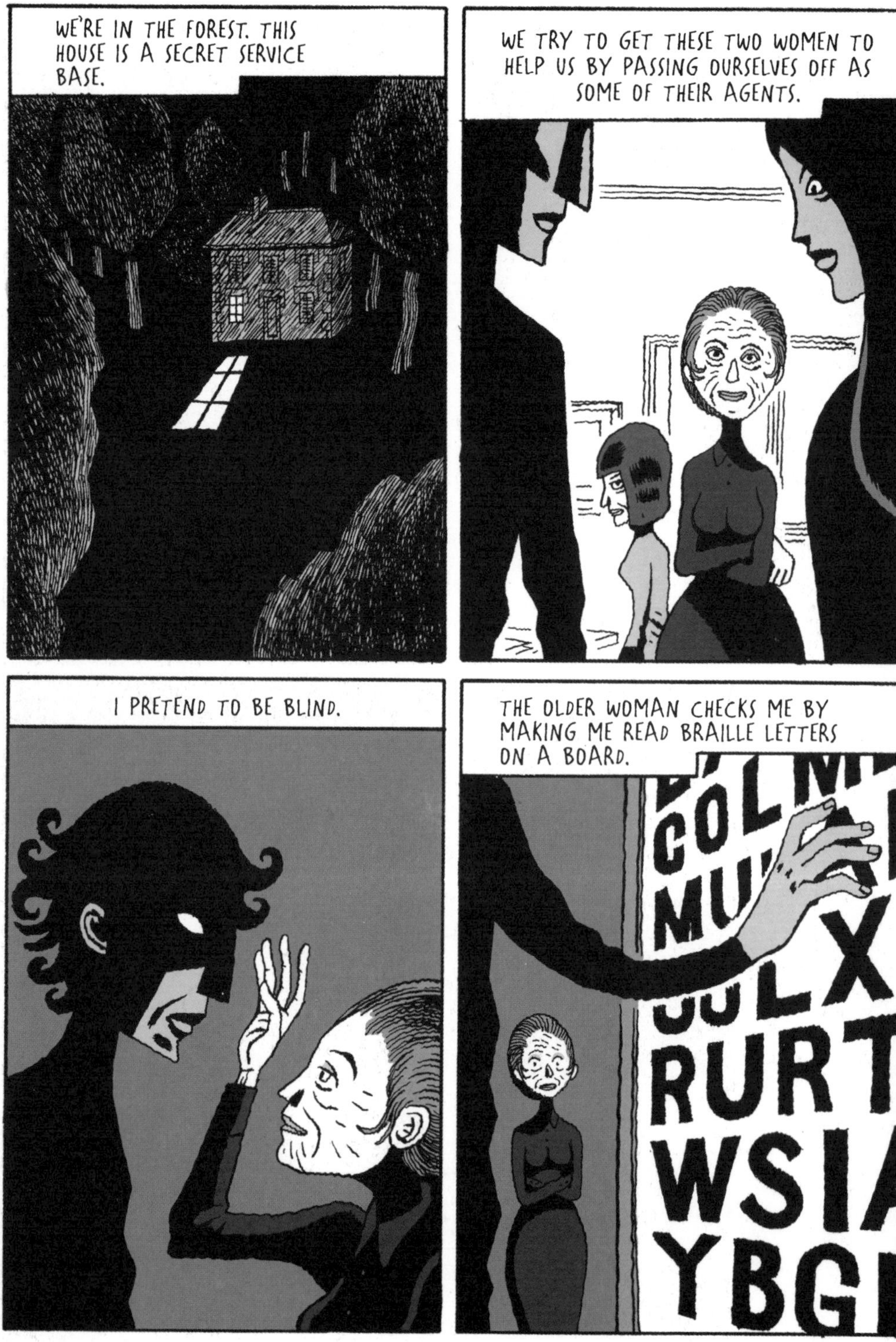
WE'RE IN THE FOREST. THIS HOUSE IS A SECRET SERVICE BASE.
WE TRY TO GET THESE TWO WOMEN TO HELP US BY PASSING OURSELVES OFF AS SOME OF THEIR AGENTS.
I PRETEND TO BE BLIND.
THE OLDER WOMAN CHECKS ME BY MAKING ME READ BRAILLE LETTERS ON A BOARD.
COL
RURT
WSIA
YBG

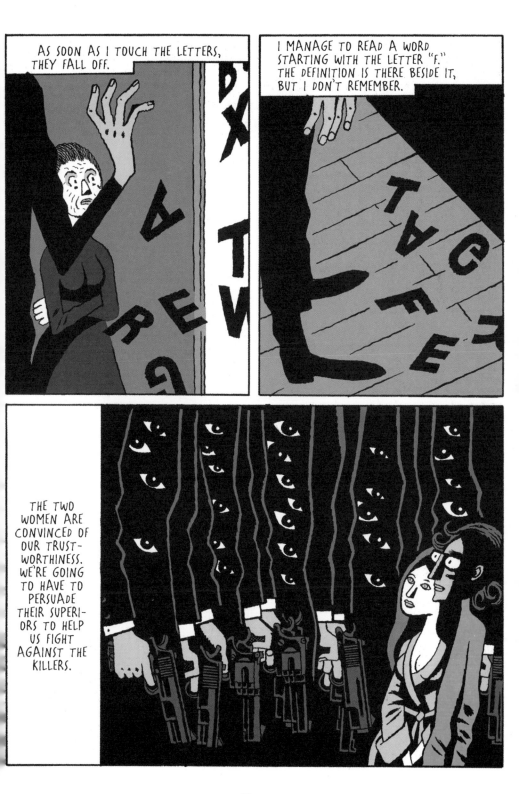

AS SOON AS I TOUCH THE LETTERS, THEY FALL OFF.

I MANAGE TO READ A WORD STARTING WITH THE LETTER "F." THE DEFINITION IS THERE BESIDE IT, BUT I DON'T REMEMBER.

THE TWO WOMEN ARE CONVINCED OF OUR TRUST-WORTHINESS. WE'RE GOING TO HAVE TO PERSUADE THEIR SUPERI-ORS TO HELP US FIGHT AGAINST THE KILLERS.

15 • The Fat Cop

A DREAM FROM FEBRUARY 13, 1993.

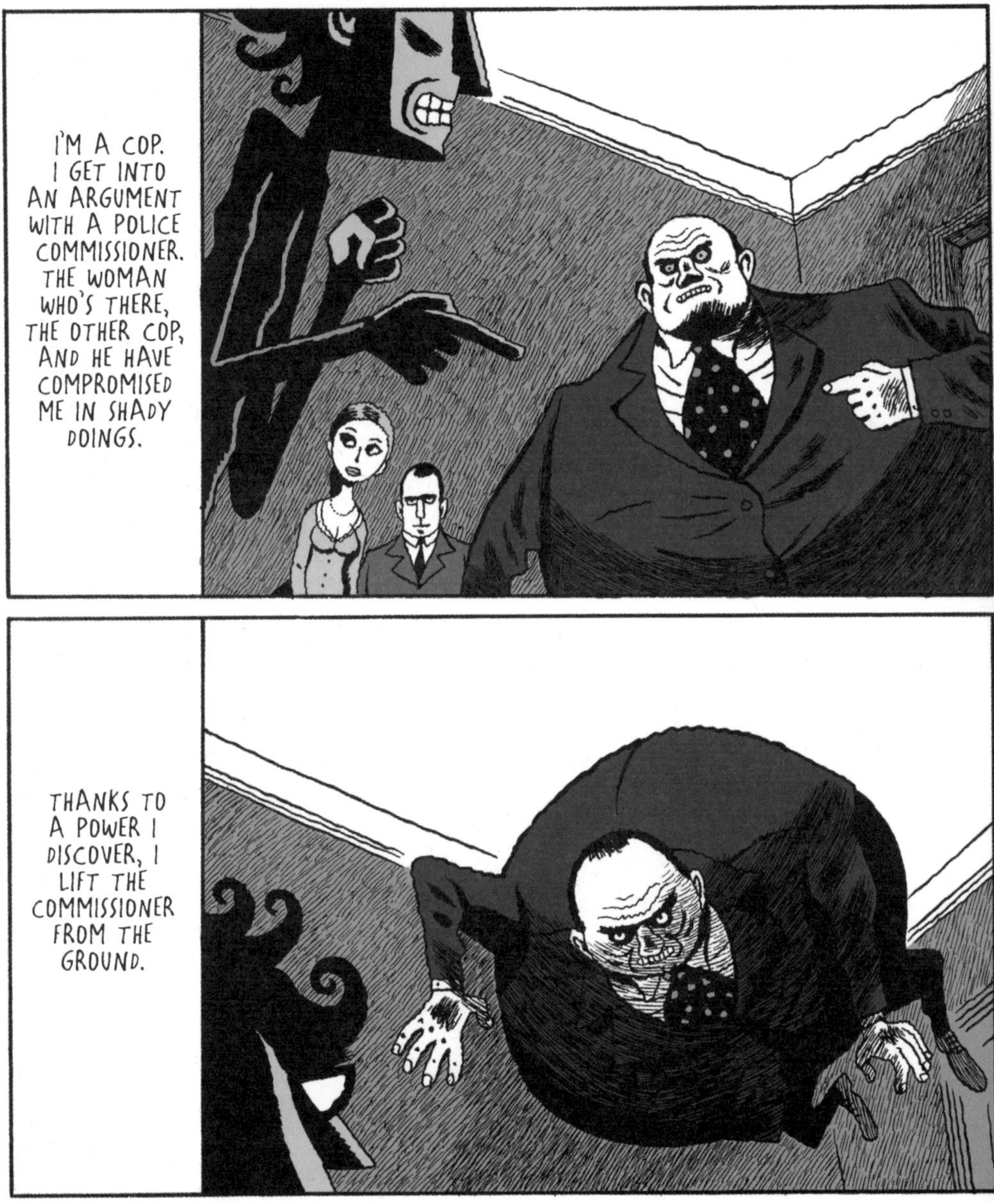
I'M A COP. I GET INTO AN ARGUMENT WITH A POLICE COMMISSIONER. THE WOMAN WHO'S THERE, THE OTHER COP, AND HE HAVE COMPROMISED ME IN SHADY DOINGS.
THANKS TO A POWER I DISCOVER, I LIFT THE COMMISSIONER FROM THE GROUND.

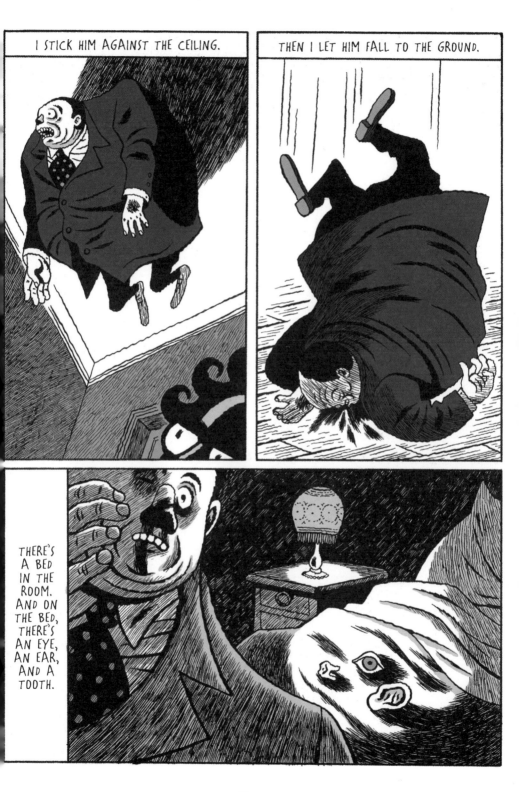

I STICK HIM AGAINST THE CEILING.

THEN I LET HIM FALL TO THE GROUND.

THERE'S A BED IN THE ROOM. AND ON THE BED, THERE'S AN EYE, AN EAR, AND A TOOTH.

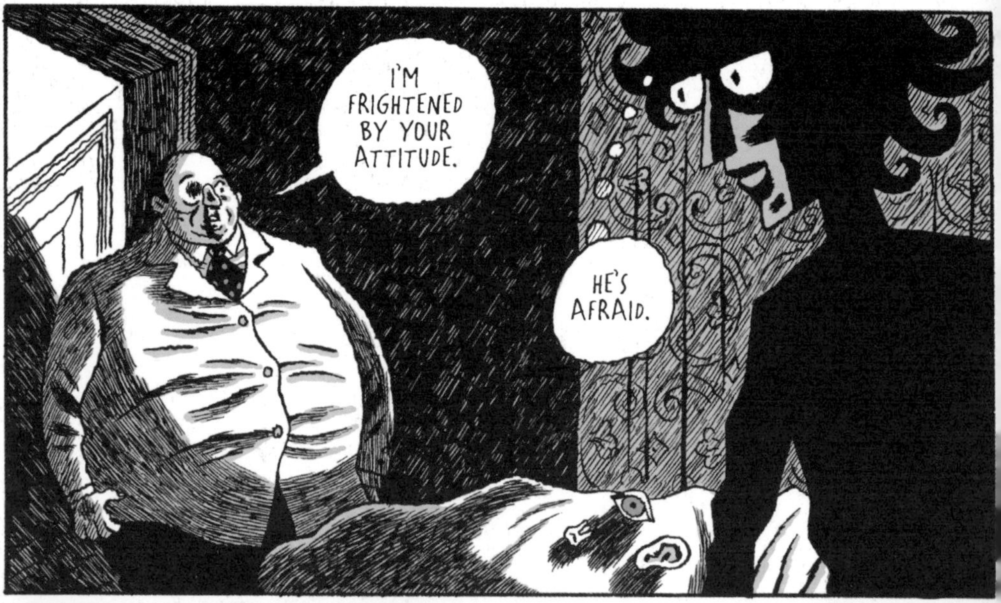
I'M FRIGHTENED BY YOUR ATTITUDE.
HE'S AFRAID.

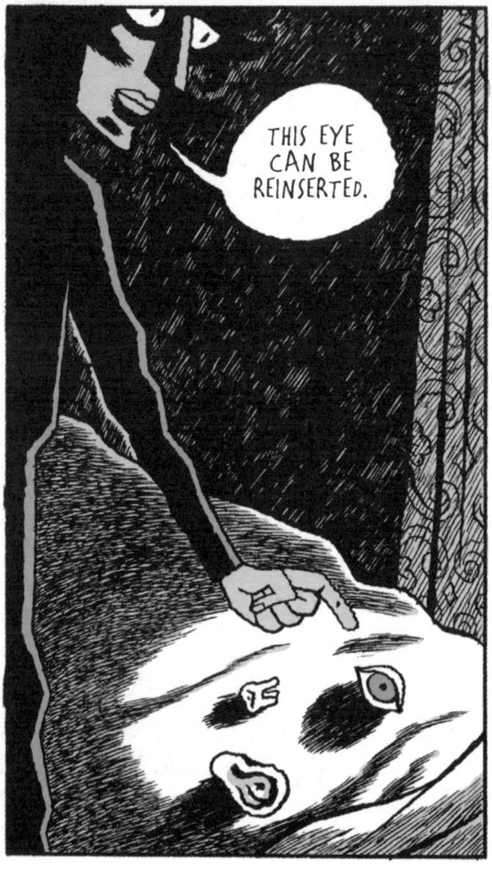
THIS EYE CAN BE REINSERTED.

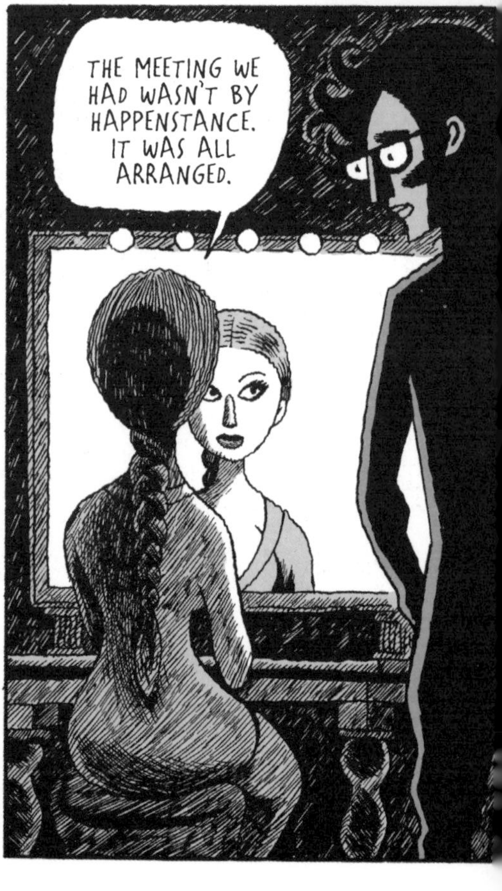
THE MEETING WE HAD WASN'T BY HAPPENSTANCE. IT WAS ALL ARRANGED.

16 • A Love Affair

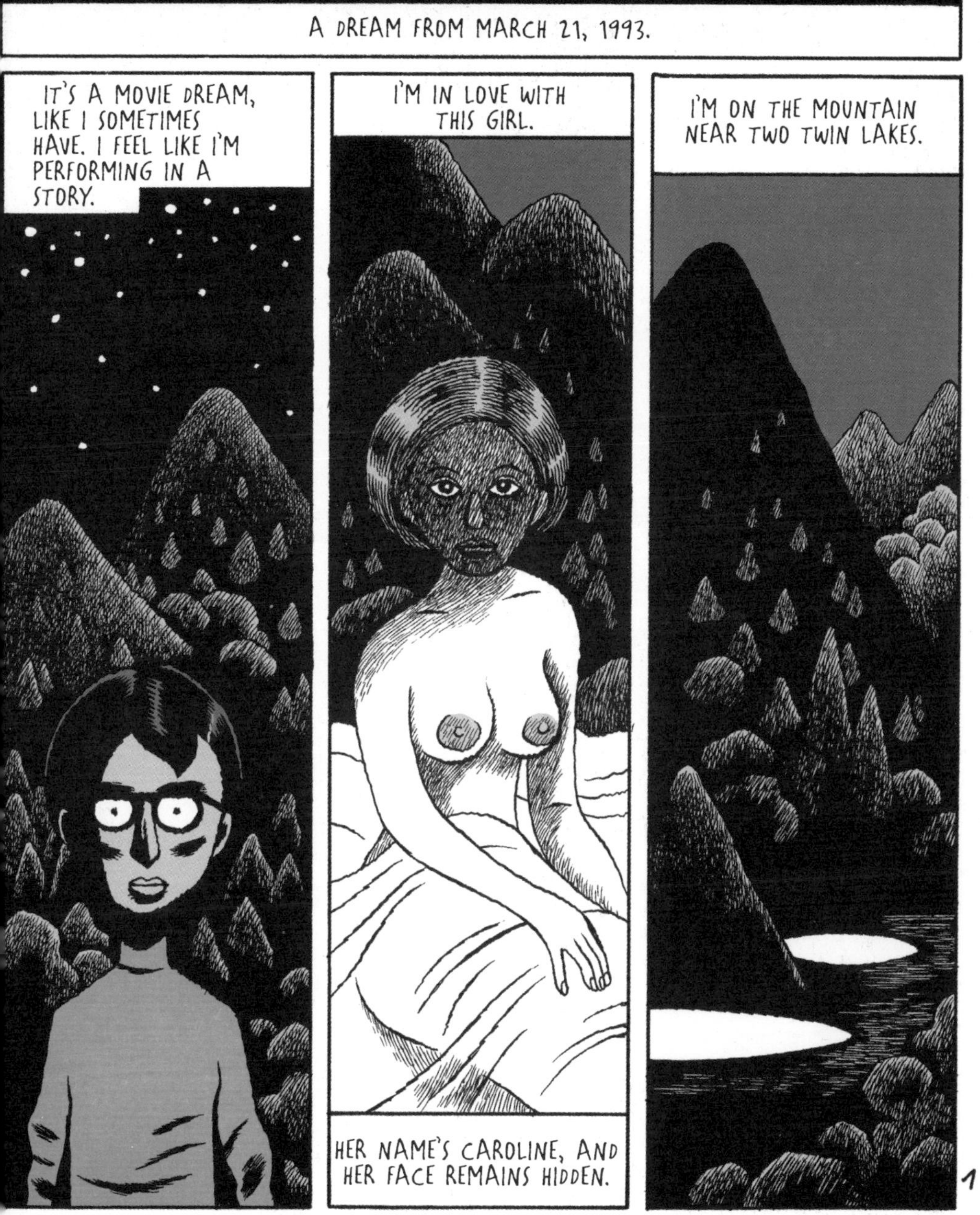
A DREAM FROM MARCH 21, 1993.
IT'S A MOVIE DREAM, LIKE I SOMETIMES HAVE. I FEEL LIKE I'M PERFORMING IN A STORY.
I'M IN LOVE WITH THIS GIRL.
HER NAME'S CAROLINE, AND HER FACE REMAINS HIDDEN.
I'M ON THE MOUNTAIN NEAR TWO TWIN LAKES.
1

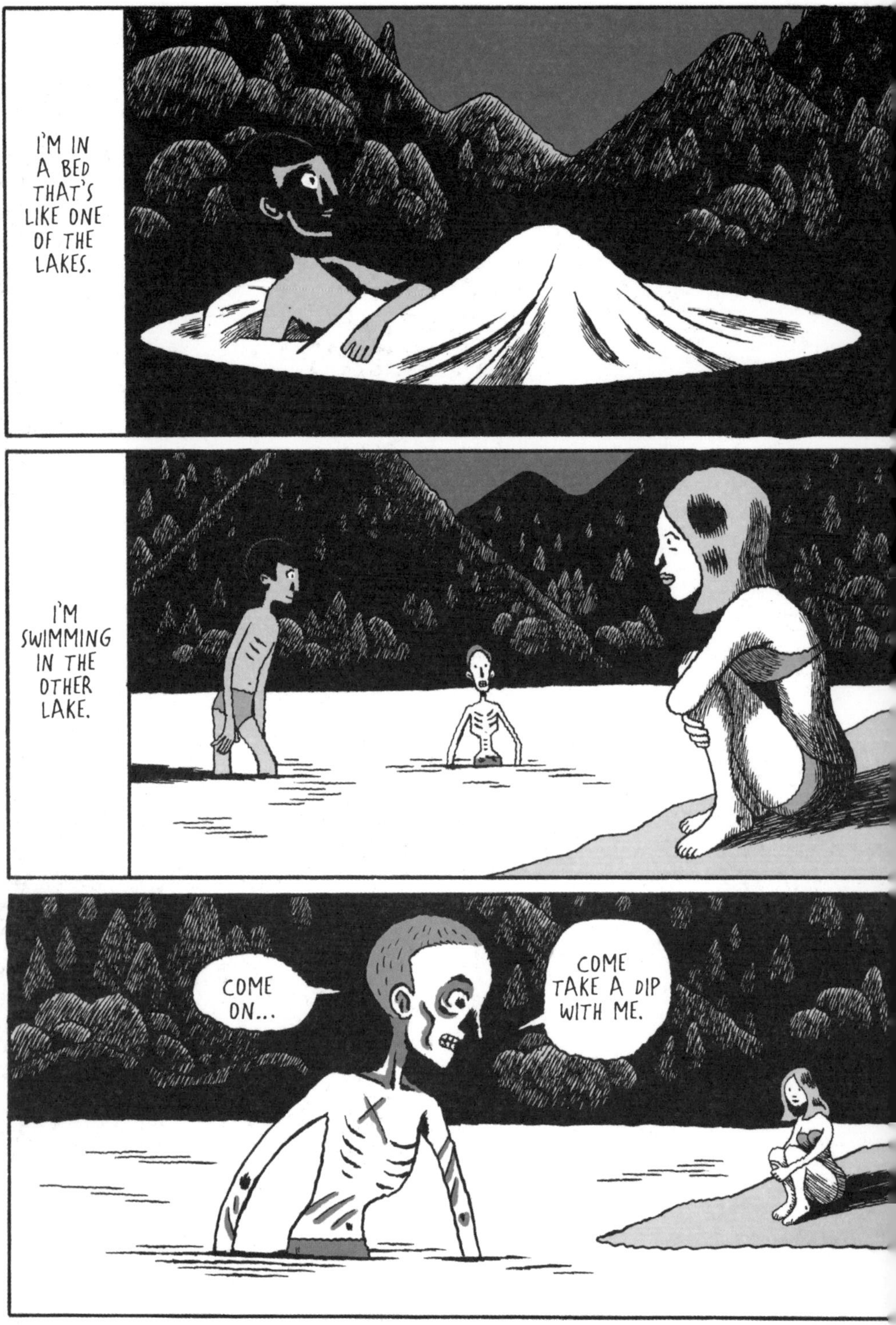
I'M IN A BED THAT'S LIKE ONE OF THE LAKES.
I'M SWIMMING IN THE OTHER LAKE.
COME ON...
COME TAKE A DIP WITH ME.

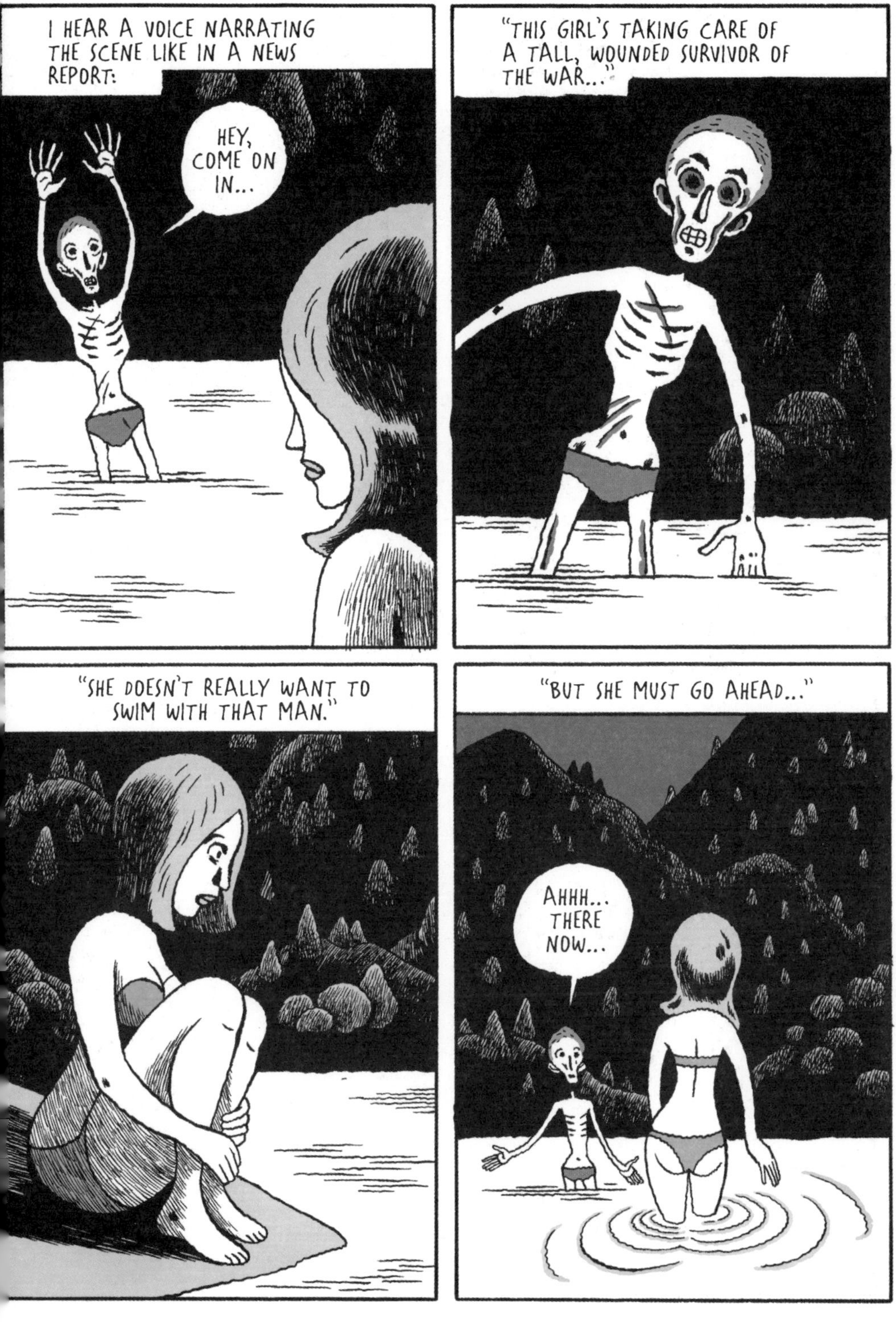
I HEAR A VOICE NARRATING THE SCENE LIKE IN A NEWS REPORT:
HEY, COME ON IN...
"THIS GIRL'S TAKING CARE OF A TALL, WOUNDED SURVIVOR OF THE WAR..."
"SHE DOESN'T REALLY WANT TO SWIM WITH THAT MAN."
"BUT SHE MUST GO AHEAD..."
AHHH... THERE NOW...

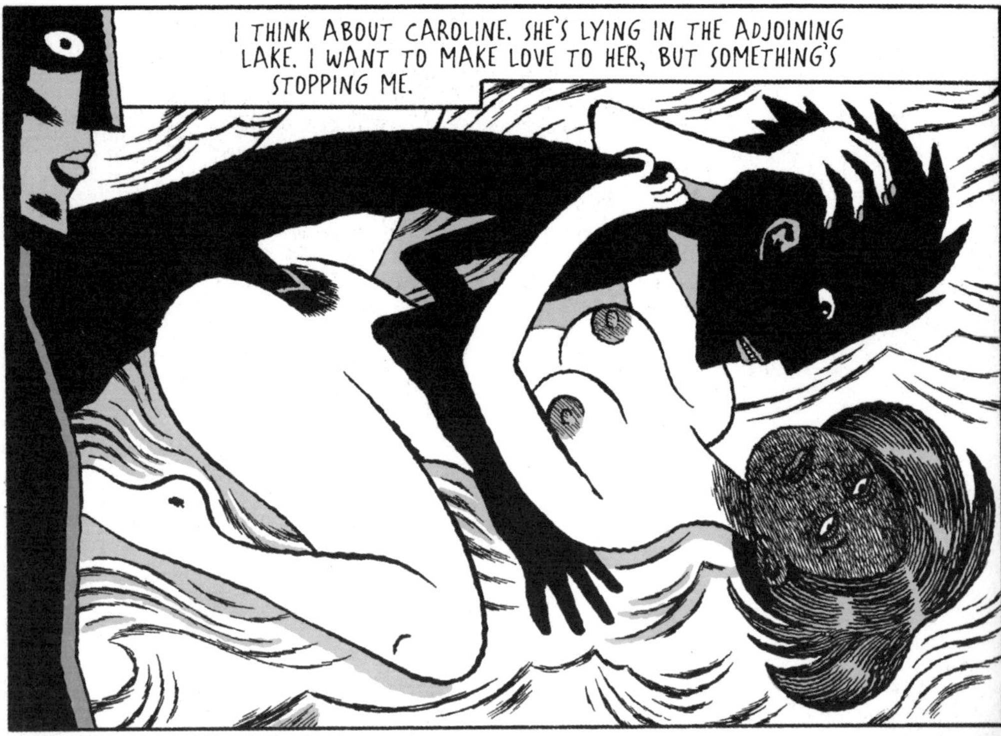
I THINK ABOUT CAROLINE. SHE'S LYING IN THE ADJOINING LAKE. I WANT TO MAKE LOVE TO HER, BUT SOMETHING'S STOPPING ME.

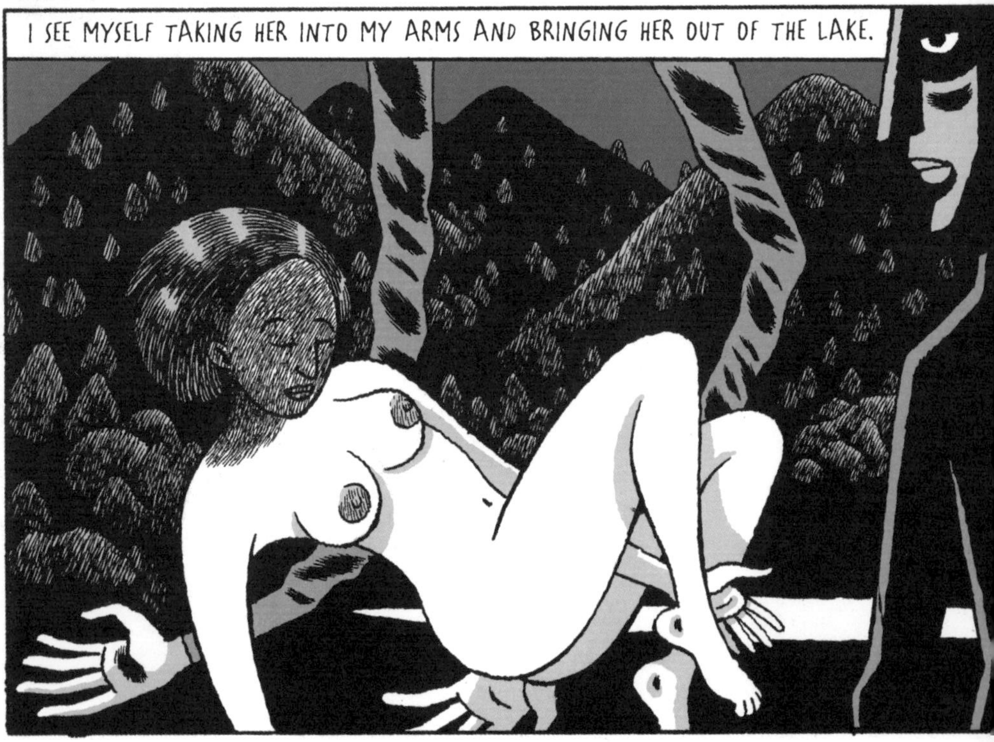
I SEE MYSELF TAKING HER INTO MY ARMS AND BRINGING HER OUT OF THE LAKE.

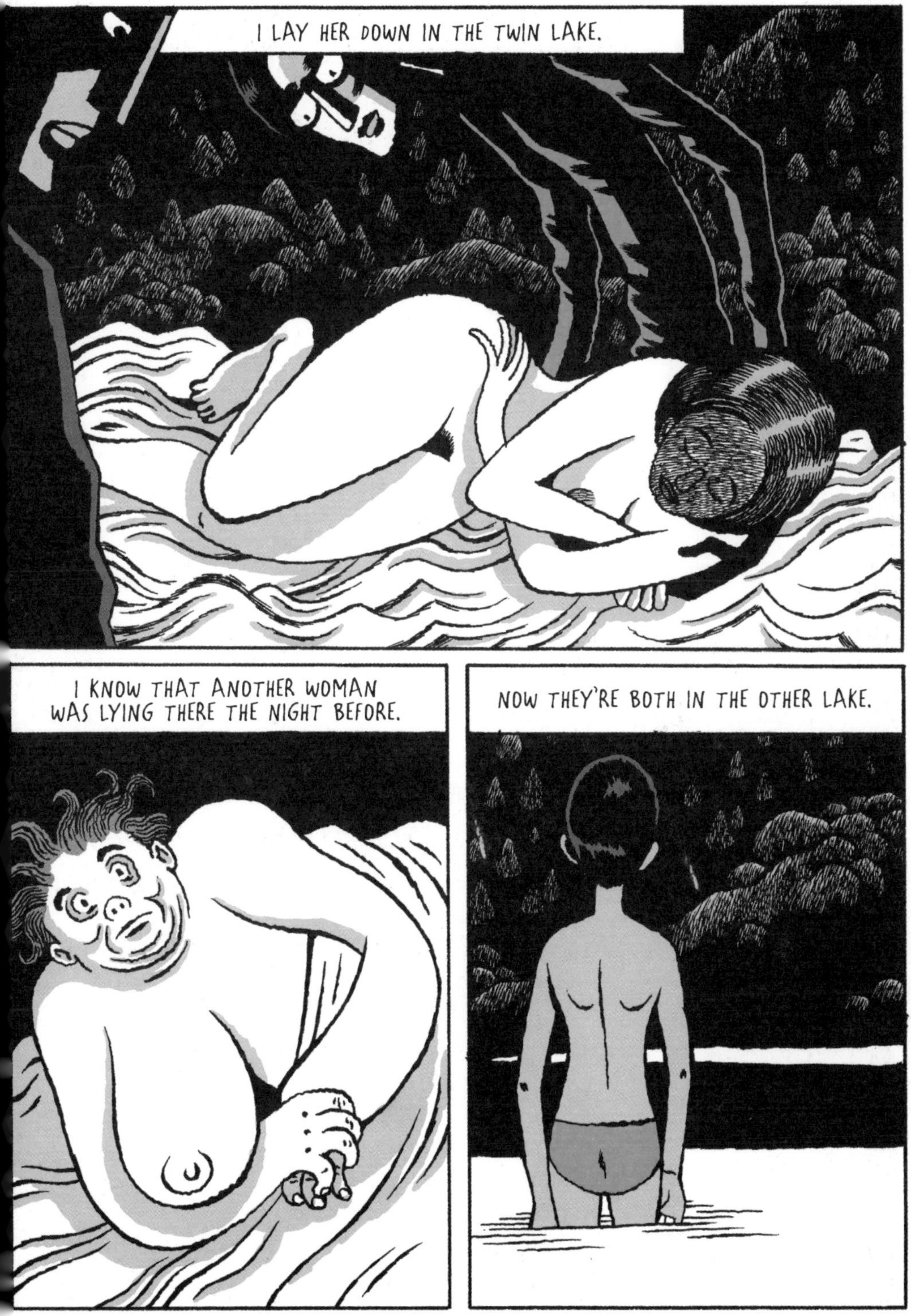
I LAY HER DOWN IN THE TWIN LAKE.
I KNOW THAT ANOTHER WOMAN WAS LYING THERE THE NIGHT BEFORE.
NOW THEY'RE BOTH IN THE OTHER LAKE.

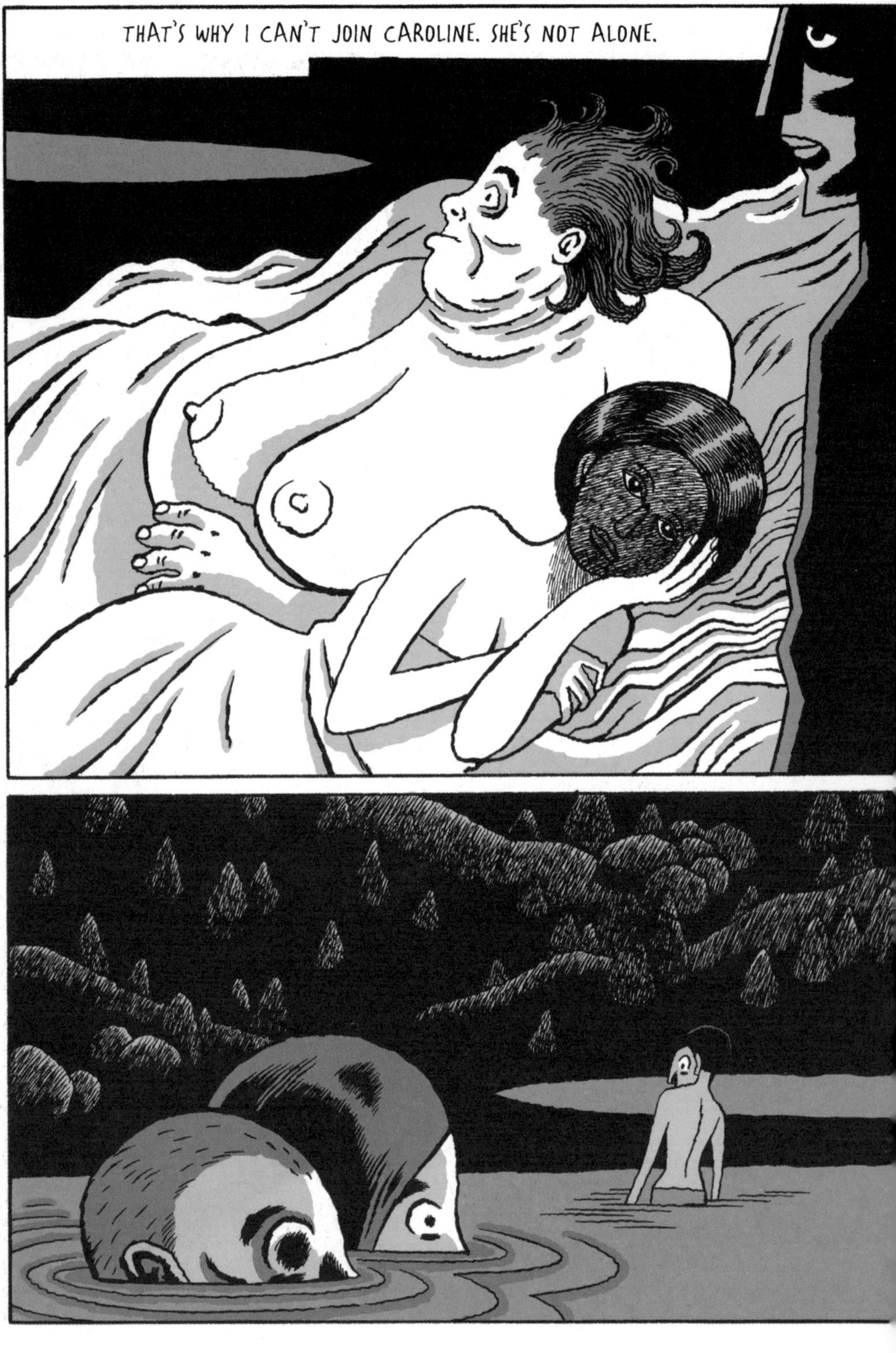
THAT'S WHY I CAN'T JOIN CAROLINE. SHE'S NOT ALONE.

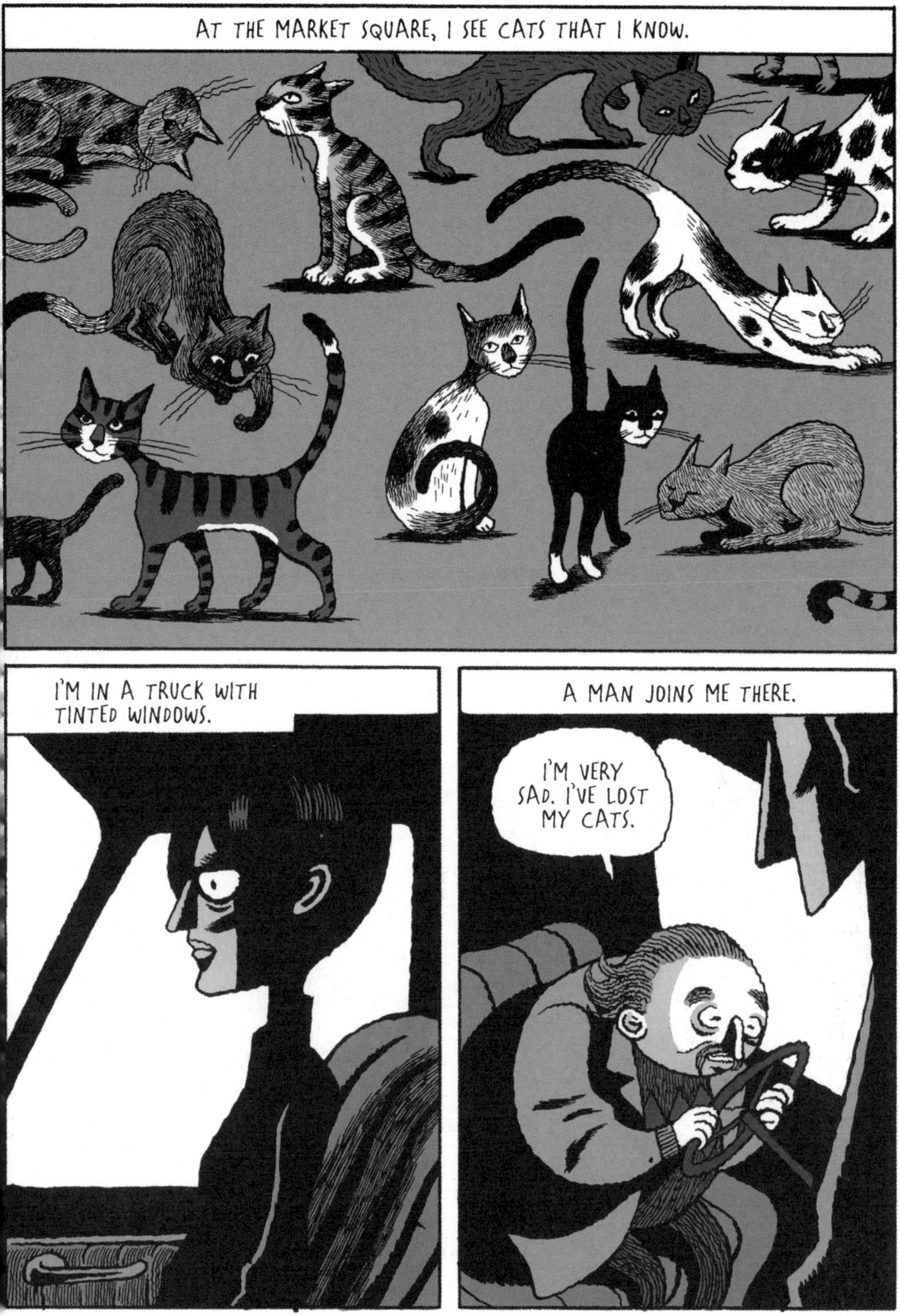
AT THE MARKET SQUARE, I SEE CATS THAT I KNOW.
I'M IN A TRUCK WITH TINTED WINDOWS.
A MAN JOINS ME THERE.
I'M VERY SAD. I'VE LOST MY CATS.

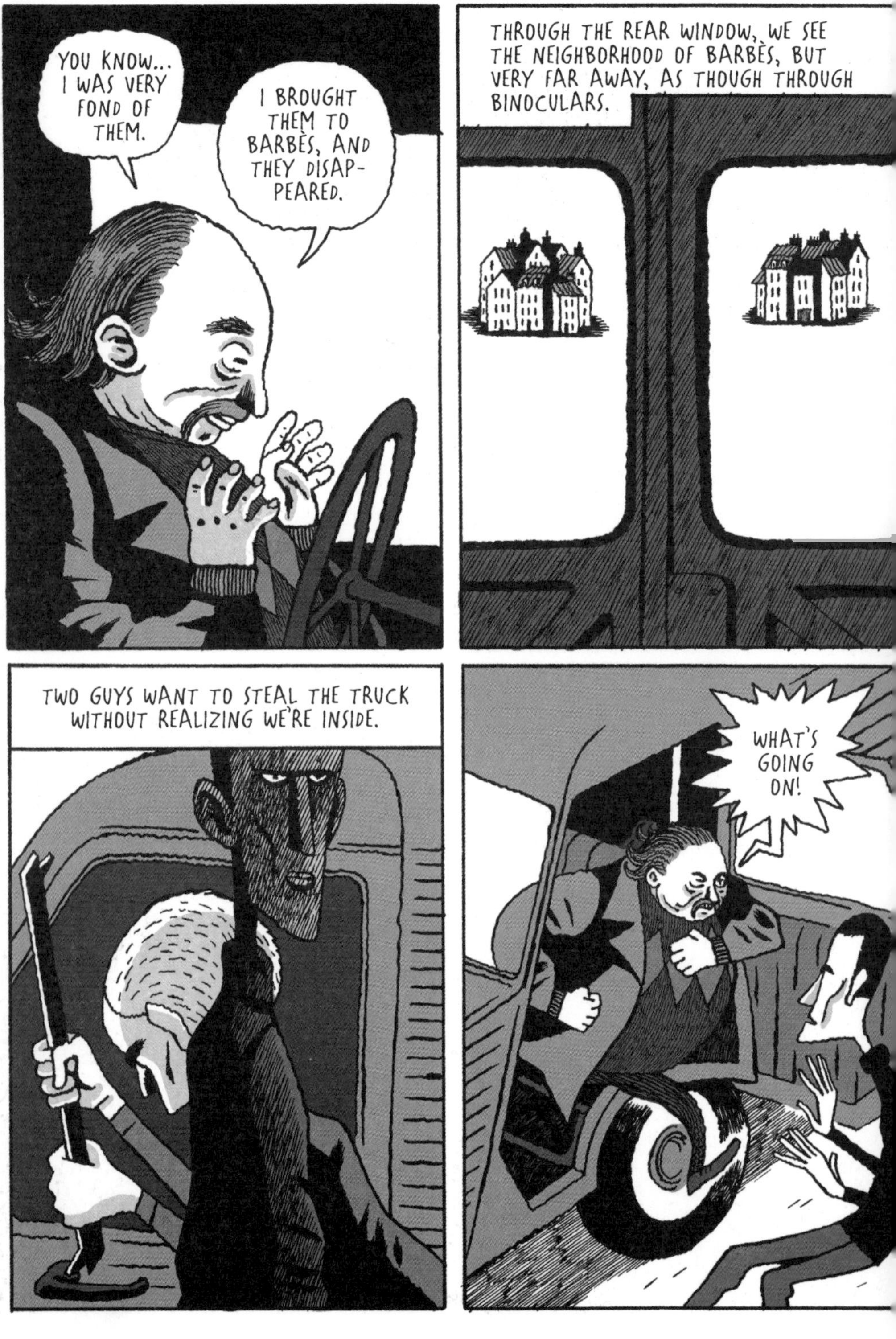
YOU KNOW... I WAS VERY FOND OF THEM.
I BROUGHT THEM TO BARBÈS, AND THEY DISAP-PEARED.
THROUGH THE REAR WINDOW, WE SEE THE NEIGHBORHOOD OF BARBÈS, BUT VERY FAR AWAY, AS THOUGH THROUGH BINOCULARS.
TWO GUYS WANT TO STEAL THE TRUCK WITHOUT REALIZING WE'RE INSIDE.
WHAT'S GOING ON!

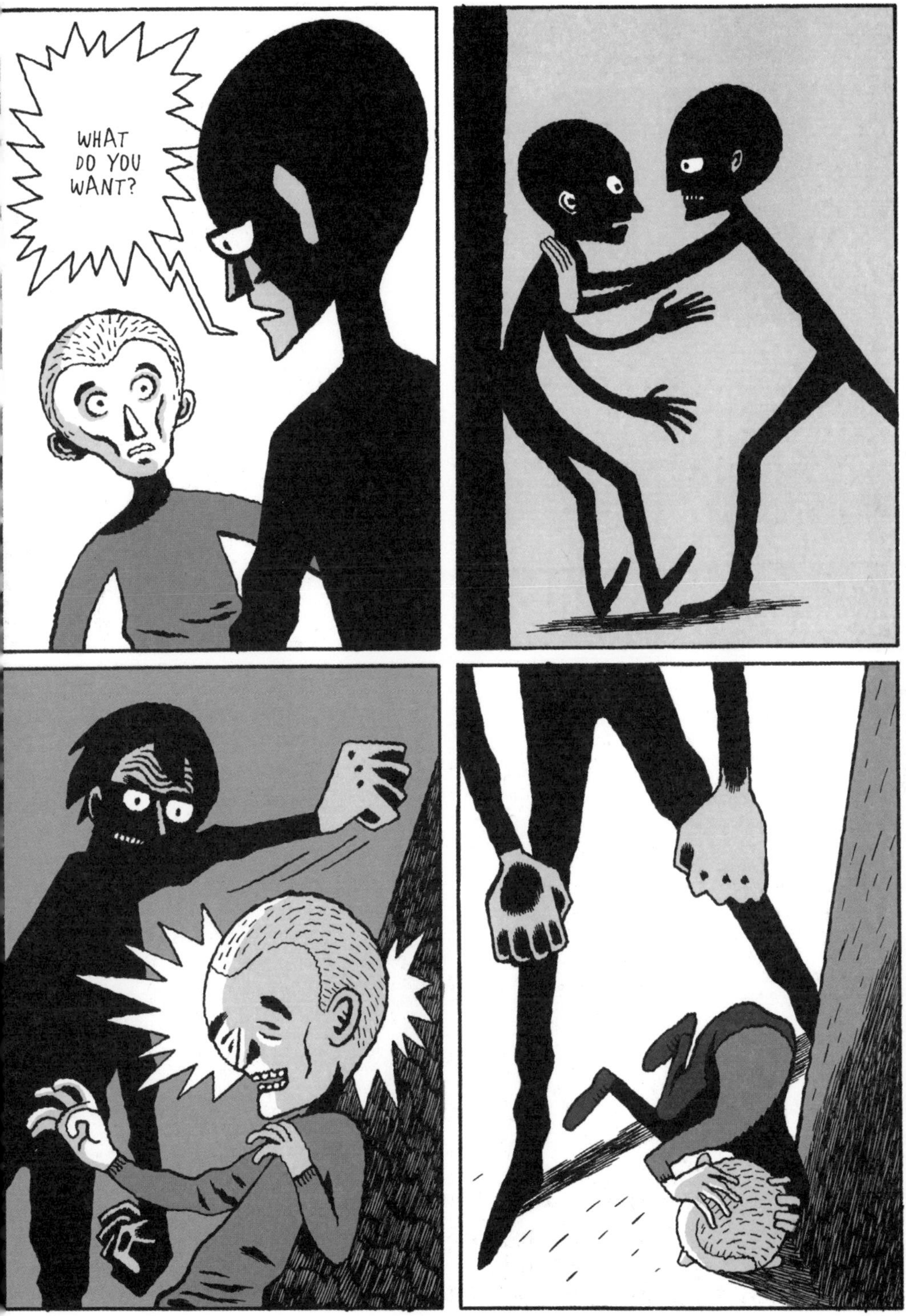
WHAT DO YOU WANT?

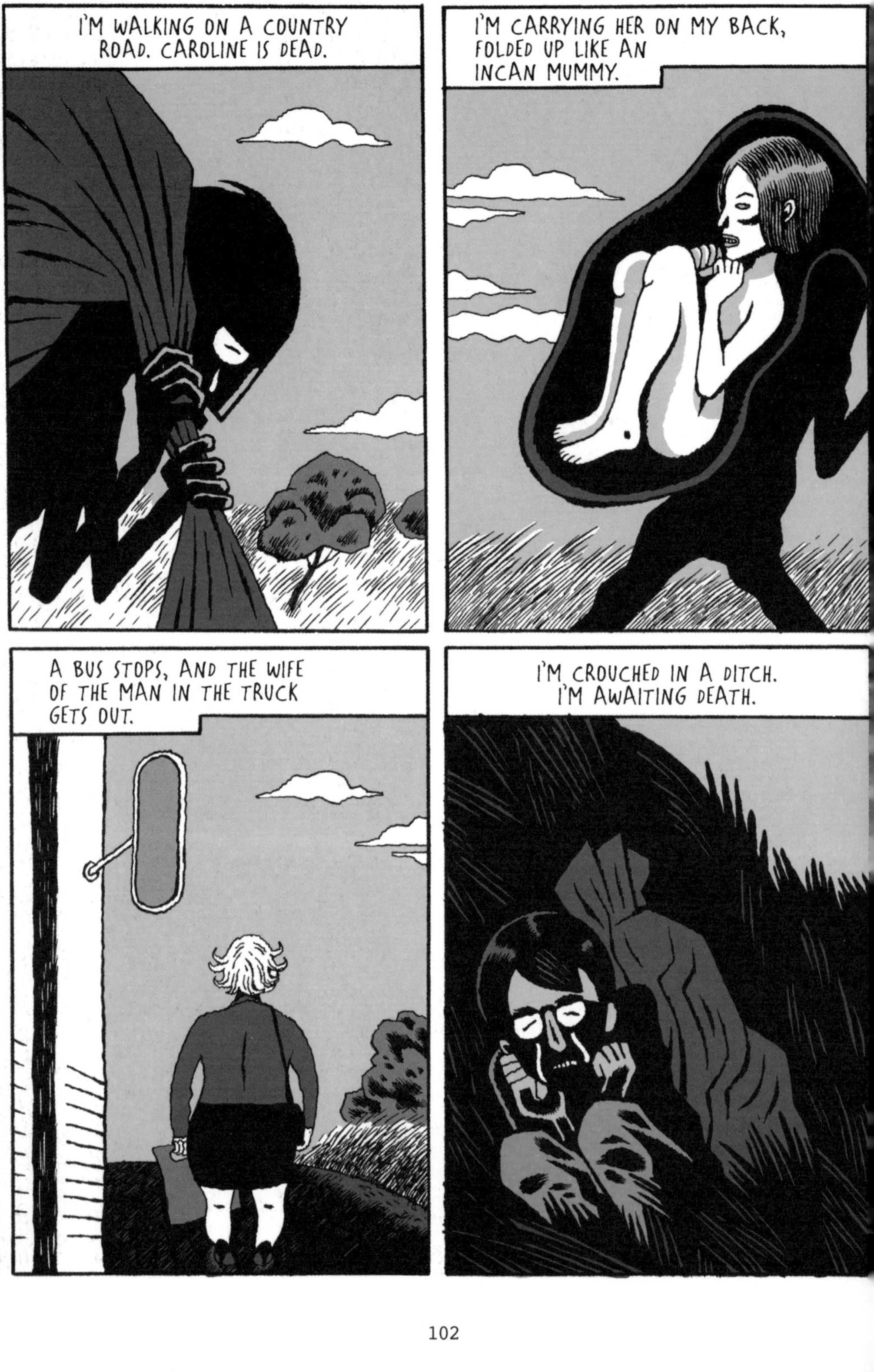
I'M WALKING ON A COUNTRY ROAD. CAROLINE IS DEAD.
I'M CARRYING HER ON MY BACK, FOLDED UP LIKE AN INCAN MUMMY.
A BUS STOPS, AND THE WIFE OF THE MAN IN THE TRUCK GETS OUT.
I'M CROUCHED IN A DITCH. I'M AWAITING DEATH.

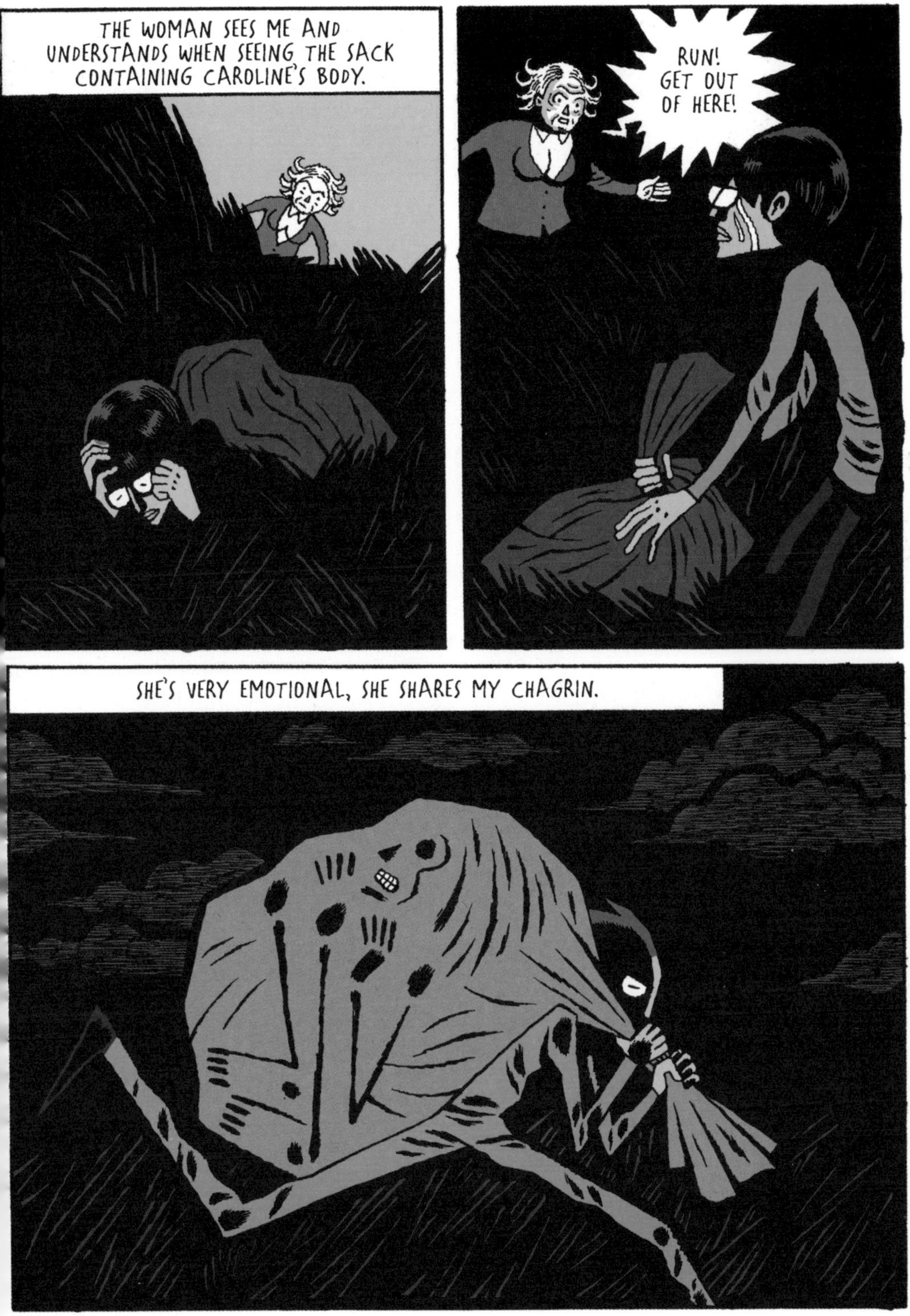
THE WOMAN SEES ME AND UNDERSTANDS WHEN SEEING THE SACK CONTAINING CAROLINE'S BODY.
RUN! GET OUT OF HERE!
SHE'S VERY EMOTIONAL, SHE SHARES MY CHAGRIN.

17 • The Heads

A DREAM FROM FEBRUARY 26, 1993 AND AN ATTEMPT
TO FINISH THE DREAM THE FOLLOWING NIGHTS.

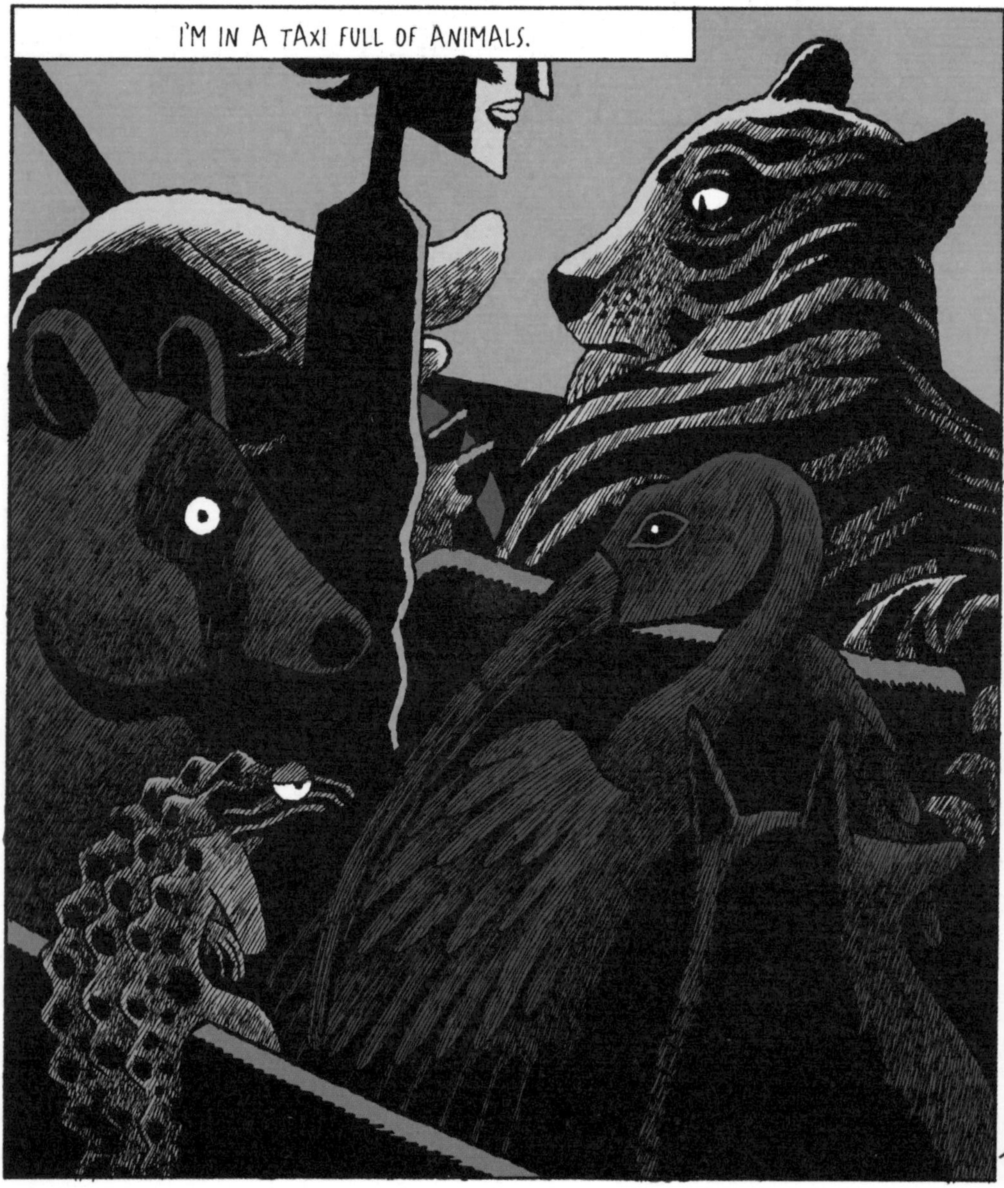
I'M IN A TAXI FULL OF ANIMALS.

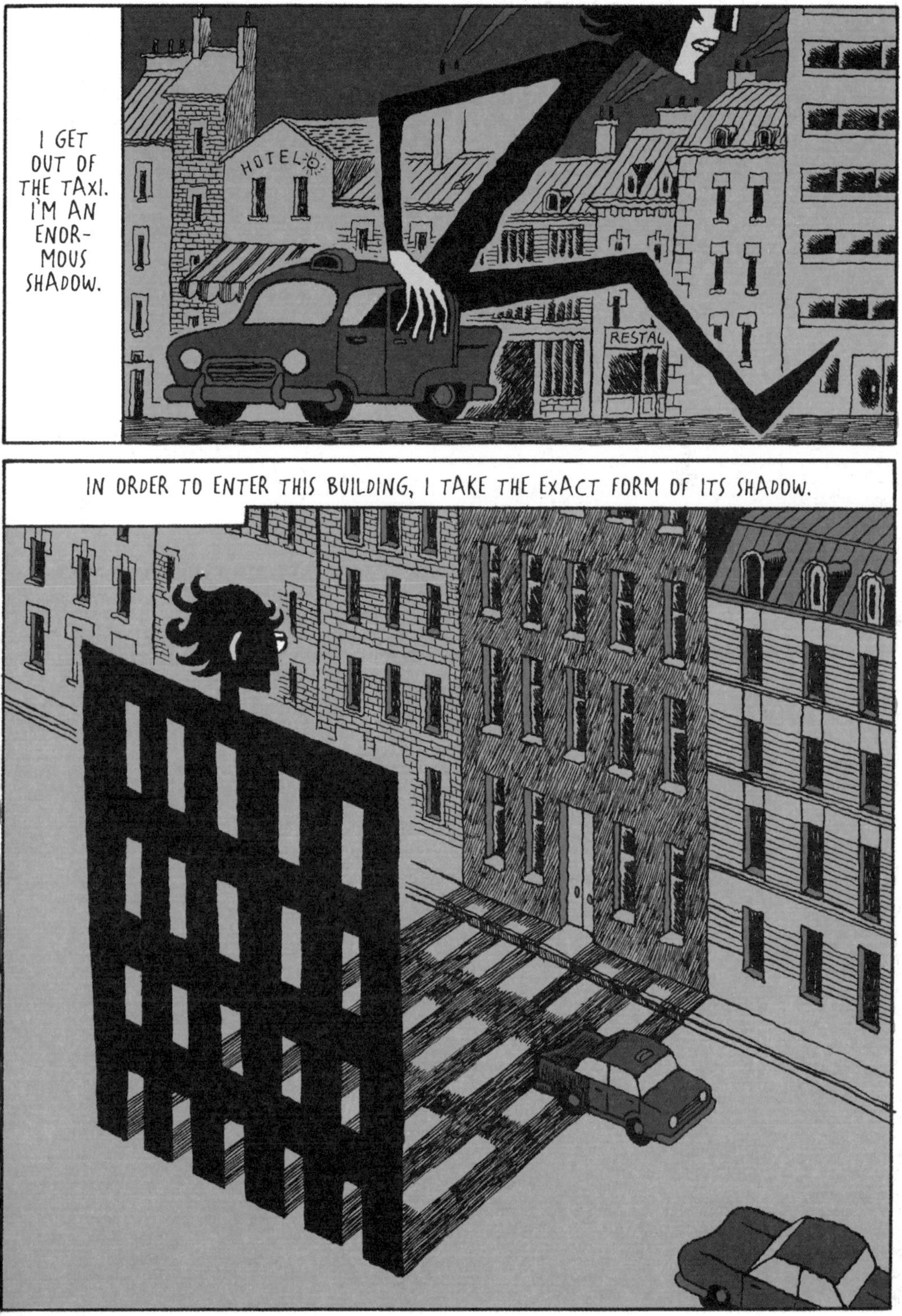
I GET OUT OF THE TAXI. I'M AN ENORMOUS SHADOW.
HOTEL
RESTAU
IN ORDER TO ENTER THIS BUILDING, I TAKE THE EXACT FORM OF ITS SHADOW.

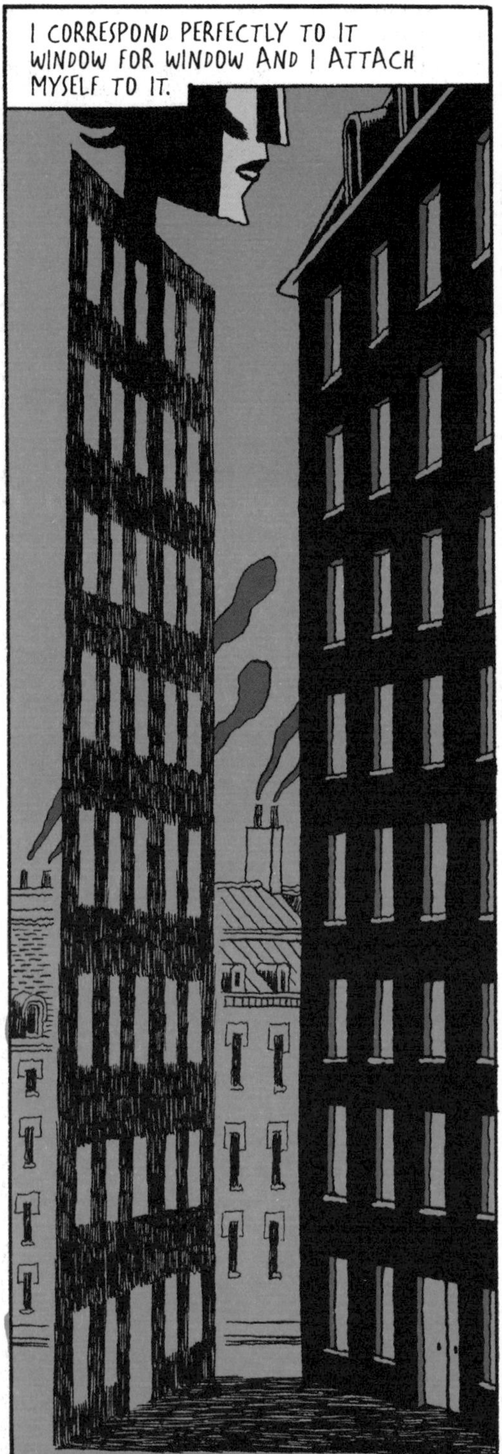
I CORRESPOND PERFECTLY TO IT WINDOW FOR WINDOW AND I ATTACH MYSELF TO IT.

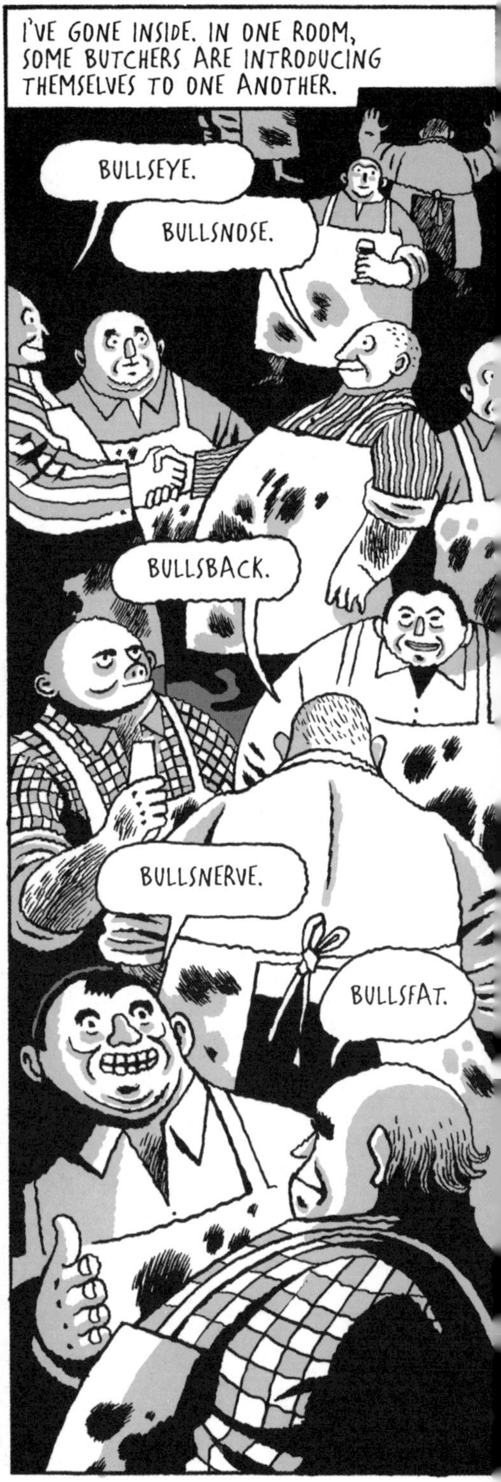
I'VE GONE INSIDE. IN ONE ROOM, SOME BUTCHERS ARE INTRODUCING THEMSELVES TO ONE ANOTHER.
BULLSEYE.
BULLSNOSE.
BULLSBACK.
BULLSNERVE.
BULLSFAT.

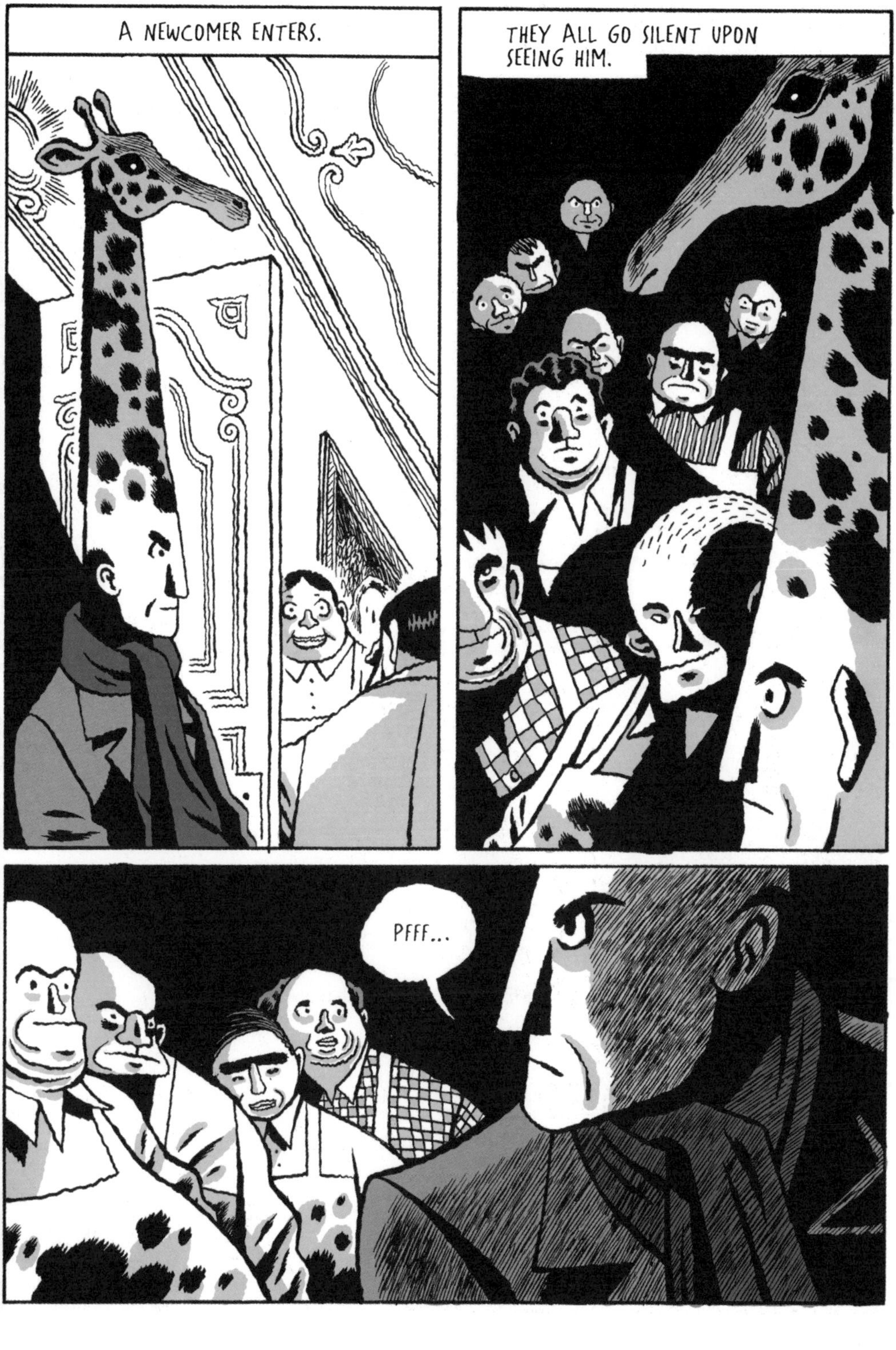
A NEWCOMER ENTERS.
THEY ALL GO SILENT UPON SEEING HIM.
PFFF...

THE MAN'S WALKING IN THE STREET BUT HE NO LONGER HAS HIS GIRAFFE HEAD.

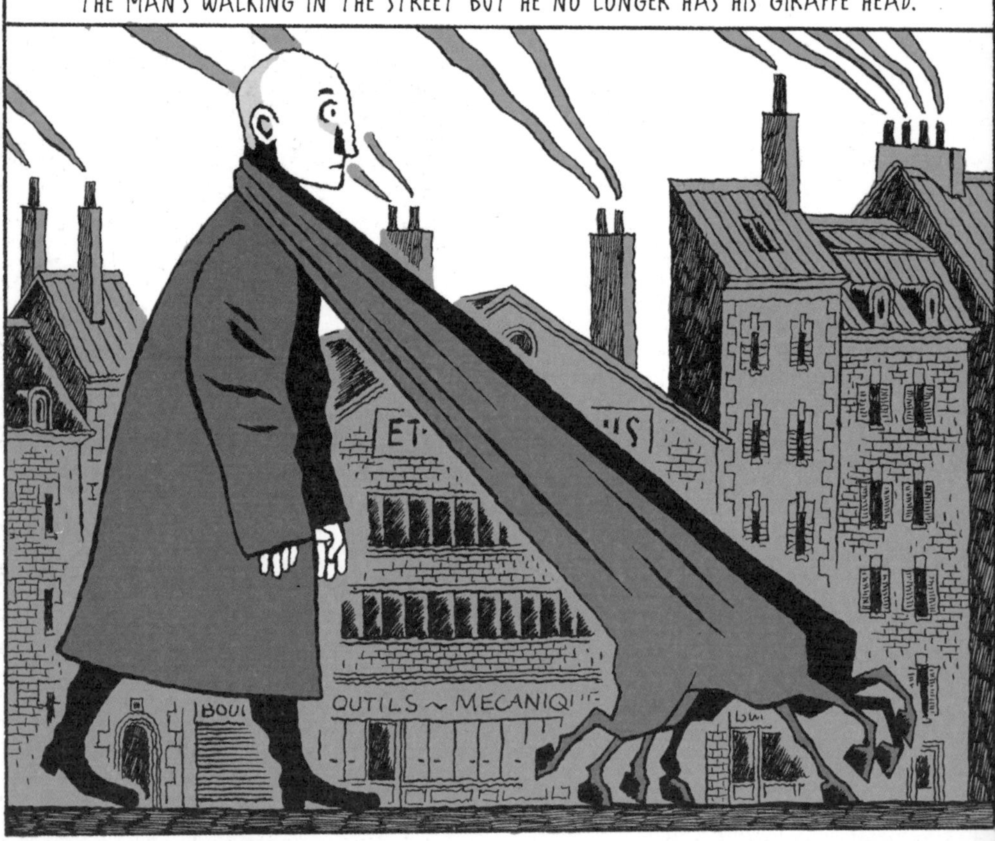

ET
OUTILS ~ MECANIQU
BOU

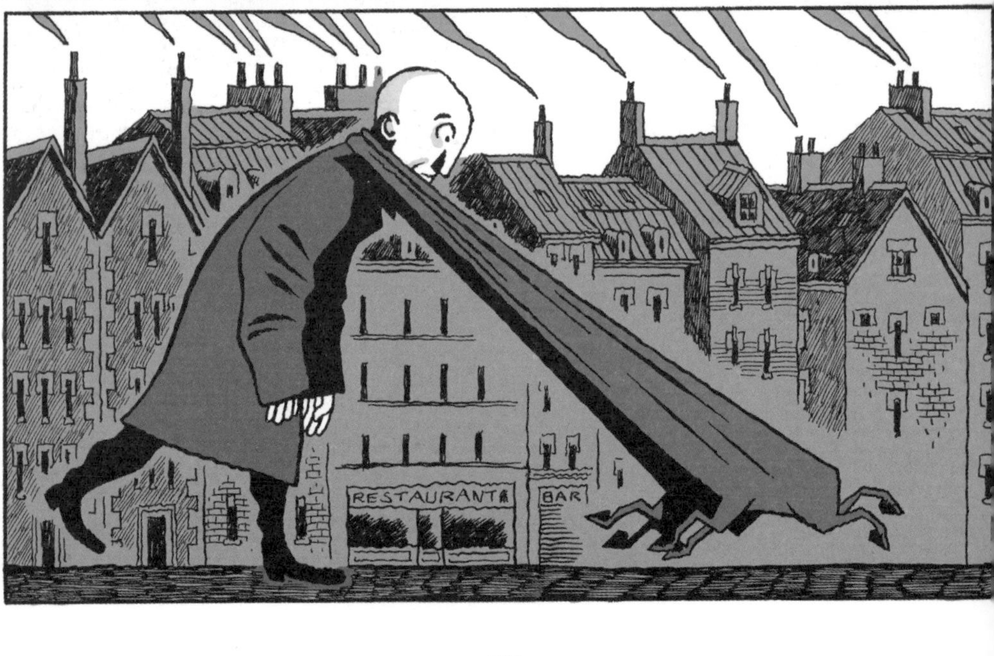

RESTAURANT
BAR

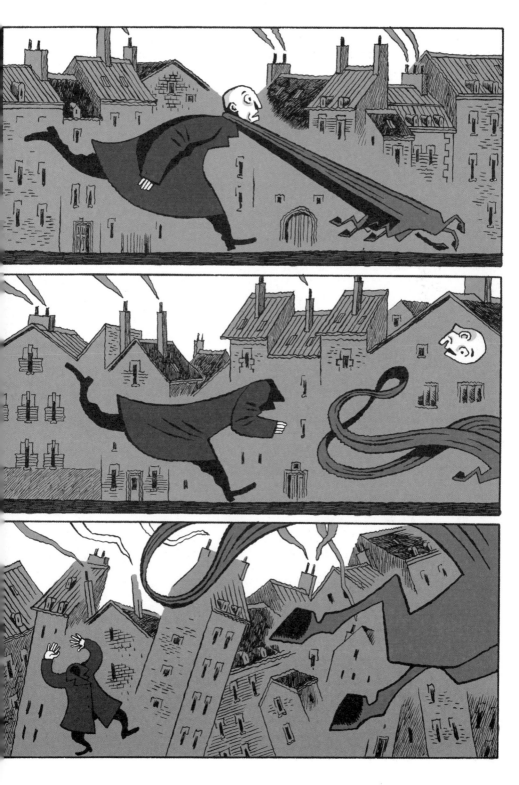

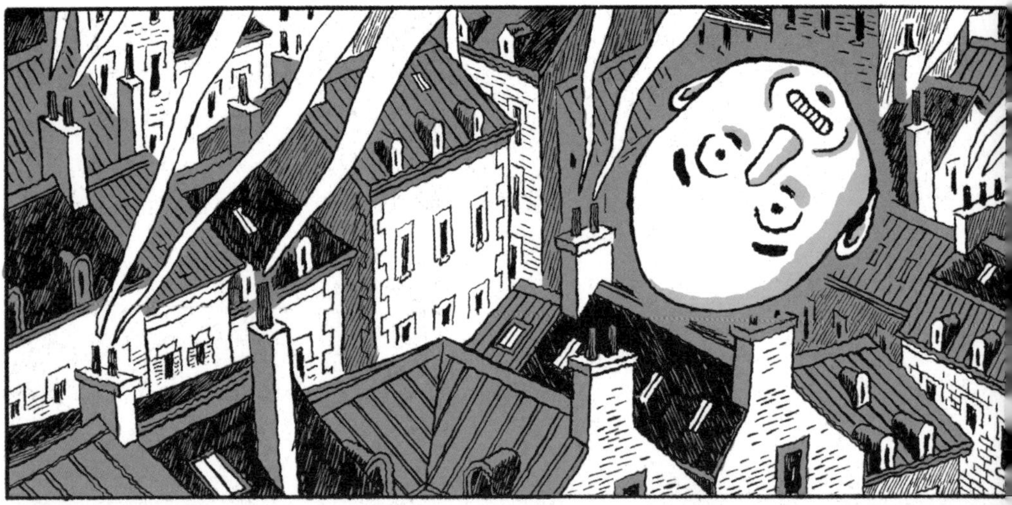

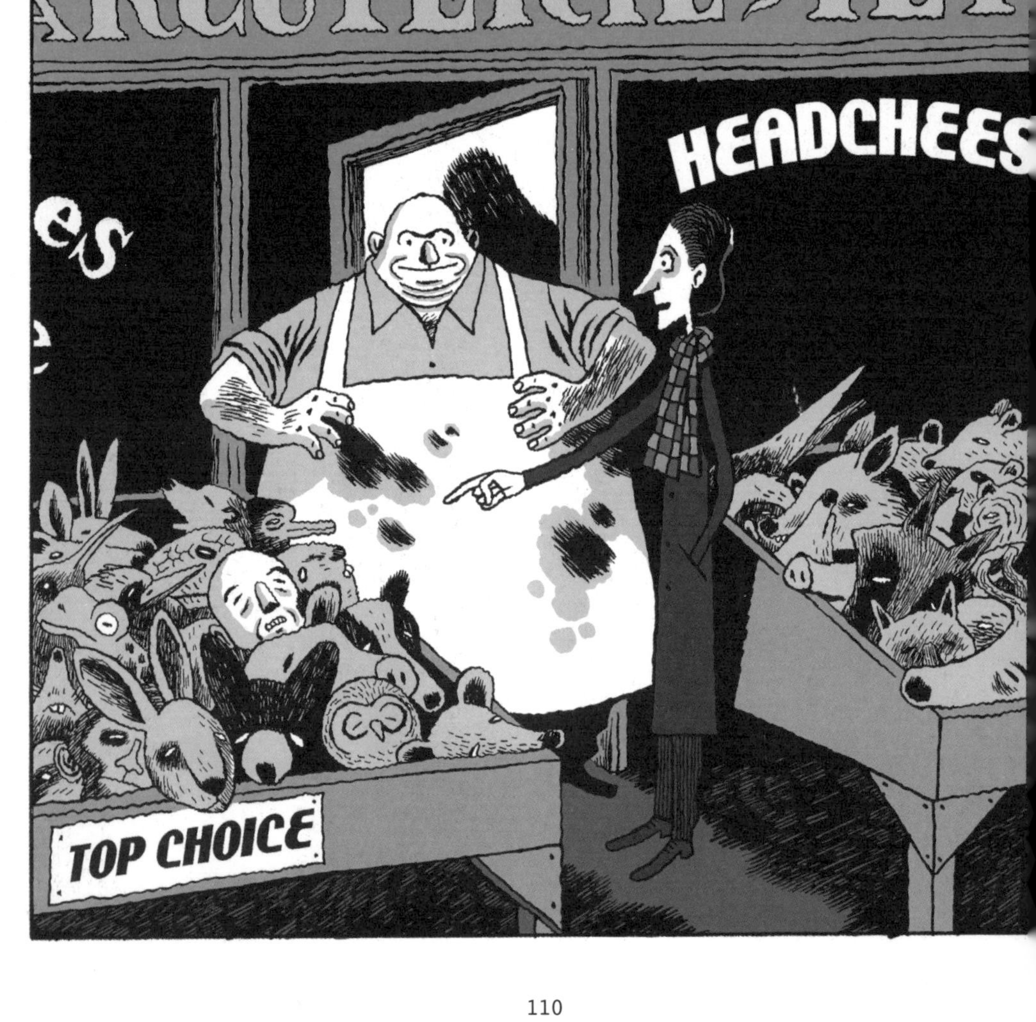
HEADCHEES
TOP CHOICE

18 • The Children

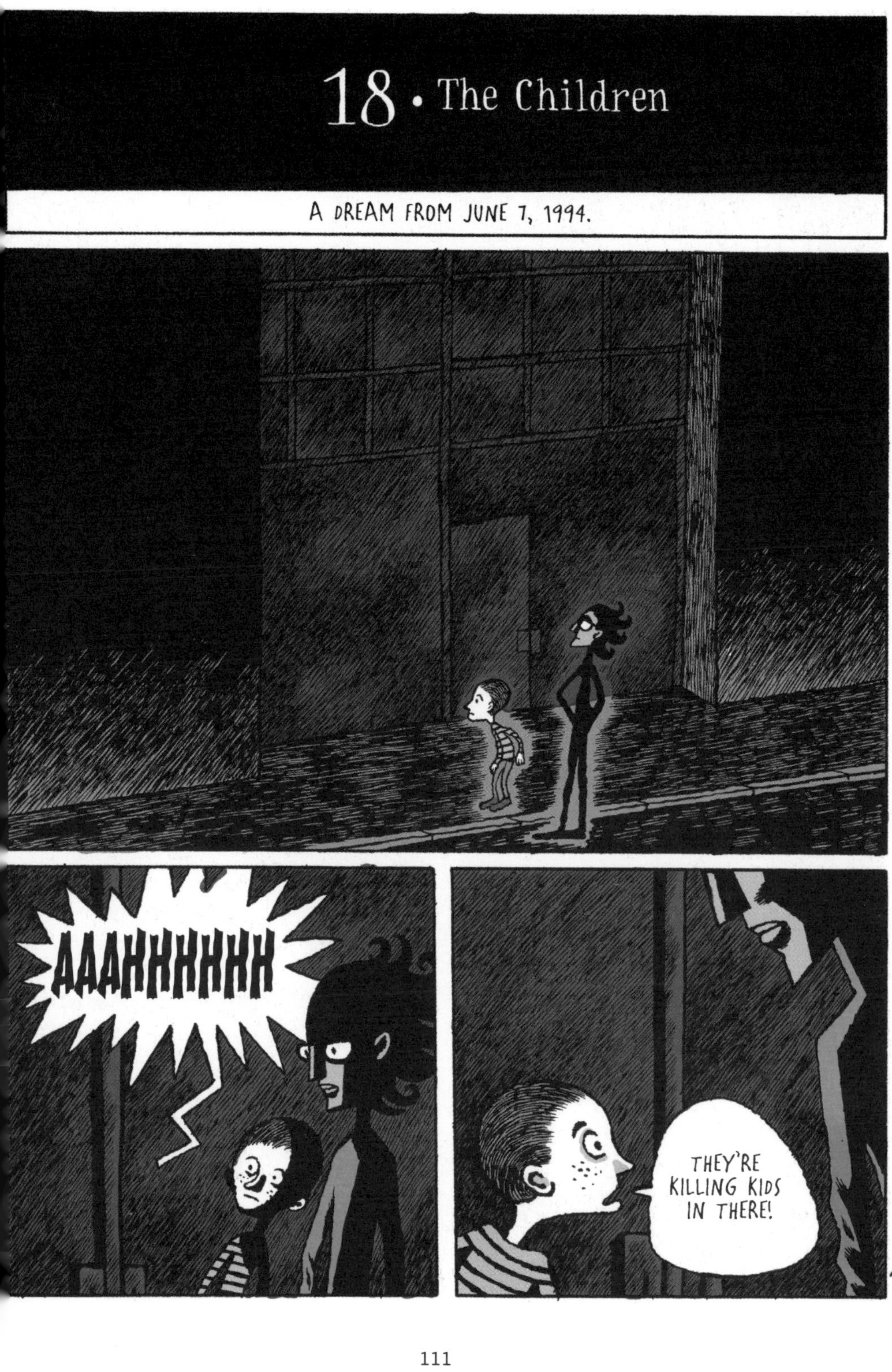
A DREAM FROM JUNE 7, 1994.
AAAHHHHHH
THEY'RE KILLING KIDS IN THERE!

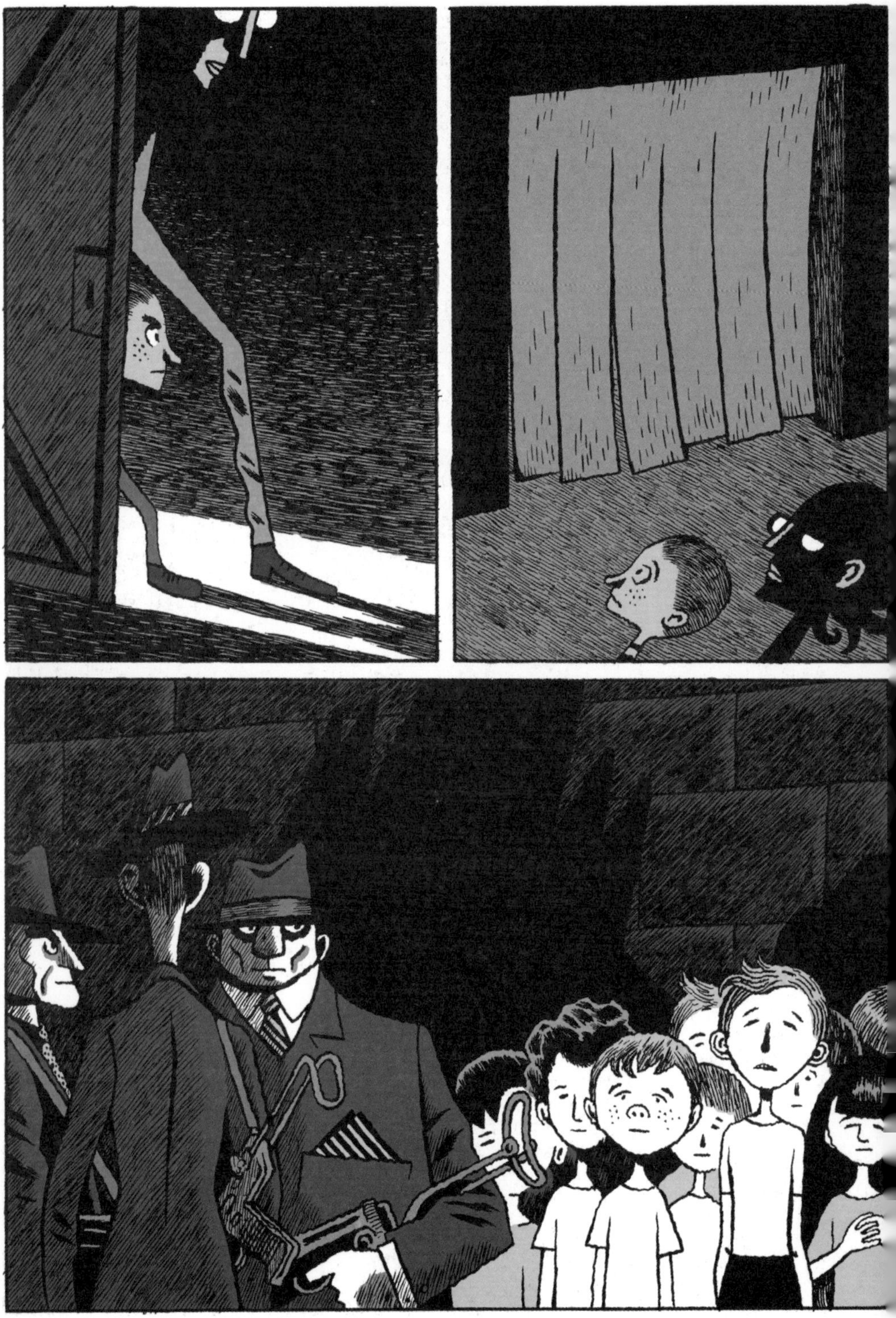

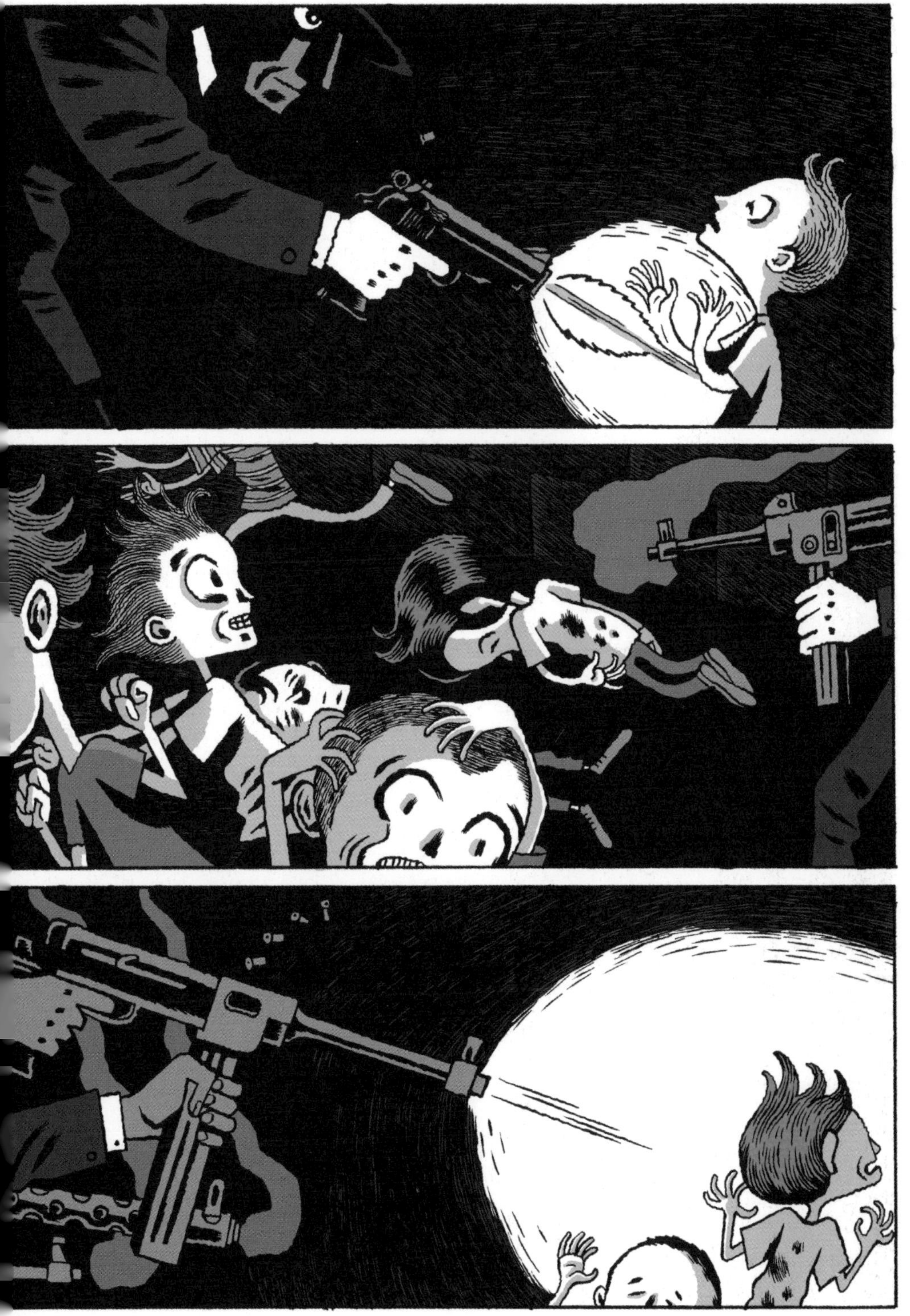

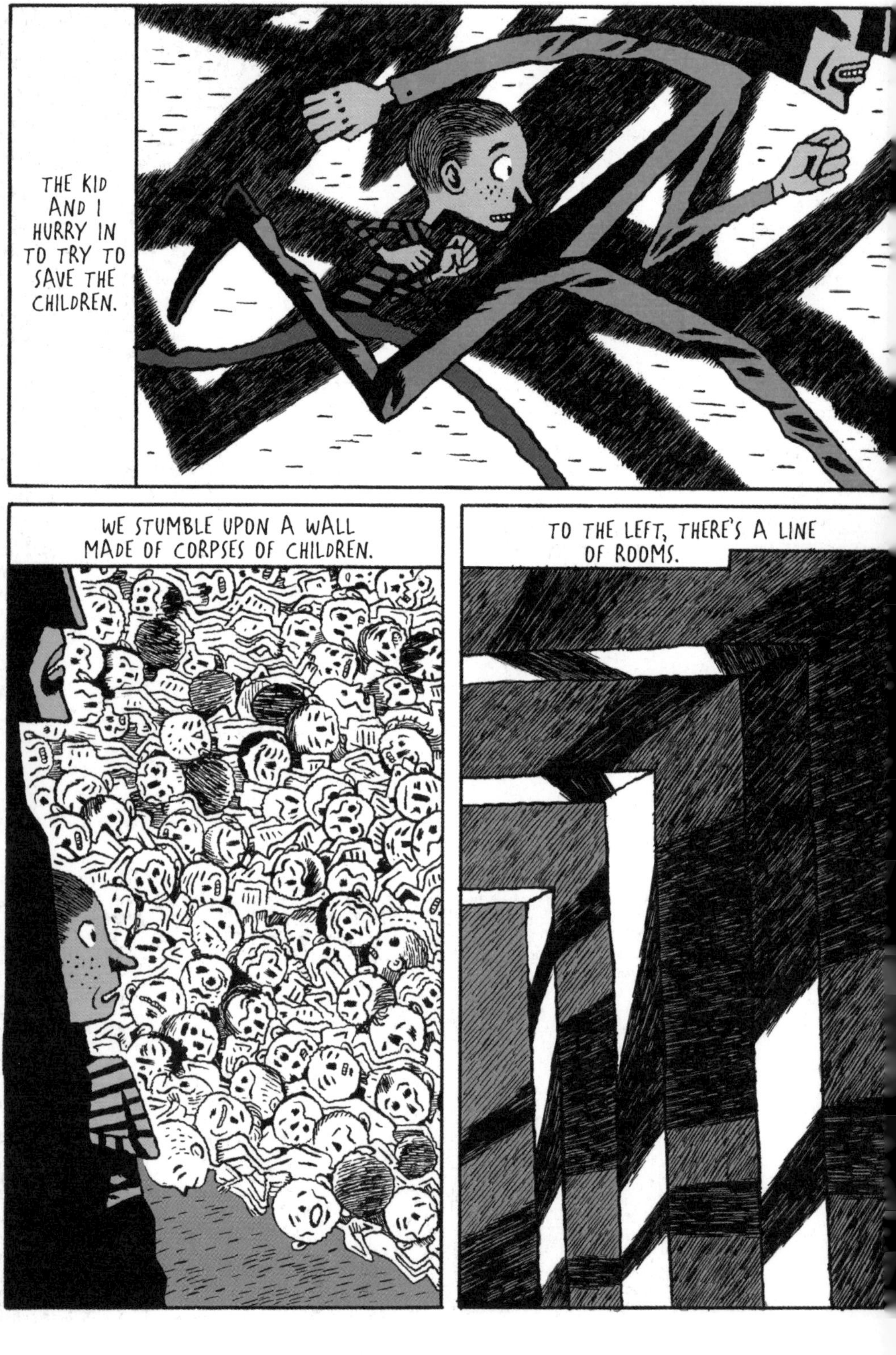
THE KID AND I HURRY IN TO TRY TO SAVE THE CHILDREN.
WE STUMBLE UPON A WALL MADE OF CORPSES OF CHILDREN.
TO THE LEFT, THERE'S A LINE OF ROOMS.

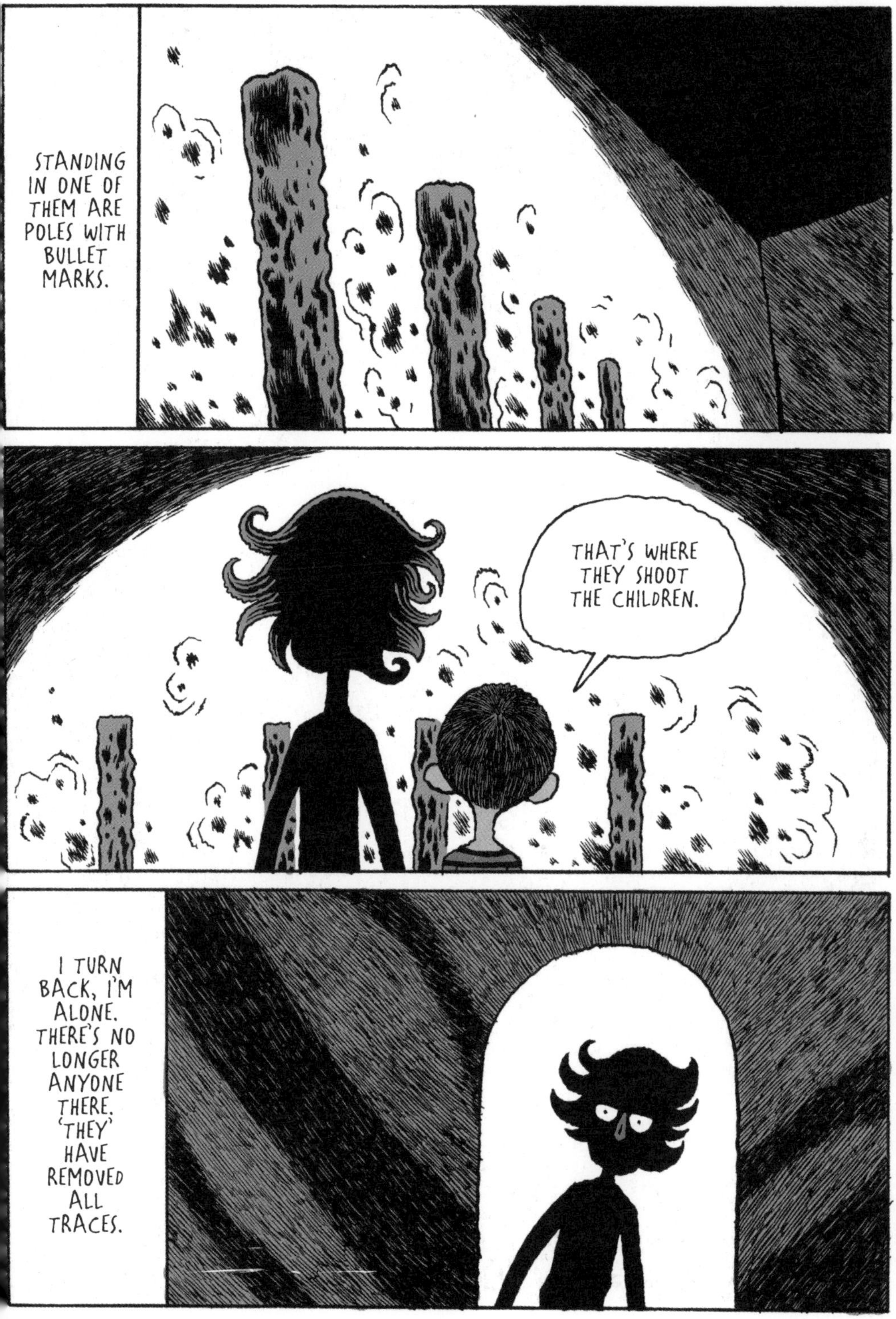
STANDING IN ONE OF THEM ARE POLES WITH BULLET MARKS.
THAT'S WHERE THEY SHOOT THE CHILDREN.
I TURN BACK, I'M ALONE. THERE'S NO LONGER ANYONE THERE. 'THEY' HAVE REMOVED ALL TRACES.

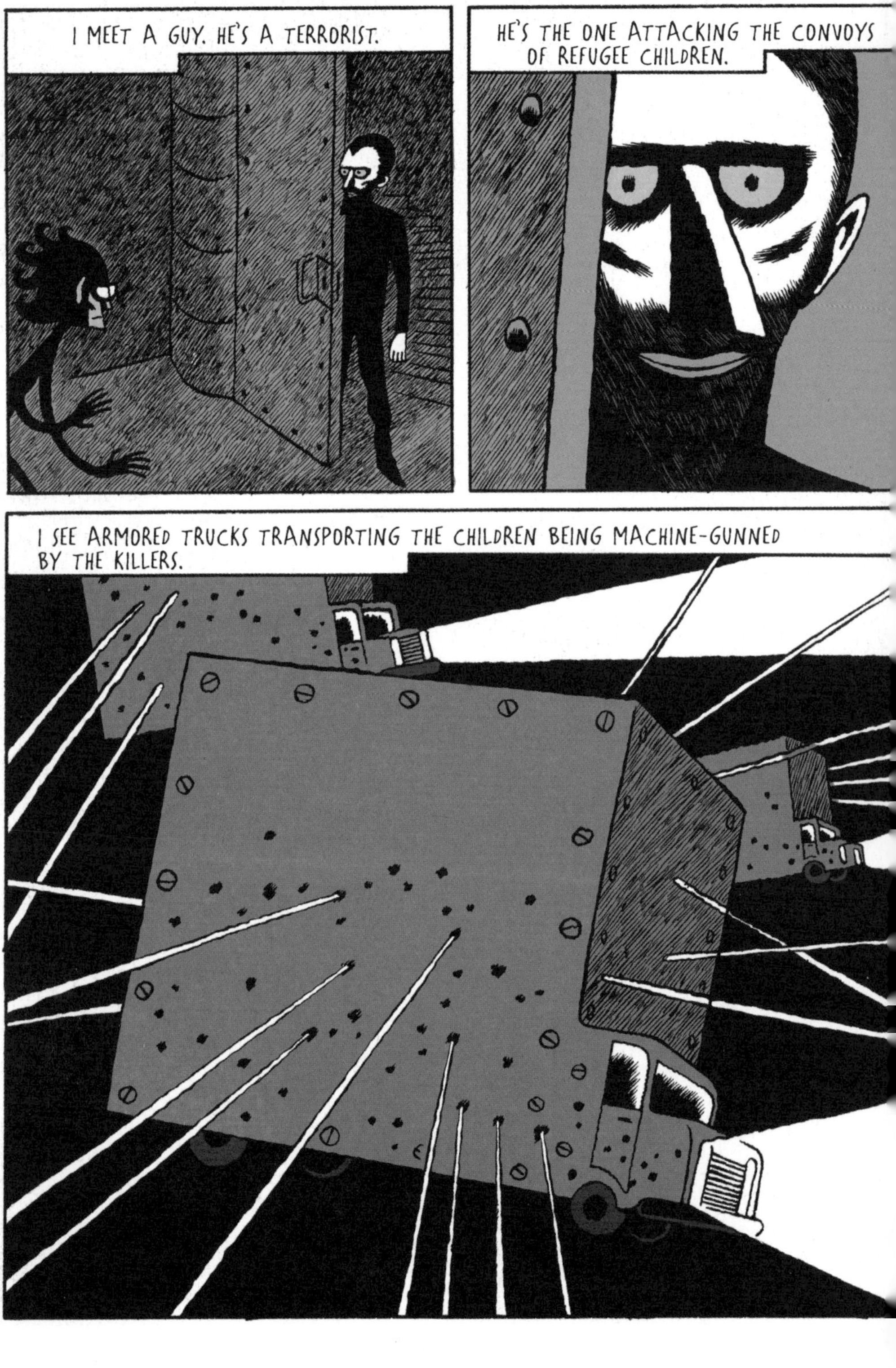
I MEET A GUY. HE'S A TERRORIST.
HE'S THE ONE ATTACKING THE CONVOYS OF REFUGEE CHILDREN.
I SEE ARMORED TRUCKS TRANSPORTING THE CHILDREN BEING MACHINE-GUNNED BY THE KILLERS.

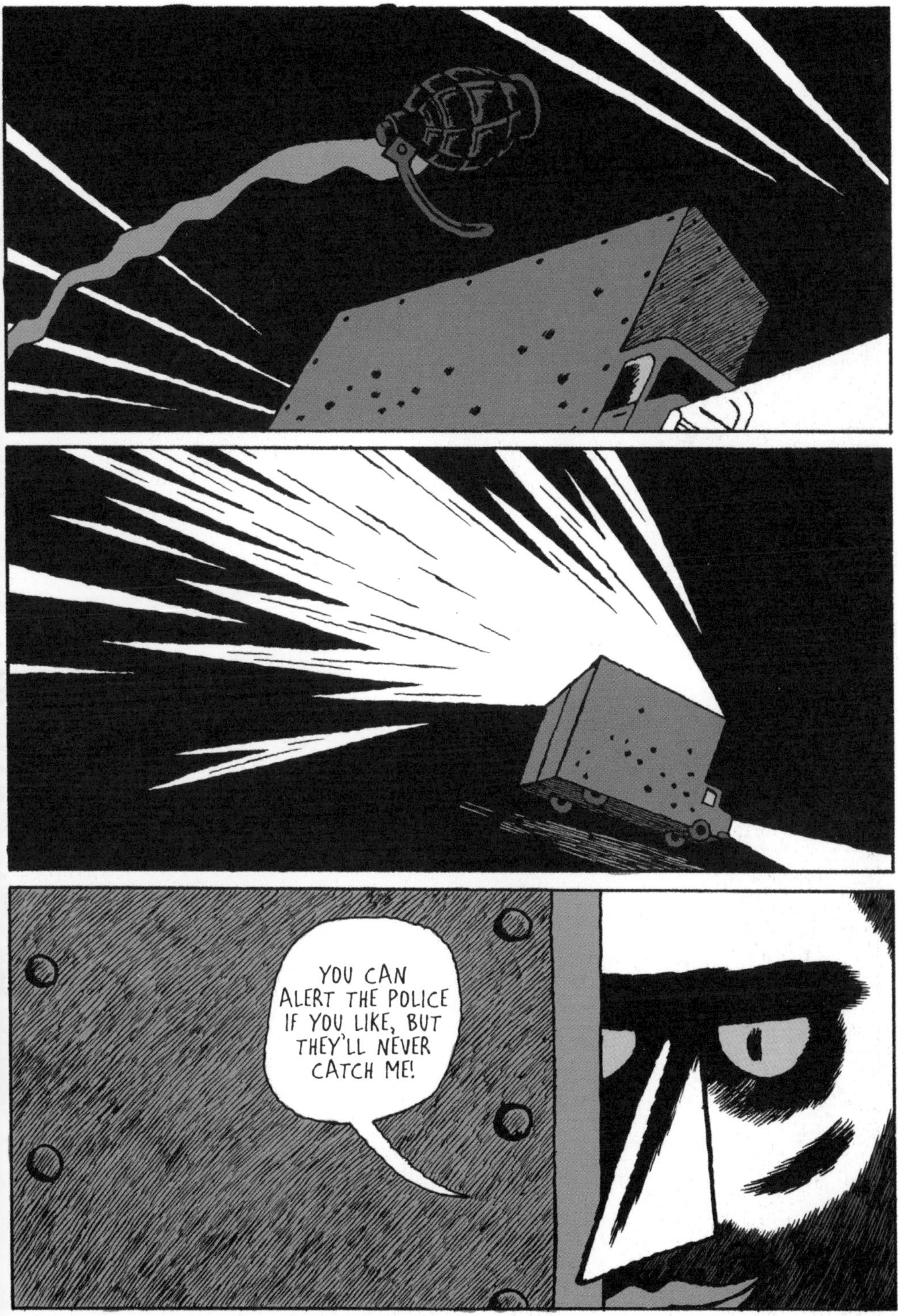
YOU CAN ALERT THE POLICE IF YOU LIKE, BUT THEY'LL NEVER CATCH ME!

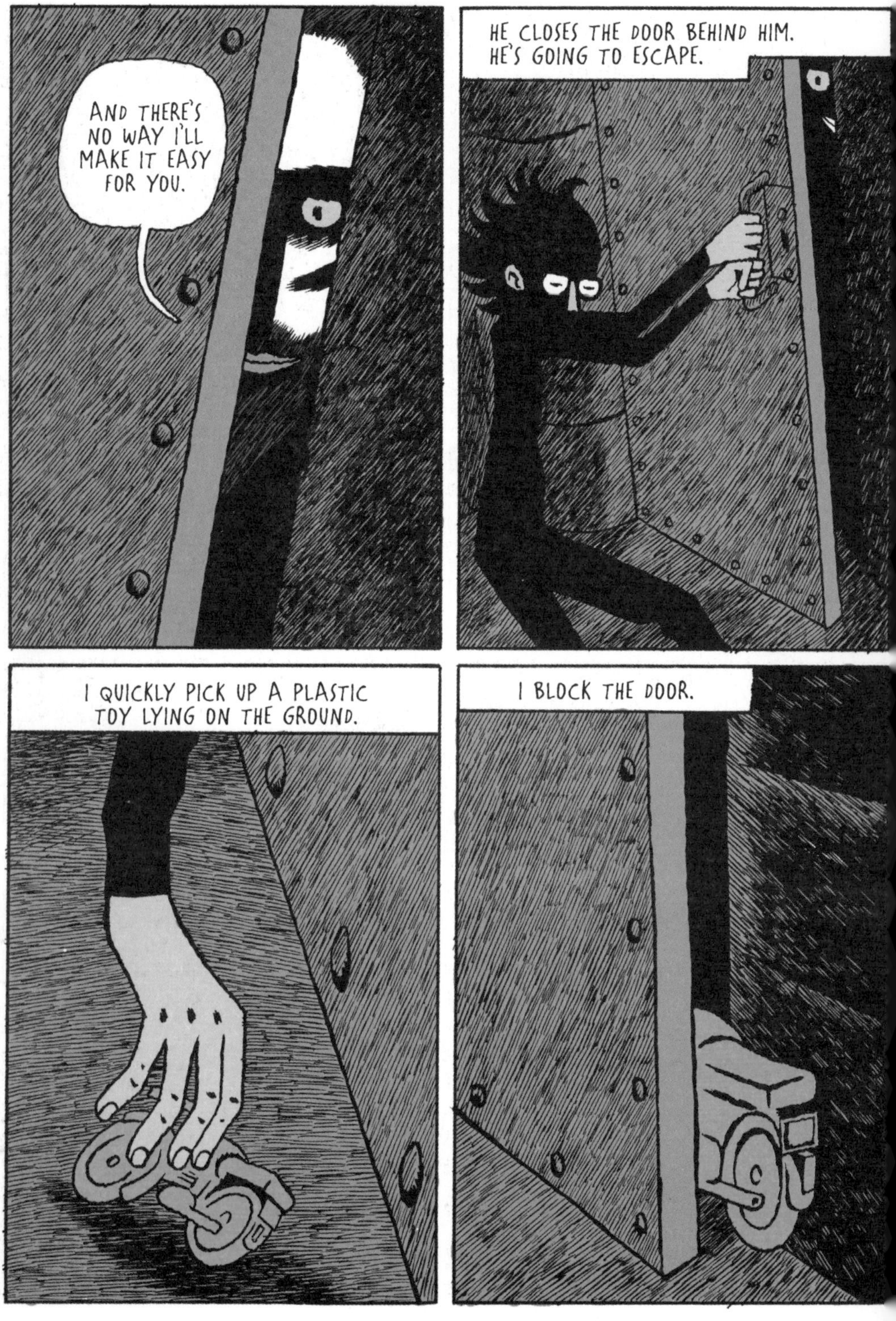
AND THERE'S NO WAY I'LL MAKE IT EASY FOR YOU.
HE CLOSES THE DOOR BEHIND HIM. HE'S GOING TO ESCAPE.
I QUICKLY PICK UP A PLASTIC TOY LYING ON THE GROUND.
I BLOCK THE DOOR.

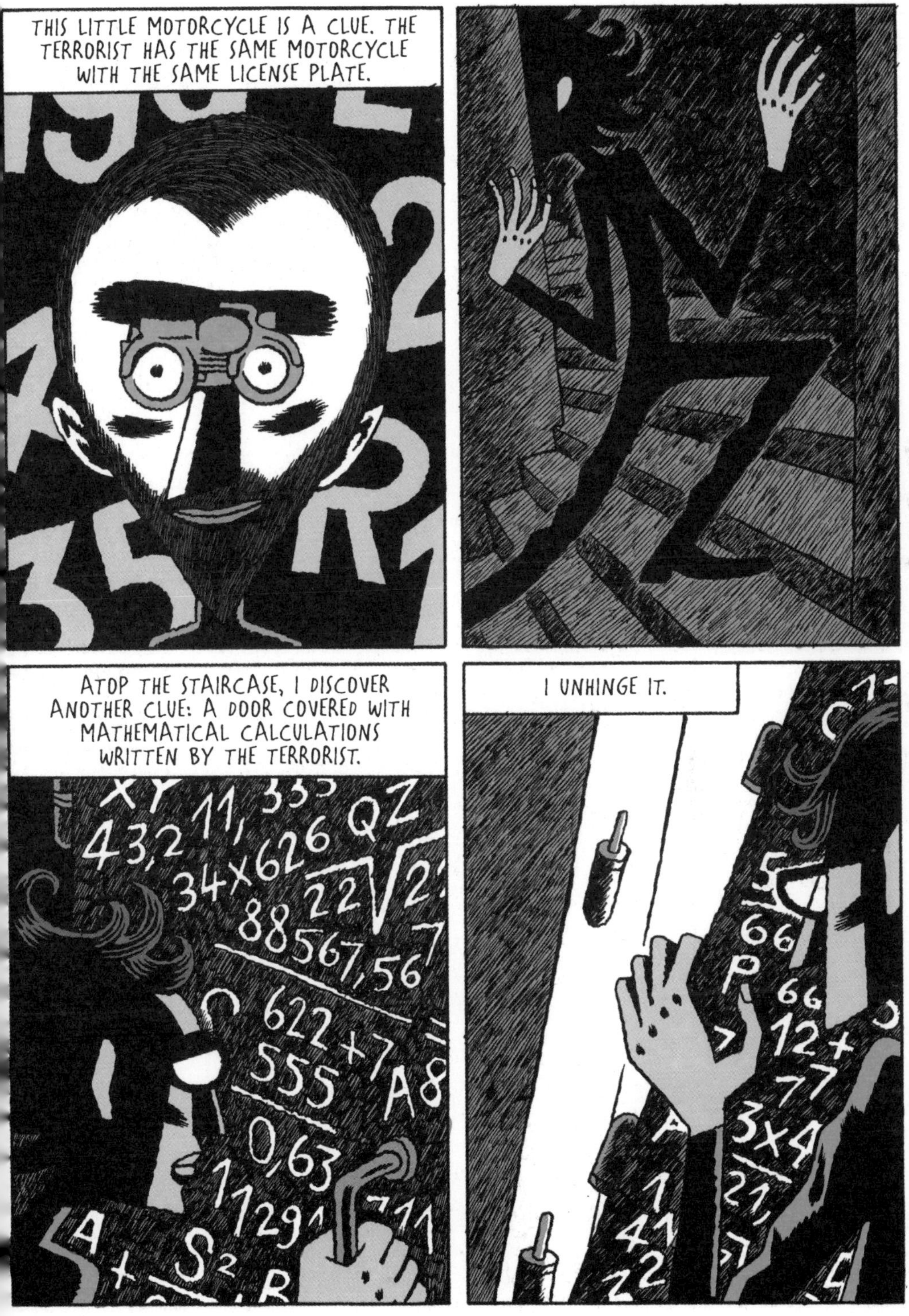
THIS LITTLE MOTORCYCLE IS A CLUE. THE TERRORIST HAS THE SAME MOTORCYCLE WITH THE SAME LICENSE PLATE.
ATOP THE STAIRCASE, I DISCOVER ANOTHER CLUE: A DOOR COVERED WITH MATHEMATICAL CALCULATIONS WRITTEN BY THE TERRORIST.
I UNHINGE IT.

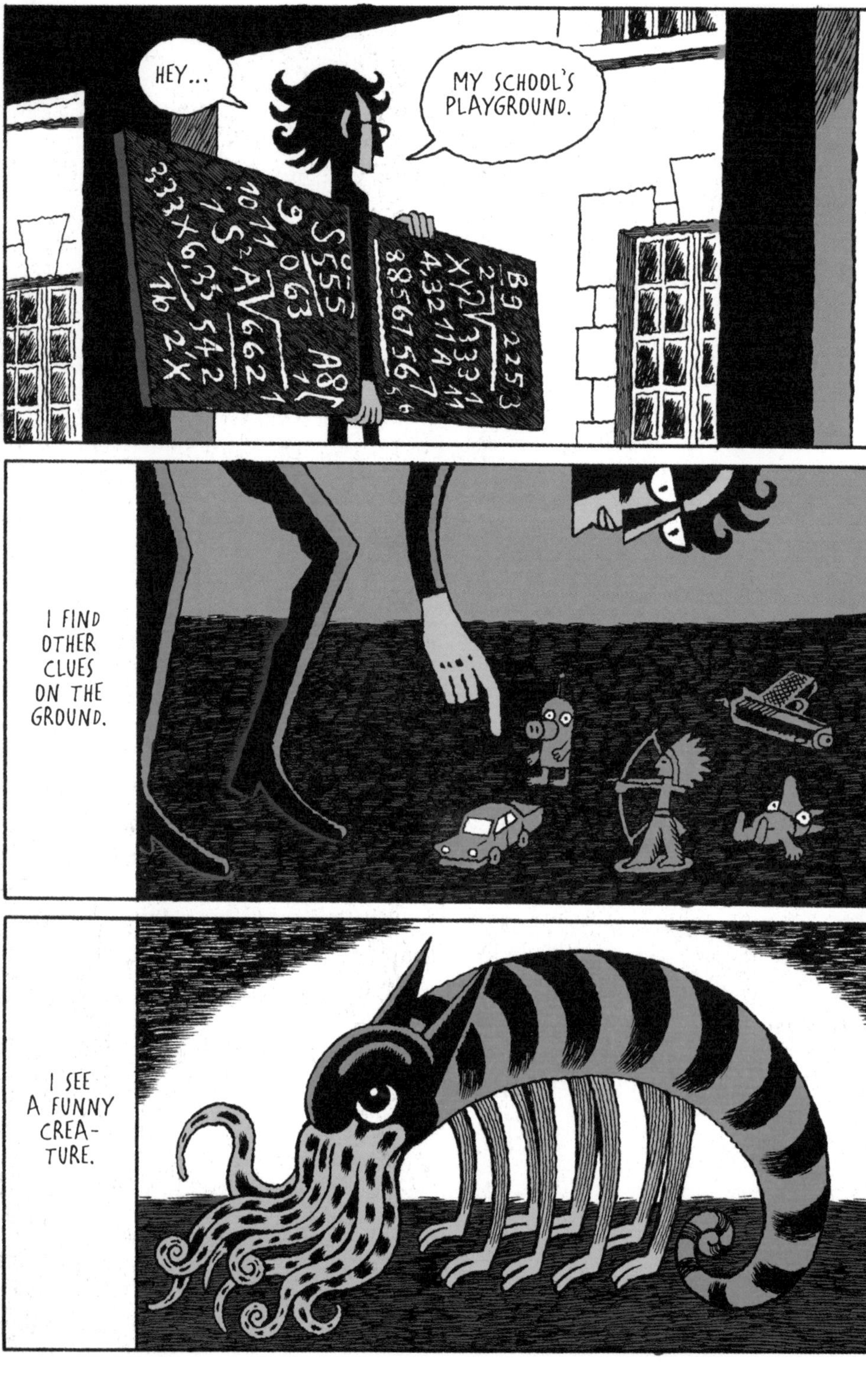
HEY...
MY SCHOOL'S PLAYGROUND.
I FIND OTHER CLUES ON THE GROUND.
I SEE A FUNNY CREA-TURE.

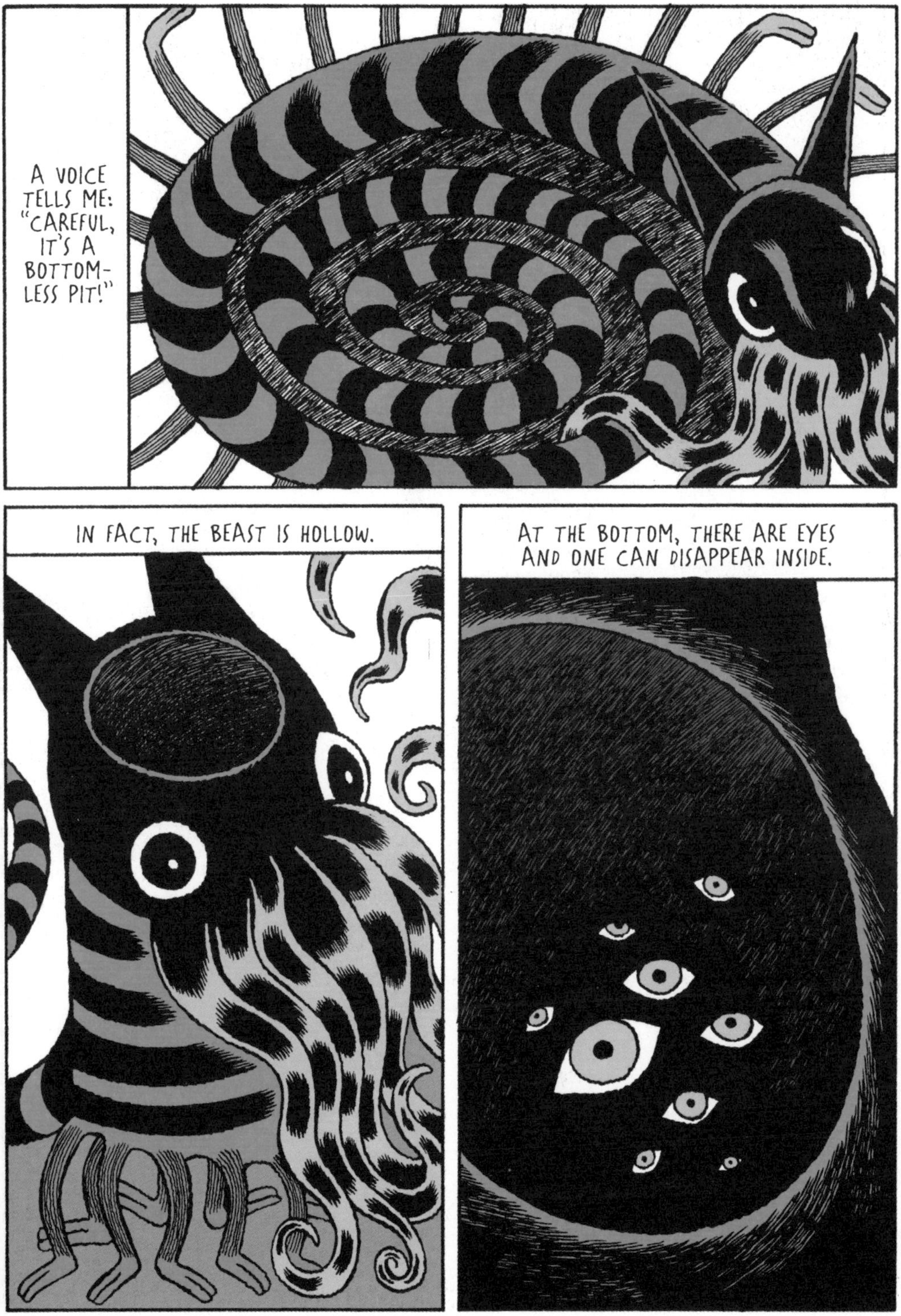
A VOICE TELLS ME: "CAREFUL, IT'S A BOTTOMLESS PIT!"
IN FACT, THE BEAST IS HOLLOW.
AT THE BOTTOM, THERE ARE EYES AND ONE CAN DISAPPEAR INSIDE.

19 • The Cowboys

A DREAM FROM SEPTEMBER 9, 1994.

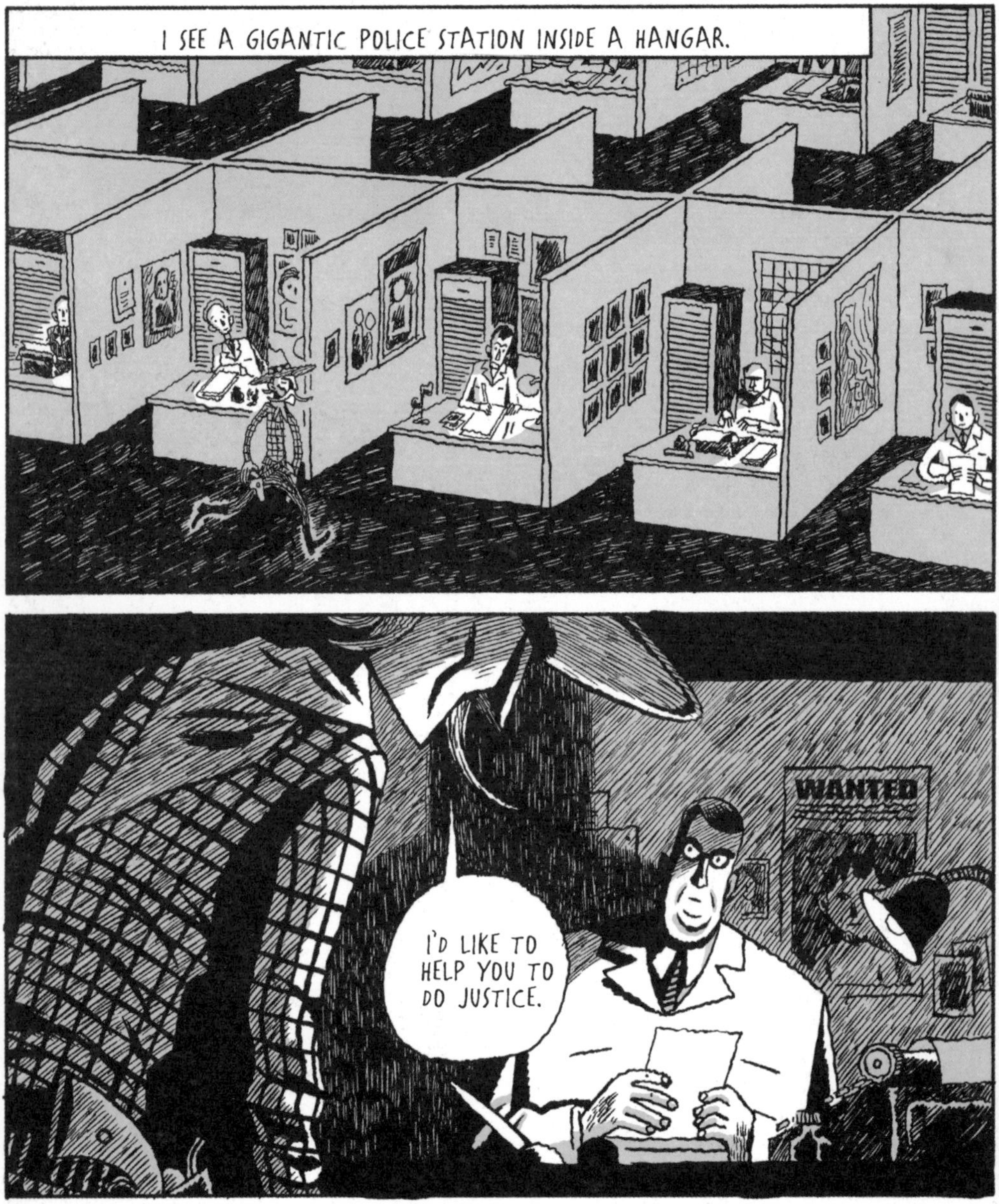
I SEE A GIGANTIC POLICE STATION INSIDE A HANGAR.
WANTED
I'D LIKE TO HELP YOU TO DO JUSTICE.

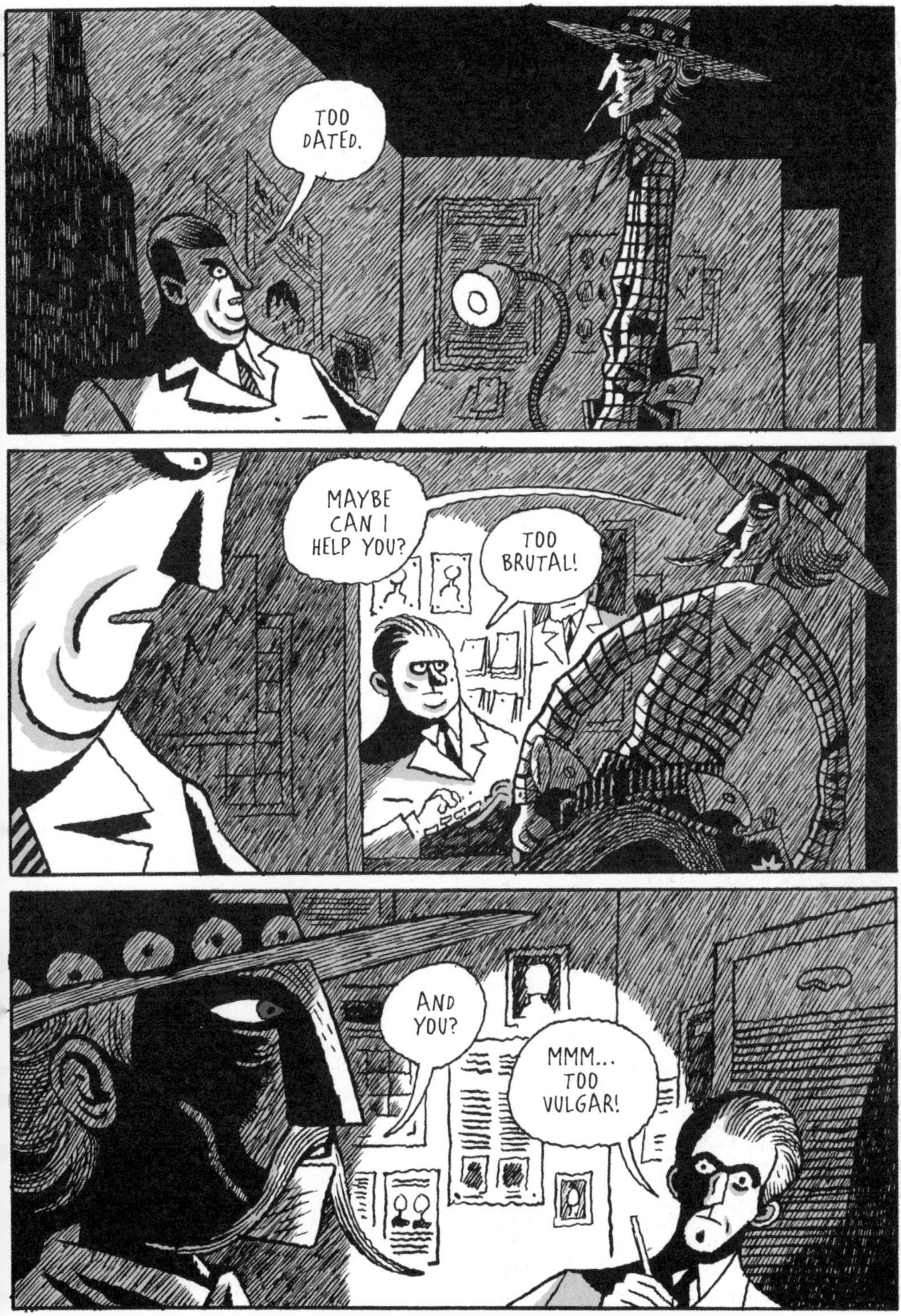
TOO DATED.
MAYBE CAN I HELP YOU?
TOO BRUTAL!
AND YOU?
MMM... TOO VULGAR!

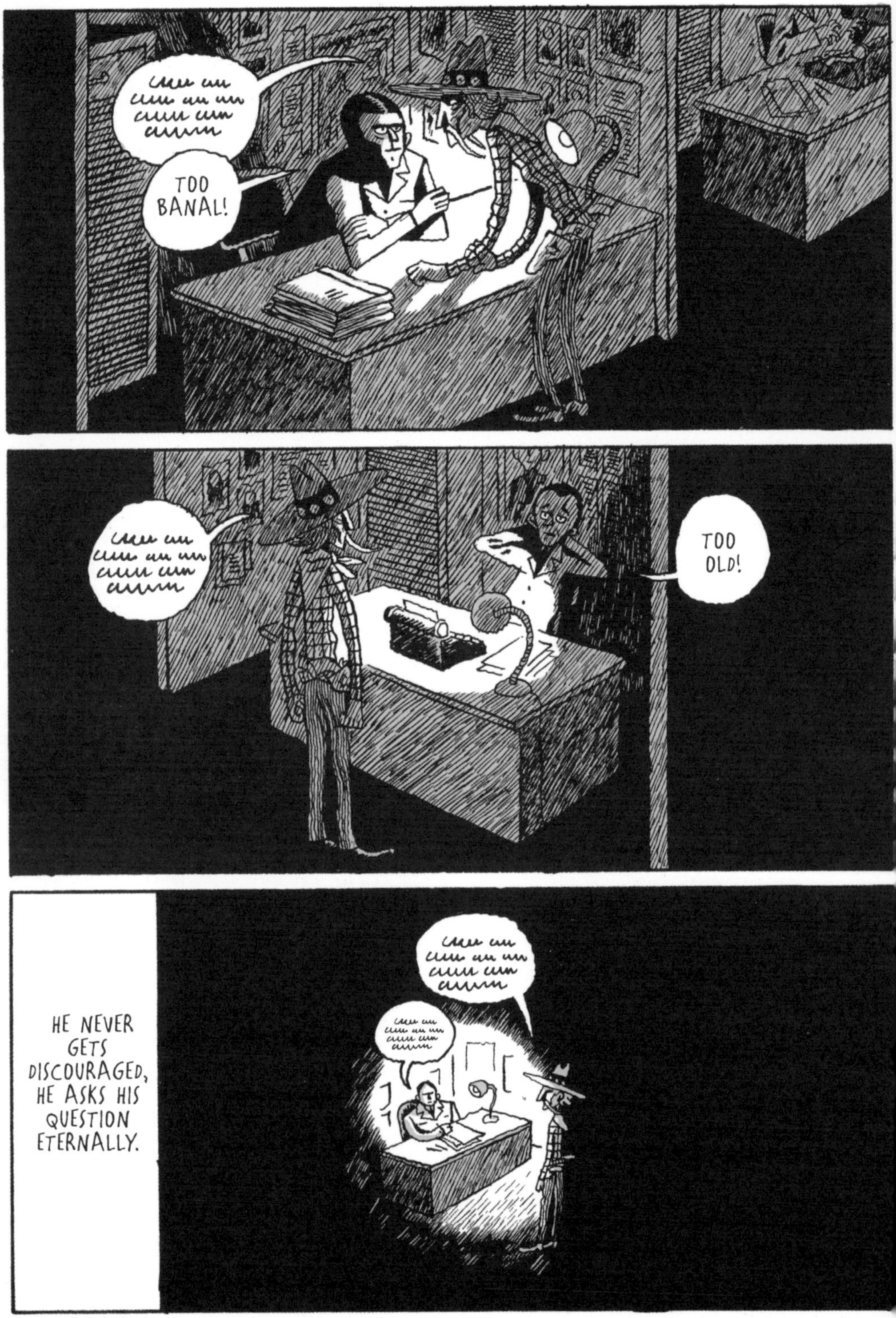
TOO BANAL!
TOO OLD!
HE NEVER GETS DISCOURAGED, HE ASKS HIS QUESTION ETERNALLY.

Also available from ComicsLit:
Little Nothings, $14.95
Isaac the Pirate, vols. 1, 2: $14.95 each
Add $4 P&H first item
$1 each additional.

We have over 200 titles, write for
our complete catalog:
NBM
40 Exchange Pl., Suite 1308
New York, NY 10005
www.nbmpublishing.com

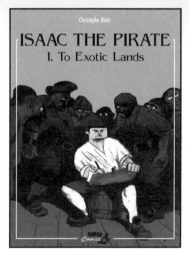